Chilean Theater,
1973–1985

for David,

still with that wee bit
of nostalgia
and, as always,
with love,

[signature]

February 1992

Chilean Theater,
1973–1985
Marginality, Power, Selfhood

Catherine M. Boyle

Rutherford ● Madison ● Teaneck
Fairleigh Dickinson University Press
London and Toronto: Associated University Presses

Associated University Presses
440 Forsgate Drive
Cranbury, NJ 08512

Associated University Presses
25 Sicilian Avenue
London WC1A 2QH, England

Associated University Presses
P.O. Box 39, Clarkson Pstl. Stn.
Mississauga, Ontario,
L5J 3X9 Canada

The paper used in this publication meets the requirements
of the American National Standard for Permanence of Paper
for Printed Library Materials Z39.48-1984.

Library of Congress-in-Publication Data

Boyle, Catherine M.
  Chilean theater, 1973–1985 : marginality, power, selfhood /
Catherine M. Boyle.
    p.   cm.
  Includes bibliographical references and index.
  ISBN 0-8386-3363-3 (alk. paper)
    1. Theater—Chile—History—20th century.   2. Chilean drama—20th
century—History and criticism.   I. Title.
PN2491.B69   1992
792'.0983'09047—dc20   88-46172
                                                            CIP

Pero mi amor ha quedado pegado en las rocas, el mar y las
                                                    montañas.
Pero mi amor te digo, ha quedado adherido en las rocas, el mar y
                                        las montañas.
                        —Raúl Zurita, *Canto a su amor desaparecido*

[But my love is pinned to the rocks, the sea and the
                                            mountains.
But my love, I tell you, clings to the rocks, the sea and
                                        the mountains.
                        —Raúl Zurita, "Song to a disappeared love"]

Contents

Introduction: Chilean Theater from the Inside Out

I came to the study of Chilean theater through a love of the performing arts, of Latin American literature, and, more immediately, through music, through contact with the dramatic qualities of Chilean song in exile. This book started life as a doctoral thesis and grew into what, in many ways, is a personal reaction to and relationship with the performing arts in Chile, developed primarily over visits to the country in 1985 and 1988. During these visits I was, much to the bewilderment of the vast majority of the people I met, writing a thesis about Chilean theater since 1973. To people outside academe, thesis writing is an inexplicable way to spend time, and those who knew what a thesis was thought that there were myriad more interesting topics in more colorful Latin American countries. But more than writing a thesis about theater in the former "Great Britain of America," I wanted to be able to study and to understand as far as possible the enormous creative force that turns simple words and images embedded in a collective imagination into powerful tokens of a real immensity of experience. Through theater—good, bad, indifferent, and absolutely awful—I knew it was possible to glimpse layer upon layer of reality, "truths," "lies," propaganda, alongside fear, terror, suffering, pain, courage. This is what I hope to be able to communicate to those who read this book.

The year 1985 meant for me piecing together a jigsaw. It meant inexpertly trying to find the pieces that would go around the edge to make the straight lines and form the frame, the guide to a picture of Chilean theater. But intuitively I knew that, despite being an outsider, the edges were not the place to start. To understand the processes of artistic creation in Chile, I had to creep into the center and, frustratingly at times, join together pieces that seemed to have no relation to one another or to the jigsaw as a whole. I don't believe that I ever had the illusion that I would be able to recreate the whole; I never felt the temptation to try to do so. I only wanted to find the keys, to be able to dig deep into the language of the theater in Chile and emerge able to enter into worlds of expression and

11

communication through art, through the essential and endlessly inventive need to say, to tell, to share lived experiences with others through words, music, painting, tapestry, dance, even writing on walls.

For most of 1985, and then again in 1988, I lived in a type of limbo between theater and reality; perhaps I came to share the limbo that theater had too often been forced into. I wandered and walked, I talked to people, incessantly it seemed, asking questions, realizing the questions I was asking were the wrong ones, starting again and learning to ask more appropriate questions. I began to learn the immense importance of the detail, of words, endlessly pummeled from left, right, and center. I also learned to be wary of some words, those whose meaning never seemed to be clear, those that you think you understand until you realize that you don't know how to use them. Then, language has to be learned again, but in a different way, alert to colors and nuances rather than defined meanings. And in the circles of theater criticism, I learned to be wary of, for example, the word "interesante," especially when pronounced with the elongated, singsong "a." I heard it on many occasions when asking theater people for their opinion on a play I had just seen. On hearing "interesante," I knew that the opinion being camouflaged was bordering on the negative, but that for certain reasons of friendship, solidarity, or the proximity eavesdroppers, I was going to hear no more.

Above all in those months, I watched and listened and, from the comfortable limbo of the visiting European, I distilled the information as best I could, using the knowledge, the insights, and the fledgling understanding of the subtle and not so subtle machinery of everyday expression.

In 1985 Chile was in a state of siege. I arrived from the United Kingdom to a situation that was totally beyond my experience: a state of total censorship of the press and the media, of the absence of civil liberties, of a curfew, of streets empty after nine o'clock in the evening, of the practical fear of not getting the last micro, or bus, home. And then there were the earth tremors, the aftershocks that followed the March earthquake, and that always seemed to be strongest at five in the morning, when the nearest threshold seemed to me to be miles away. This barrage of new experiences was confusing and exhausting, not to say bewildering and upsetting. But they are fundamental; they are the essence of a growing understanding of and sensitivity to a different society and culture. The intellectual dawning begins to take place as they settle and then filter back up from the gut to the head and we begin to see through

these experiences into images, words, symbols, metaphors that
that society uses in the artistic expression of itself, openly or
covertly, obtusely or transparently, to give tangible evidence of
existence.

On 30 March 1985 I went to see Jaime Miranda's *Regreso sin
causa* [Return without a cause]. I had been told not to miss it, for
the content of the play and the light it would shed on the common
Chilean experience of exile, for the performances of two great
actors, Julio Jung and María Elena Duvauchelle, recently returned
from exile, and because of its huge popular success. The previous
day I had thought briefly that I had lost my command of the
Spanish language when, walking in Providencia, the main shopping
paradise of the middle classes, I picked up a leaflet that told of the
shooting and abduction of two men in a school not far away at 8:30
that morning, when the school playground was full of children. At
that time, hardly three weeks in the country, it was something I
could barely take in. I reread the leaflet convinced that I must have
misunderstood. Of course, I hadn't. Later that day it was revealed
that these two men, along with one other—all prominent in the
Communist party and associated with the Church solidarity movement, La Vicaría de la Solidaridad—had gone missing. At the
beginning of *Regreso sin causa*, Julio Jung read out a message of
condemnation of these disappearances, and a message of support
for the families of the missing men. And at the end of the play, he
made another announcement, of news that had been received in the
interval. The three men had been found *degollados*, with their
throats cut, in the outskirts of Santiago.

I can only say that I felt physically sick. Reality was penetrating
the theater with too great an insistence. My first visits to the theater
were alone, and I spent a long time during some of the performances wondering how such overtly political productions could be
allowed. With my European sensibilities and fantastic notions of
dictatorship, I awaited some action against the companies—a raid
perhaps? I had never expected this kind of brutal intrusion. As I
was watching *Regreso sin causa*, not far away, in the center of
Santiago, in the Teatro La Comedia, home of Ictus, Chile's longest
running and most committed theater group, Roberto Parada, father
of one of the assassinated men, was acting in *Primavera con una
esquina rota* [Spring with a broken corner], playing the role of a
man in exile whose only son is a political prisoner in Uruguay, in a
prison called "Libertad," Freedom.

The events of those days taught me a lot about actions, reactions,
counteractions, about rage and its accompanying "certainty" that

something must happen, that they (and everyone knew in whose hands the blame could be laid) could not possibly outlive this latest cynical atrocity. And I witnessed the fading of another illusion of the long-awaited fall of the general, an illusion born of the most repeated, perverse, and obscene of circumstances. I began to learn then to read the pages of the official press and to stop trying to read always between the lines. For some declarations are absolutely blatant; they do not need any decoding. These pages said that Chile was in a state of siege, that there was an internal war that had been waged since the coup, and that the methods used were legitimate. They said too that the murderers may even have been members of the Communist party. During all this, I began to learn that, in order to read, understand and be able to relate any insights I may have, it is also necessary to look at the obvious and to give credit to what is before our very eyes. The foreigner in me learned that the sounds of sirens, of helicopters, that the mention of disappearances and fear in the theater were not merely theatrical codes.

At rehearsals for different plays, both in 1985 and 1988, I was witness to different forms of working, from collective creation to directorial theater, and I saw processes of discussion, trial, and error; of frustration, failure, and success. I experienced the physical circumstances in which all this was happening, with no state support, with actors who could not hope to begin to make a living from acting, who survived with help from friends, acquaintances, sometimes with nothing, when the results would become "muy artesanal," home-made. The trees are still there for the posting of publicity for the poorest, and the independent professional groups hope for exemption from the state imposed tax on works that are not deemed to be culturally significant.

And I asked the same questions over and over again. What does that mean? Who comes to see this? Why do they come? How can you say this on stage? Are you scared? I ended up, they said, "empapada," soaked in everything I was trying to squeeze out of the short time I had to write this "thesis," to gather the information that would help me to read a country through the long and complex process of making theater.

The other part of my research was, inevitably, carried out in libraries and research institutes. In the small Theater Library of the Theater School of the Universidad Católica I spent long hours going through their excellently catalogued newscuttings from the late sixties to the present day. Sitting in the library, accompanied by an electric fire, against a penetrating cold that even my Scottish blood had never experienced, I carried out a central part of my research. Through these clippings I learned more than I could have thought possible, reading the impressions of critics; finding out their particular point of view, their favorite topics; seeing the role they play in the shaping of a public awareness of theater. Here was a play-by-play account of the history of theater in Chile, sometimes sleepy, sometimes frantic, often beautifully productive. And always, it seemed, in the specter of a crisis. This taught me to look beyond the themes of the plays in a sociocultural analysis of the theater, to the criticism, the reasons, the protagonists' own perceptions of what they are trying to do and what they are, in fact, achieving.

And the final part of the research, which like the others still goes on, was the hunting for manuscripts, which were begged, borrowed, and photocopied. Things were definitely easier once the realization that manuscripts generally do not exist had sunk in. Then it is time to ask more questions, read more reviews. When a manuscript does exist, life becomes a long process of phoning, making appointments to collect the only existing one, and—when it is safely in your hands (and this does not always turn out to be the case), and after swearing on your own grave that you will protect it from all evil—photocopying it. This must be the most frustrating aspect of the whole business. I lost count of the number of times I was stood up—in the nicest possible way, I think—but it did teach me the old Chilean art of how to "fregar" (politely translatable as "to pester").

This book has grown out of this experience; out of observing, reading, collecting information and material; and it has grown from an unfinished process of assimilation. In it I have aimed to trace the development of Chilean theater from within, from what the plays and their productions suggest and/or demonstrate. The central part deals with theater after the military coup of 1973, in which the Popular Unity government of Salvador Allende was overthrown and the regime of General Augusto Pinochet was brutally installed. The first chapter, however, takes the form of a history of theater in Chile since 1941, when the Teatro Experimental de la Universidad de Chile was formed, and places a special emphasis on the period since 1968 when, with the political radicalization in society, many artists embarked on the task of making theater more accessible to larger and wider sectors of the community. Without the groundwork of the years since 1941, theater would not have occupied the central, if at times problematic, space it has done since 1973.

When talking of theater in Chile since 1973, it is difficult to avoid the notions of rupture and continuity, the former generally perceived as negative, the latter as positive. Through providing a longer perspective on theater, I want to create a sense of the multiple threads of creation and thought, artistic and political, that have been woven together, and I want to implant the idea that these threads are forever being teased through the continuum of creation, some leading nowhere, some lost to be picked up again, some, stronger or more productive, carrying through. And some deliberately and brutally severed.

After the coup, activity in the theater was seriously curtailed. Apart from the almost total disappearance of popular and amateur theater, there were blacklists of actors and actresses prohibited from appearing on the television. Many actors and directors went into exile, often after periods of repression and/or imprisonment, and there was brutal censorship of the tiny number of overt expressions of resistance. This must be seen within the context of the regime's program of "cleansing" society, of curing it from the Marxist "illness" it had suffered under the Popular Unity government. Any form of expression that evoked the ideology of Popular Unity was wiped out. In 1976, however, the presentation of new Chilean plays that referred overtly to contemporary problems such as unemployment opened an extremely productive period in the theater. In the reduced space for communication and the transmission of information, theater began to assume a special role providing a space for commentary on the state of the country. As a result of its peculiar capacity for coded language and its ability to reach an audience in an environment in which acts of community, meetings, and gatherings were prohibited, it took on a role that would otherwise have been performed by the media. In some cases theater has been the first medium to comment openly on the issues of the day.

One of the major reasons for this leniency in the regime's approach toward censorship in the theater may be that the audience is notoriously small, about 1 percent of the Santiago population, so that the damage that can be done by a dissident voice in theater is seen to be minimal. Another reason often offered is that the regime must be able to point to some form of freedom of expression. Yet the answer to why theater should be treated with relative indulgence is more complex and lies in the nature of its development since the middle of this century and in its role as a form of artistic expression of the urban middle class, which is politically a vitally important sector of the community.

There are many concepts that have been taken for granted in the analysis of this period of cultural history in Chile. Among these is that of the "cultural blackout," the *apagón cultural.* They have been repeated over and over again until their sense is lost in cliché.

In Chile I found out that there cannot be a real cultural blackout. Like so many other people, I talked about it, I looked for it, I searched for signs of defeat. And like so many others, I could see these signs, in a seeming debris of things past. But it was this very debris that was blinding me to the fact that it could not exist if there really were a cultural blackout. For, how could it be, then, that I was able to discover the signs, the symbols, the images that whispered and screamed from all sides? It was in the writing, the performing, the theater, the songs—in which, as so many said, "the voice had become tremendous"—that I was able to decipher the core of the society that had taken me in.

One thing is certain, the phrase cultural blackout is one of a set of phrases that were coined in moments of great despair, when perceptions of negation, loss, and defeat dictated a series of interpretations of the period that emphasized and were based in an "awareness" of sterility. Yet the real and lasting beauty of the experience in Chile is that the creative impulse and its results did not die, that even in the moments when the cultural blackout seemed to be at its bleakest, the search for the ways to express this experience surfaced time and time again. If political impotence was matched by a seeming cultural impotence, then this was heightened by the lack of awareness of what was actually being created, of the ways individuals were reacting to the violence of the long months and years that followed 11 September 1973. It was then that the images, the sounds, the scenes and words that would be the source for, especially, song and theater were playing on the individual imagination and sensibility. Yet there could be no collective sense of this, for the process by which these are changed slowly, imperceptibly into "works" was only just beginning.

If the phrase "cultural blackout" was coined to express a lack of artistic activity, what, in retrospect, it really expressed was the invisibility of the arts, so evident in the previous years. While recognizing the contemporary relevance of such terms, I have tried to put them in the perspective of the moment by stepping back, perhaps as only an outsider can do, and looking at the way people have built on this period and given life through the theater to the most human reactions to the basest actions man can be capable of.

For a long period after the coup, the theater community sought a way out of a period of impasse. In plays about work and marginality, power relations, and finally exile—the basis for the chapters in this book—writers, actors, directors presented an overall image of a society that was paralyzed, where the conflict of the sixties had been eradicated. The characters did little; there was little conflict,

development or resolution; things happened far away, they were
suggested, rarely made explicit, but they defined the lives of the
characters on stage, who lived awaiting the moment of resolution of
a prolonged period of stalemate. Especially in the first period, the
characters echoed the general disorientation about the place of
theater in society: ". . . the protagonists didn't know what to do or
what to say, they had no one they could legitimately talk to, they
turned in circles, longing, remembering. . . ."[1] The very act of
creating these plays, usually through collective creation, was a way
out of the artistic impasse, but it was not without its problems. For,
all too often, the political role becomes an expectation, a demand
even, of the audience. Theater long accepted this political role,
"justifying" what had always been perceived in many sectors to be
an idle, unproductive existence. But this role is restricting, it becomes another form of inhibition, for demands for political expression do not always go hand in glove with the search for effective
artistic expression. And by the early eighties, a sense of "crisis"
began to emerge again. The questions being asked then revolved
around the central point of how theater could begin to cope with the
opening toward democracy, what space theater could occupy now
that the media was being allowed a louder voice and fulfilling its real
role. Recently, the search has become one for a new theater language, adequate to the late eighties, and in line with the constant
need for artistic exploration and renewal. I hope that through this
book, Chilean theater can speak to those who have not sat in the
theaters and that this in turn can tell of a world of experiences that,
while lived in a specific circumstance of dictatorship, do not belong
exclusively there. So often they are based on the individual experience within the collective.

In 1988 I returned to Chile and carried on a similar process of
observation, conversation, theater-going, and collecting information. Although this book does not deal with the period after 1985,
the visit added to the understanding of the development of theater
there, since in 1988 the regime's days seemed finally to be really
numbered. In September "la alegría ya venía," happiness was on its
way, the Plebiscite in which the Chilean people were to vote yes or
no to Pinochet was held. The No campaign used the simple, optimistic and recognizable images of the rainbow and spring. The Yes
campaign, like the characters we will see in *Baño a baño* [Bath to
bath], tried to turn spring on its head and make their own this
perennial symbol of renewal. They failed. The faces of blacklisted
actors and newscasters were seen again on television and, in a
fulfilment of Salvador Allende's last words to the nation from the

bombarded palace of government La Moneda, the great avenues of Santiago were filled with people demonstrating. Demonstrating their political preference and their sheer, pure, incredulous happiness.

In 1988 the Chilean people imbued the word *no* with hope and made it positive. And perhaps that is the most eloquent metaphor for the development of theater in Chile since 1973.

Acknowledgements

The funding for a research trip to Chile in 1985 was provided by the Scottish Education Department, and for a second trip in 1988 by the British Academy.

I wish to express my gratitude to all those who helped and encouraged me during my stays in Chile: to Dr. Ricardo Couyoumdjian for his initial support in, among other things, arranging access to the library facilities of the Universidad Católica in Santiago; to the librarians in the research centers and institutions I visited, especially to Isabel in the excellent theater library of the Drama School of the Universidad Católica, for their assistance in the search for material; to those people in CENECA (Centro de Indagación y Expresión Cultural y Artística) who offered help, friendship and advice; to the playwrights, actors, and directors who gave up their time to talk to me, answer my questions, and provide manuscripts of their largely unpublished work. The friendliness and cooperation of all these people have made my time in Chile memorable and productive. If they are not named individually here it is because they are present in every chapter of this book, and present in my memory, in my admiration for their work and their courage.

Two people have guided me through, first, my thesis and, then, my continuing study of theater in Latin America. They are James Higgins and María de la Luz Hurtado, who have given so much to the study of Latin American culture.

This book is dedicated with love to my parents.

Chilean Theater,
1973–1985

1
Historical Perspectives

Before 1941

It has long been undisputed that 1941 is the key year in the history of modern Chilean theater. This is the year of the founding of the Teatro Experimental de la Universidad de Chile by a group of students from the Instituto Pedagógico in Santiago, whose first productions, of *La guarda cuidadosa* [The cautious warden], a Cervantes entremés, and *Ligazón* [Liaison] by Valle Inclán, have been regarded as signifying the beginning of a new era in Chilean theater.[1] Before entering into the study of theater in Chile since 1973, I want to trace the steps taken before then, for they provide important insights into roles that theater has both played and defied. I want to explain why 1941 was so important and what made years like 1955, 1968, 1973, and 1978 significant in their turn. The answers to these questions lie in the historical, political, social, and cultural circumstances, both national and international, that led firstly to the formation of the Teatro Experimental and later to the central place of the university theaters as the "driving force" behind contemporary Chilean theater.[2]

In 1941 one of the determining social factors was the growing strength of the middle classes. Since the turn of the century, the power of the old land-owning aristocracy had been in decline, and economic power and wealth had been moving to new sectors, notably in the mining centers, industry, and commerce. In an article in 1930, the historian Ricardo A. Latcham pointed to the distance of the aristocracy from the reality of Chilean life, accusing them of a "spiritual mummification." He spoke of the emergent "studious" middle classes, made up of teachers, writers, journalists, lawyers, still effectively and comfortably marginalized from the political life of the nation, but alongside whom were emerging, "legiones más audaces, del mismo estrato social, que avanzan resueltas a la conquista del poder."[3]

By the 1920s there was a new generation of artists that was

composed substantially of people of middle-class extraction who were, by profession, teachers, journalists, civil servants.[4] Political power was "conquered" by these sectors in 1920 when Arturo Alessandri won the presidential election at the head of the Liberal Alliance, a coalition formed by the Radical and Democratic parties and some sectors of the Liberal party. From then the middle sectors grew in political strength until 1938 and the election of Pedro Aguirre Cerda and the Popular Front, when, "the state aparatus passed completely into the control of the middle sectors," who were organized through and linked primarily with the Radical party and socialism.[5]

How important was this in terms of theater? Hugo Montes and Julio Orlando, authors of *Historia y antología de la literatura chilena* [History and anthology of Chilean literature], provide a clue when they say that the dramatic form emerges most authentically and naturally in developed cultural circumstances, when there is a real dialogue between the art and the environment in which it is created.[6] The concentration of power in the middle sectors was accompanied, even preempted, by a search for dramatic expression that went beyond the superficial and picturesque costumbrism that had predominated in the early twentieth century. Opera and the facile hispanified dramas or foreign fare of touring companies may have satisfied the elitist, europeanized outlook of the old oligarchy, the hackneyed themes epitomizing their "mummification" and distance from Chilean reality, but by the thirties, the middle sectors, urban and educated, were actively seeking, demanding, and creating artistic expressions that were in tune with the Chile they were building politically, socially, and economically.

The environment in the late 1930s and 1940s was one of great cultural dynamism. Essayists such as Benjamín Subercaseaux and Ricardo Latcham turned their attention to the national character of the Chilean; Gabriela Mistral's work was gaining international acclaim, not always matched by national recognition, prior to her winning the Nobel prize for literature in 1945; Pablo Neruda, Chile's second Nobel prize poet (1971), produced his most famous early works; the writers Fernando Alegría and the generation of 1938 were exploring new forms of expression in prose; in 1938 the journal *Mandrágora* was founded in the Instituto Pedagógico de la Universidad de Chile, dealing not only with literature, but with art and philosophy. Education was the key to the rise of the middle classes, and the universities were to become the natural place for the fomenting of talent, of literary groups, of magazines. In the Universidad Católica, the School of Architecture became the

breeding ground for artists and sculptors such as Nemesio Antúnez
and Roberto Matta. And the two university theaters were founded
in the Instituto Pedagógico of the University of Chile and the
School of Architecture of the Universidad Católica.

Theater had floundered miserably since the 1920s.[7] Many commentators blamed the advent of the moving picture in 1929 for
tempting away the audiences and encouraging the empresarios of
the stage to convert their theater halls for the more lucrative cinema
business, but this was not the only cause (indeed, as Julio Durán
Cerda says, it did have a positive side since the architectural plans
for many of the city center halls made provision for small theaters,
which were later to be used as *teatros de bolsillo*"[8]). In fact,
productions in the theater were of bad quality, too often still the
products of a worn-out costumbrism, and did not satisfy audiences
in search of expression such as could be found in painting, sculp-
ture, poetry, and the novel. The decline of the Chilean theater in the
years from 1928 to 1938 was notorious:

> Desde *La viuda de Apablaza* no se adelanta un paso en esa senda
> naturalista. Ni en otras. Viene un interregno en el que el teatro chileno
> arrastra una existencia anémica, sostenida por una producción
> mostrenca y rutinaria, encaminada únicamente a la obtención de un
> pronto lucro económico de empresarios, actores cabezas de compañías
> y autores. La depresión financiera mundial desatada por aquellos
> aciagos años del 30 se conjuraba también en esa mengua artística. Con
> frecuencia, los propios directores de conjuntos arreglaban una pieza
> ajena o la escribían ellos mismos, aprovechando circunstancias de la
> actualidad política, todas de ínfimo valor, con que medraban en aquel
> marasmo. Proliferó un tipo de obras menores, de mezquino aliento
> costumbrista que solían integrar programas de variedades o de comple-
> mento de alguna obra mayor, incapaz de llenar por sí sola una función,
> o, en fin, acababan presentaciones radiofónicas de auspicio comer-
> cial.[9]

> [After *The Widow of Apablaza* not one step is taken along the path of
> naturalism. Nor along any other path. There is an intervening period in
> which Chilean theater leads a dull, anemic existence, sustained by
> monstrous, routine productions, aimed only at swift economic profit by
> entrepeneurs, actor-directors and authors. The international economic
> depression of those fearful years of the thirties also contrived to add to
> this artistic low. Often, the directors of companies adapted another
> author's work, or they wrote one themselves, that took advantage of
> contemporary political circumstances; all of these works were of the
> lowest level, and with these they thrived in that period of stagnation.
> There proliferated a kind of minor work with a slight costumbrist

leaning, that would appear in variety shows or would accompany a more important work that could not on its own make up a complete program, or else they were involved in radio productions under commercial auspices.]

In 1935, in an attempt to provide incentives for national drama, a law was passed creating the Dirección Superior del Teatro Nacional, designed to protect authors' copyrights, to promote theater through prizes, to subsidize foreign companies performing Chilean works, to form touring companies and, perhaps most importantly, to free from taxes those companies whose cast was 75 percent Chilean and that performed primarily Chilean works.[10] These measures are an important indicator of the general cultural atmosphere, but for the immediate reasons behind what can only be called the birth of modern theater in Chile in 1941 we have to look to direct artistic influence.

The outstanding source of inspiration for theater in the thirties was the exodus of many artists from Spain in the throes of the Civil War.[11] Among these was Margarita Xirgú, whose company arrived in Chile in 1938. The tour was a revelation to the Chilean audience, exposing the underdevelopment of Chilean theater, the unadventurous use of the stage, and the dated treatment of themes. Nothing could compare with the combined talents of García Lorca, Margarita Xirgú, and Savador Dalí. It was this unveiling of the failings of the Chilean stage that finally prompted the founding of the university theaters.

1941: The University Theaters

According to Carlos Miguel Suárez Radillo, by 1941 it had become "indispensable" to create "un movimiento teatral de extracción culta y proyección auténticamente nacional."[12] The members of the Teatro Experimental were acutely aware of the task before them, a task they saw in terms of breaking the old mold of theater in Chile and revitalizing the national stage as a true reflection of society. They set out four aims: "Difusión del teatro clásico y moderno; formación del teatro escuela; creación de un ambiente teatral; presentación de nuevos valores."[13]

The first aim, the diffusion of classical and modern theater, was intended as a return to the roots of drama, especially of the Hispanic tradition, in the belief that the only way to learn about theater was to start from the beginning. Productions of the classics and modern drama were, furthermore, part of the education of the theater-going public, and as such they have remained in the repertoires of the university theaters until the present day. The founding of a drama school was intended as a means of ridding the stage of the "monstruous" productions of old by creating professional actors, directors, scenographers. A school was first founded by Agustín Siré in 1949. Initially it had no financial backing and the courses were given by "profesores ad honorem," who did the best they could to provide a three-year course. It was not until 1959 that a school was formally established and became the Instituto de Teatro de la Universidad de Chile (ITUCH).

The third aim, the creation of a theater atmosphere, was based in the ideal of attracting an audience from sectors other than the old theater and opera-going elite, that is, from the middle and working classes. This was done partly through the *teatros carpa,* mobile theaters that performed primarily Chilean works in working class districts both in the capital and the provinces. Amateur groups were encouraged through festivals—the first of which, the Festival de Teatro Aficionado, was held in 1955—held every two years until 1968. But the real success of the creation of this atmosphere in which theater could thrive is to be found in the founding of other university groups and schools. The Teatro de la Universidad Católica, TEUC, was founded in 1943, in the innovative School of Architecture. This was followed by the Teatro de la Universidad de Concepción, TUC, in 1947, and the theater and school at the Universidad Católica in Valparaíso in 1958; in the same year TEKNOS, the theater of the recently founded Universidad Técnica del Estado, was established; and in 1962, a theater was set up in the Universidad de Antofagasta in the north.

The "presentation of new values," the fourth objective, refers to the encouragement of a new, professional approach to the theater, and new "men of the theater," especially dramatists. This was promoted through an annual drama competition, the winning work of which would be produced in a collaboration between the author and the group. During the forties, dramatist such as Zlatco Brncic (*Elsa Margarita,* 1943) and Enrique Bunster (*Un velero sale del puerto* [A sailing ship leaves port], 1943) presented prize-winning dramas, favored for their innovative qualities. Julio Durán Cerda talks of their "atmósfera alegórica, de alta ficción poética, de fantasía, de ensueño, de personajes interesantes, de acontecimientos mágicos."[14] The theater of these dramatists was a step away from the purely Chilean themes portrayed in costumbrism; they sought to be universal and absorbed the influence of the modern greats, of García Lorca, Eugene O'Neill, Maeterlinck.

If 1941 is the year of the emergence of the university theaters, then 1955—when three "women of the theater," María Asunción Requena, Gabriela Roepke, and Isidora Aguirre, presented their first works—is the year of the emergence of the university dramatists. In the early fifties, there was a resurrection of the Chilean classics that reached its highest point in 1954, "sin duda una de las fechas de la escena chilena moderna,"[15] when the Teatro de Ensayo de la Universidad Católica presented Santiago del Campo's adaptation of *Martín Rivas,* the nineteenth-century novel by Blest Gana. Martín Rivas is a classic Chilean hero, the embodiment of the highest Chilean values; the novel is set in a period of the awakening consciousness of the middle classes and culminates in the Liberal uprising of 1851. After a ten-year parade of the wealth of international drama, both classic and modern, the stage was set for a return to the exploration of the essence of being Chilean, a search that has to this day remained at the heart of the country's drama.

The University Dramatists

The greatest testimony to the importance of the university dramatists lies in the fact that their work, old and new, continues to fill a significant part of the theater repertoire. While I do not intend to enter into a long discussion of these playwrights, I do want to introduce some of the key plays, suggesting shared thematic trends and preoccupations and illustrating the wealth of productivity that, soon after, made the years between 1955 and 1970 seem like golden years.[16]

The names that occupy the greatest space during these years are Isidora Aguirre, María Asunción Requena, Luis Alberto Heiremans, Egon Wolff, Fernando Debesa, Sergio Vodanović, Jorge Díaz, Alejandro Sieveking. What did these dramatists, born of the conditions that the university theaters had created, write about? Julio Durán Cerda talks about three main trends, the historic, the sociopsychological, and the poetic. The historic was represented by dramatists like María Asunción Requena, whose first play, *Fuerte Bulnes* [Fort Bulnes] (1955), was a historical drama about the lives of the colonists of the region of Magallanes in the extreme south in the nineteenth century. Her *El camino más largo* [The longest road] (1959) is the story of Chile's first woman doctor, Ernestina Pérez;

and *Ayayema* (1964) studied the lives of the almost extinct "alcalufe" Indians of the south in their fight for survival, and the conflict between them and the corrupting influence of the white traders. Fernando Debesa's *Mama Rosa* [Nanny Rosa] (1955) dealt with the life of an aristocratic family over the first half of this century, and that of their *mama*, the traditional nanny who becomes an integral part of their family life. It is fundamentally the story of the decline of the old aristocracy, of the family conflicts involved in their adaptation to the changing structures of society, and of the fate of the servants, which was intrinsically linked to that of the family. His other play of this period, *Bernardo O'Higgins* (1961), is a dramatization of the life of the great libertator, of the wars of Independence, and his death in exile in Peru.

Both Egon Wolff and Sergio Vodanović studied the middle classes in realist and psychological drama. All of Egon Wolff's output—*Discípulos de miedo* [Disciples of fear] (1958), *Mansión de lechuzas* [House of owls] (1958), *Parejas de trapo* [Rag couples] (1959), *Niñamadre* [Childmother] (1962)—was related to the middle classes, to their inherent limitations, linked, above all, to the deep fear of the loss of their position in society. His best known works of the period up until 1973, *Los invasores* [The invaders] (1963) and *Flores de papel* [Paper flowers] (1970) are nightmare renderings of this fear and its realization, *Los invasores* dealing with a dream of the invasion of the dispossessed into a wealthy home, a dream, it is suggested in the last moments of the play, that will turn into reality.

Sergio Vodanović studied problems of individual integrity and social justice in *El senador no es honorable* [The untrustworthy senator] (1953) and *Deja que los perros ladren* [Let the dogs bark] (1959), and then to social satire in *Viña: Tres comedias en traje de baño* [Viña: Three comedies in bathing suit] (1964). And Fernando Cuadra's plays also fell into a psychological realist mold, with such works as *La niña en la palomera* [The girl in the attic] (1966), based on the true story of the kidnap of an adolescent girl, in which the author studies the impossible dreams and aspirations of a teenage girl from a lower-class family.

Other dramatists wrote in a more poetic style. Gabriela Roepke's small output, including *Las santas mujeres* [The holy women] (1955) and *Una mariposa blanca* [A white butterfly] (1955), verges on the absurd. Alejandro Sieveking's work has involved the psychological study of tense human relationships in *Mi hermano Cristián* [My brother Christian] (1957), *Parecido a la felicidad* [Something like happiness] (1962), and the poetic folklore of *Animas de día claro* [Spirits by daylight] (1962) and *La remolienda* [Rave-up]

(1965). The most acclaimed poetic dramatist was Luis Alberto Heiremans, who died of cancer in 1964 at the age of thirty six. He was the author of the first musical comedy, *La señorita Trini* [Miss Trini] (1958), to be performed in Chile. The protagonists of his major works, *Sigue la estrella* [Follow the star], *Los güenos versos* [The good verses] (1958), *Versos de ciego* [Verses of the blind] (1960) and *El abanderado* [The outlaw] (1962), inhabit a poetic world of popular tradition and religious symbolism. Heiremans had looked forward to a dramatic form that would "stylize" realism by delving into the symbolic depths of the individual, and create existential studies of "the anguished condition of man".[17]

Jorge Díaz was the first Chilean dramatist to exploit the theater of the absurd. As in the case of Wolff and Vodanović, his frame of reference is the world of the middle classes, but while being based in this external reality, his plays of this period do not aim at psychological interpretations. Rather, they lay bare the emptiness of the social values accepted by the middle classes, his audience. In *El cepillo de dientes* [The toothbrush] (1961) he attacked the standard, sterile world of modern man, the vicious circles of ritual and incomprehension, the inherent absurdity of life. *El velero en la botella* [The ship in a bottle] (1965) ostensibly looks at youth in society (the theme of *La niña en la palomera* (1966), *El wurlitzer* [The jukebox] (1964) by Juan Guzmán Améstica), through the protagonist, a boy born into a world where communication is impossible, but essentially it is a play about the power or impotence of language as expression. In other works, notably *Topografía de un desnudo* [Topography of a naked man] (1966), Díaz joined other dramatists in a study of the marginal sectors of Latin American life, namely those who live on the rubbish tips, whose lives and deaths are of no import to anyone and who live sunk in endless misery. His is a drama of the coherence of the absurd in a world such as that created around the interests of the Latin American bourgeoisie.

Isidora Aguirre, whose first plays had been light comedy such as *Carolina* (1955), also turned to social comment in *Población Esperanza* [Shanty town called Hope] (1959), which deals with the growing problem of the *poblaciones callampas,* shanty towns that had begun to spring up around the major cities in the fifties as a result of the incapacity to accommodate the growing number of migrants from rural areas. And *Los papeleros* [The paper gatherers] (1963) is a brechtian play about the miserable life of the people who live on the rubbish tips, gathering paper that they then sell for miserable rates to the owner, who, in turn, sells it to factories as raw material. As in *Población Esperanza,* the central theme is the need for the deprived sectors of the community to fight together for a better way of life, a fight that is undertaken in the shanty town but that is impossible in the rubbish tip of *Los papeleros.*

One of the most successful theater productions of all time in Chile has been *La pérgola de las flores* [The flower market] (1960) by Isidora Aguirre in collaboration with Francisco Flores del Campo. It is a musical comedy that deals with the flower sellers whose market was beside the San Francisco church in the Alameda, the central avenue through Santiago. In 1929 their market was threatened with demolition and removal to another site when a plan to widen the Alameda was proposed. The proposal was supremely unpopular and the level of public protest, allied with the fight put up by the flower sellers, won the market a respite of 15 years. The play had an unprecedented run of 976 performances and was a huge success in Europe when the Teatro de la Universidad Católica went on tour in 1961. The success of *La pérgola de las flores,* light entertainment in the tradition of the Spanish *zarzuela,* is proof that a wide audience was in existence, for it is wrong to suppose that the theater of the university dramatists existed in isolation. Alongside it, in the halls of Santiago, what came to be regarded as pre-university companies continued, catering for a public that sought light entertainment, melodramas, farces.

The actor, director, and dramatist Lucho Córdoba's main aim— from 1937, when he set up his own company with his wife Olvido Leguía, until his death in 1980—was to provide simple entertainment. His comedies were in the old mold, centered around a principal character usually played by himself (the principal character in the plays aged at the same speed as the actor), and his works were generally in the *sainete* form. While his plays took place in a never-changing vacuum, humorous social allusions to contemporary events were never far from his work, which was firmly rooted as a stationary "afirmación de la clase media acomodada . . . en su mejor momento".[18] Another husband and wife team, Américo Vargas and Pury Durante, who survived until 1980, provided a similar style of light entertainment, again involving lighthearted satirical commentary and also including high comedy from the international repertoire. These companies and a few more—the most famous being the companies of Alfredo Moya-Grau (1956–66) and of Silvia Piñeiro and Miguel Frank—provide a constant in Chilean theater, on the margins of and largely impervious to the political upheavals of later periods. The theater-going audience in

Santiago has never been exclusively composed of conscientious, politically active leftist middle-class intellectuals, for there is always an audience for musicals and comedies.

By the fifties, Chile was widely held to be at the forefront of the theater in Latin America. Willis Knapp Jones, writing about the theater season in 1957, declares that finally "Chilean dramatists had come into their own" and adds: "Of all the countries I visited in my winter theater circuit, I could put Chile at the top for abundance and excellence of plays, and when it comes to a national theater, in the sense of playwrights and themes that are products of the country, there is no other South American nation even near to it."[19] The themes in Chilean theater were still primarily a treatment of local reality, but now with a greater emphasis on the study of the psychology of the middle classes. By the sixties, the social face of Chile was changing rapidly and new sectors were calling for power. These were the sectors that began to provide the newest characters and situations for the stage.

1967: The University Reform

The diffusion of theater in Chile had never been so great or so seriously undertaken as in the fifties and sixties; there had never been so many good dramatists. Yet between 1966 and 1969 the number of original works began to diminish.[20] By 1966 the perennial problems that heralded impending "crisis," those of the relevance of Chilean theater to the immediate social environment and of the diminishing size of the theater-going public, were again being named. Two factors serve to explain this. Firstly, in 1962, television had made its debut for the coverage of the World Cup, held in Chile that year. The immediate impact was hardly noticeable, for television was too expensive for a large sector of the population, but as prices fell and savings and credit plans became more common, it soon began to affect theater audience numbers.

The other reason has to do with the very nature of the theaters created through the universities. The sixties were years of rapid social change. The Christian Democrats were elected in 1964 under the leadership of Eduardo Frei, with a far-reaching social reform program, the "revolution in liberty." They were in power until 1970, when the Popular Unity coalition won the general elections and Salvador Allende was elected president. Their program was the radical "Chilean road to Socialism," and the revolutionary intent of Popular Unity satisfied the anti-imperialist, Cuba-inspired ideology of the intellectual left wing by promising a greater commitment to a Chile free from political, economic, and cultural domination. This involved the rejection of foreign cultural domination, which was seen by the prevailing ideology as an essentially alienating force that had moved from a general "extranjerización" to the more perfidious "norteamericanización."[21] The universities were both a mirror of and an agent for change in society, and university theater was far from immune to the political polarization of these years. The most important cultural/political event of the late sixties was the University Reform of 1967.

The process of university reform began in 1967 in the Universidad Católica de Valparaíso and culminated in the occupation of the central building of the Universidad Católica de Santiago in August of the same year. Rooted in the ideal of active democracy, the main objectives of the university reform were the democratization of the university system in order to halt the exclusion of large sectors from access to education, and a demand for academics to step down from the ivory towers they traditionally inhabited. These goals were broadly summed up as "external democratization" and "internal democratization."

University theater schools became part of inter- or multidisciplinary academic structures. In 1968, ITUCH became DETUCH (Departamento de Teatro de la Universidad de Chile), which in 1969 became part of La Facultad de Ciencias y Artes Musicales y de la Representación that grouped together music, dance, and theater. As part of this new faculty, DETUCH defined an outlook that went hand in glove with the dominant antidependency leftist ideology and sought to create "un teatro nuevo que responda a la ideología de la Nueva Universidad: anti-imperialista y anti-burguesa."[22] Theater was regarded as an instrument for the promotion of social change and almost without exception works were chosen for their relation to the political and ideological atmosphere.

A brief look at the plays performed by DETUCH during the period provides ample evidence of the policy in practice. In 1969 *El Evangelio según San Jaime* [The Gospel according to Saint James] by Jaime Silva became one of the few plays by a Chilean author to have provoked a real public outcry. It is a grotesquely ridiculous version of the New Testament written in verse in *huaso* Chilean,[23] set in the feudal land system. God the Father is "un tirano y un patrón" governing earth through fear, while Jesus Christ is a revolutionary hero whose mission on earth is to incite rebellion among the peasants and bring down the tyranny of his Father. Mary's Immaculate Conception is announced after her meeting in the garden with an absurdly phallic "Gallo Intrusivo," Joseph is referred to throughout as "El Sordo José," and Mary's marriage to such a man is greeted by one of her neighbors with the words, "De sólo verlos/ me dan ganas de llorar" (p. 16). *El Evangelio según San Jaime* touched the fragile sensibilities of the middle-class audience. Hans Ehrmann details some of the attacks the play received: outrage from the Opus Dei, attacks on provincial tours, tear gas and stink bombs on the opening night, demonstrations, and masses to ask divine forgiveness. The vehemence of these attacks led the critic to conclude, "Chile is free, easy and democratic on the surface, but once God and Country are touched on aggressively, the silent majority comes to life."[24] The intensity of the middle and upper classes' defence of God and Country would later be seen in more concrete terms in their support of the military coup.

The same year DETUCH presented Isidora Aguirre's *Los que van quedando en el camino* [The ones left by the wayside], which tells of the massacre of peasants in Ranquil in 1934. Set in 1969, it uses a peasant woman as the vehicle for the narration of the Ranquil massacre. By juxtaposing these two dates, the author sets out to compare two periods of agrarian reform,[25] with the accompanying expectations and ultimate disillusion of the peasants. The play is divided into two parts, "Los días buenos" and "Los días malos." The peasant women tries to remember only the good days, when the battles against the limitations of the peasants—illiteracy, fear, lack of unity, faith in paternalism—were undertaken and the peasants began to set up their own movements. But she is haunted by the "ánimas," the spirits of those who had died during the bad days, which began with the change of government and the ensuing retreat on the agrarian reform and culminated in the revolt, when the peasants found themselves isolated and without support. The "ánimas" represent the need for organization and solidarity, and through them the didactic message of the play is presented: that even those who seemingly died for nothing and with no awareness of the worth of their sacrifice gave their lives for the revolutionary cause: "De los que van quedando en el camino también se hacen las revoluciones."[26]

In 1971 DETUCH productions showed a preoccupation with the decadence of the middle classes. *El degenérisis* (1971) by Edmundo Villarroel and Jorge Rebel was described by one critic as "un estudio teatralizado de la alienación de la clase media chilena," but its impact on critics and public was minimal.[27] Their other production that year, Chekov's *The Cherry Orchard,* was interpreted by its Uruguayan director as dealing with the theme of "un mundo muerto, agotado, que va hacia otro más feliz, hacia una nueva realidad",[28] an interpretation that reflected the hoped-for demise of bourgeois society to be replaced by Popular Unity's "nueva sociedad." Another review is very definite about this, seeing the play as dealing with the problems of a failing regime in its last days:

> Sus personas están aferradas a un mundo que comienza a declinar desplazado por la clase trabajadora y el despertar de la lucha social. La tierra deja de ser, desde el momento en que se vende el jardín de los cerezos, propiedad y dominio de una minoría inconsciente que sufre por la pérdida de sus bienes.[29]

> [The characters cling to a world that is in decline, displaced by the working class and the stirrings of the social struggle. From the moment the cherry orchard is sold land ceases to be the property and domain of a socially unaware minority that suffers because of the loss of its possessions.]

Gerardo Werner's *La gran prescripción* [The great prescription] (1972) was based on the case of the Nazi war criminal Walter Rauff, who found refuge in Chile, where he could not be brought to justice, partly because Chilean legislation does not contemplate the crime of genocide and also because too long a period had elapsed since his crimes for him to be tried under Chilean law. It was intended by the author as a warning against the ever-present danger of fascism (read, the forces of the opposition against the Popular Unity peaceful road to socialism).

Also in 1972, María Asunción Requena's *Chiloé cielos cubiertos* [Chiloé, gray skies] dealt with a community in the island of Chiloé, in the south of the country, composed primarily of women who await with resignation the return of their menfolk, who are forced to leave the island in search of work and rarely return. It assumes the poetic mix of myth and reality peculiar to Chiloé, when the young protagonist resists "woman's destiny" by abandoning her husband on their wedding day and surrendering her love to the ghost of a young shipwrecked sailor. In this way she chooses love in death, defying the "defeat" that marriage would mean for her, and seeks instead hope and happiness. Through this mythical element Requena evoked the limited fate and alternatives of the women of Chiloé, and through elements of social realism, such as representing fledgling development projects, she exposed the problems of an island in a state of dire economic underdevelopment.

In the Universidad Católica during this period, similar changes were under way. In 1967 the Teatro de Ensayo had been dissolved, and became the Centro de Teatro of the newly organized Escuela de Artes de la Comunicación (EAC), which united teachers, researchers, and artists from the fields of theater, film, and television. The aim was to enrich the contact between those involved in the communicating arts and to put an end to the traditional isolation of one from the other. Between 1968 and 1969 a new group, the Taller de Experimentación Teatral, presented three works, and in 1970–71 another group, the Taller de Creación Teatral, worked under the direction of Eugenio Dittborn, former director of the Teatro de Ensayo.

Whereas the Universidad de Chile displayed a radical thematic line in tune with the ideal of motivating political change, in the Universidad Católica above all in the Taller de Experimetación Teatral, the "democratization" called for in the university reform was internalized in their preference for workshops and collective creation, a form that involved greater collaboration between all the members of the creative team and that was deemed to end the "tyranny" of the director. The first workshop production was *Peligro a 50 metros* [Danger at 50 meters] (1968), based on texts by Alejandro Sieveking and José Pineda. The first part, *Obras de Misericordia* [Works of Pity] by José Pineda, takes the form of a "symposium" in which seven corporal and spiritual acts of charity as practised by the bourgeoisie are analysed. This idea gives unity to the ensuing systematic denunciation of the bourgeoisie, attacking repressive education, hypocritical attitudes to sex, the generation gap, hippies and Christian duty; bourgeois society and North American imperialism are allotted the blame for the greatest part of the suffering in the world. The second part, *Una vaca mirando el piano* [A cow watching the piano], by Sieveking, repeats the oversimplifying pattern and is a parable on apathy and individualism in a world where luxury and depravation usurp the public imagination, leaving nothing but indifference for real social problems.

In effect the work is far from "revolutionary", for it falls into the trap of much theater that aims to be revolutionary. As Domingo Piga put it:

En esta búsqueda de nuevas formas, se ha llegada a la falacia de creer que un teatro es popular y revolucionario en la medida que lo es formalmente, por sobre toda otra consideración. . . . se ha caído en el formalismo de conceder más importancia a la forma, a la estructura nueva de una obra, al valor externo revolucionario, aunque su contenido sea débil.[30]

[In this search for new forms, people have mistakenly come to believe that a theater is popular and revolutionary insofar as it is in the formal sense, over and above any other consideration. . . . People have fallen into the convention of giving more importance to the form, the new structure of a work, to its external revolutionary worth, even though its content may be weak.]

The revolutionary message of *Peligro a 50 metros* was no more than a regurgitation of views that were clichéd even by then.

The next production, *Nos tomamos la universidad* [We occupied the university] by Sergio Vodanović, deals with the occupation of the central building of the Universidad Católica at the height of the university reform in 1967. Although this is an "obra de autor," it lends itself to collective work and improvisation. The author's notes advocate sparseness of decoration and restraint in the use of effects to separate scenes, in order to achieve openness of the stage; they suggest the use of the actors' Christian names; and invite a fair amount of ad-libbing throughout the play.[31] The play revolves around the activities of one group of students who take part in the sit-in and whose task it is to make a "monigote" (puppet) of the old rector to be burned on the day of triumph. The characters are, on the whole, poorly defined stereotypes whose value lies in that they represent different personal motives for taking part in the occupation, ranging from the need to belong, a reaction against a strict upbringing, the longing to remain young, the search for the renewal of past, betrayed ideals. The "monigote" they make is essentially a symbol of decay. This is dramatized through the process of its creation: Sylvia, its artist, first draws an angelic face and then transforms it: "Subrayé los rasgos. La sonrisa pasó a ser una mueca. Lo que era armonioso se convirtió en una caricatura" [I underlined all the features. The smile became a grimace. Everything that was harmonious became caricature]. (p. 91). The transformation the puppet undergoes is a parallel to their experience: from a picture of idealism and unity, it becomes one of disillusion and disunity. The protagonists' disillusion is born when they find out that political and personal interests have joined to work out a compromise with the university authorities and that the puppet must not be burned, lest an act of such overt symbolism offend. The final scene juxtaposes the triumphal "Himno de la Toma" with the despondent words of the group of students who know they have been failed, and, through a character who, as a child, witnessed his elders suffering similar deceptions, the play suggests that history repeats itself in rounds of illusion and betrayal.

In 1970 the Taller de Creación Teatral presented *Todas las color-inas tienen pecas* [All redheads have freckles], a work in three acts based on *Obra gruesa* [Gross work] by the poet Nicanor Parra. On the whole, *Todas las colorinas tienen pecas* was lukewarmly received. As with other works that Parra has written in collaboration with theater groups, there is an inherent contradiction in theme, presentation, style, and attitude toward the audience. Parra's anti-poetry resists political classification, for it does not profess revolution in partisan terms, but aims to subvert accepted codes of thinking and behaving by gnawing away at the linguistic edifice that houses the status quo by revealing the emptiness of the staunchly guarded petit bourgeois world. The inconsistency arises from the fact that he has often been part of a creative team that imposes narrowly defined political messages, working within the kind of conventional political framework that is the target of Parra's attack. This leads to a certain unevenness in the work, as a result of which the audience is alternatively cajoled with familiar, conformist political views, or *épaté* by a poet who seeks to undermine the very foundations of their cultural being.

After the dismal failure of the next production, *Paraíso para uno* [Paradise for one], based on stories by Alfonso Alcalde, the Taller de Creación Teatral was dissolved and the Centro de Teatro returned to the directorship of Eugenio Dittborn and a run of "obras de autor": two Latin American works—*La gotera en el comedor* [The drip in the dining room] by the Uruguayan Jacobo Langser, examining the attitudes of the Latin American middle classes in times of political crisis; and *Tres de última* [Three of the best] by the Argentinian Alberto Paredes, focusing on questions of love in a revolutionary atmosphere—and two works by Chileans of the pre-university generation, *Alzame en tus brazos* [Lift me in your arms] by Armando Moock and *Almas Perdidas* [Lost souls] by Antonio Acevedo Hernández. In effect, this followed the original Teatro de Ensayo policy of introducing Latin American theater and popularizing Chilean authors.

In the other university theaters, the pattern is broadly similar. The Teatro de la Universidad Técnica del Estado, TEKNOS, was one of the most dynamic groups. In 1968 TEKNOS produced *Pan caliente* [Hot bread] by María Asunción Requena. *Pan caliente* deals with the tensions created in the community of a *población callampa* when one person introduces exceptional social aspirations. The central character is a teenage girl, Marisela, who has lived and attended school outside the shanty town. She has grown to have great expectations from life, her driving force being the illusion of moving on in the world away from the squalor of her origins. The central conflict is between her and a young man, Juanucho, who dreams of organizing the shanty town dwellers to fight for their rights, and the central tension derives from the disdain these two characters have for each other's dreams. The drama develops around the saga of the white dress Marisela must have for her school-leaving ceremony and that her mother has made at great cost. When her drunken father finds the dress, he hugs it, believing it to be an angel, and soils it so much as to destroy it. The community clubs together to provide another dress and the fare for a taxi to take her to the ceremony, and Juanucho contributes, despite his disdain for Marisela's upward aspirations. Marisela, having experienced the kindness of her own people, begins to understand "the soul of these miserable, bad-smelling people."

The moral of *Pan Caliente* is made explicit toward the end of the play in the words of an old man who tries to help Juanucho understand why such poor people should choose to spend their money on a dress rather than on the necessities of life. He compares their reward to bread, "hot bread, fresh from the oven," one of the simplest, but best things in life: instead of buying food for their hunger, they feed their reserves of community and caring. On one hand, the destroyed dress is a symbol of the impossibility of surviving without stain in such an environment, but on the other, it is a symbol of the possibility of triumph through community spirit.

The adherence to a politically defined thematic content found expression as agitprop in the works of the Teatro Nuevo Popular, founded in 1971 in the Universidad Ténica del Estado as a pilot group of the Central Unica de Trabajadores (CUT). It aimed to defy the theatrical norms of the professional stage by taking theater to working-class areas all over the country, producing works with the minimum of stage clutter, and opening theater to all by not charging an entrance fee. *La maldición de la palabra* (The curse of the word), by Manuel Garrido, dealt with the attempts of a group of peasants to form a trade union and focused primarily on the limitations of their ability to do so as a result of their lack of education. Like Isidora Aguirre's *Los que van quedando en el camino, La maldición de la palabra* explores the need for the peasant and the worker to be in control of their own means of expression. In 1972, with the same theme and aims, the Teatro Nuevo Popular presented *Tela de cebolla* (Onion skin), written by Gloria Cordero after a period of observation and research undertaken with the actors in a textile factory that was taken over by the workers in a *toma*.[32] *Tela de cebolla* uses a historical perspective to expose the process through which the workers become aware of the levels of political, economic, and sexual exploitation they suffer and gradually, with the Chilean road to Socialism, become the owners of what they produce. When it was presented to the workers who actually took part in the *toma,* it caused a good deal of argument, with the actors being accused of missing out important details. One critic points to the advantages to be gained from such an experience: "La confrontación de esta experiencia con el juicio de los obreros espectadores enriquecerá sin duda a los artistas para evitar el esquematismo, la caricatura fácil, el mensaje político con-signístico, desligado de la imagen artística" [The confrontation between this experience and the judgment of the workers in the audience will undoubtedly enrich the artists so that in the future they avoid schematism, facile caricatures, simplistic political messages disconnected with the artistic image].[33]

In the Universidad de Concepción the efforts to promote theater were well coordinated, but they were not without problems.[34] While the more traditional plays were boycotted by some because, in the opinion of one critic, "TUC se quedó al margen de la reforma . . . carece de una línea artística definida . . . no es un grupo 'compro-metido.' " The new works, often by the Taller Experimental, such as *La revolución nuestra de cada día* (Our daily revolution) by Juan Curilem, were, on the other hand, boycotted by those with a more traditional attitude because, the same critic suggests, the opinion was that "se dan puras obras para rotos."[35] A traditional middle class audience obviously felt insulted by the propaganda being presented them.

An integral part of the place of theater in the "new" society was the importance given to amateur theater. Universities had first shown interest in the promotion of amateur theater in 1955 when the Universidad de Chile, in line with its policy of creating "un ambiente teatral," organized the first Festival Nacional del Teatro Aficionado e Independiente, which was subsequently held every two years until 1969. In 1961 Orlando Rodríguez noted the growing strength of the festival and suggested that amateur theater was more innovative and adventurous than professional theater. Out of sixty-five works presented that year, thirty-six were by authors of Chilean origin and fifteen were original Chilean plays. Psychological realism, which was the most popular form in professional theater, did not figure as prominently as works dealing with social, political and regional problems, dramatized in forms that used collective creation and showed the influence of Brecht and Ionesco.[36]

By 1968, when the call for radical change was gaining momentum, critics of the paternalistic organization of the festivals began to see the links with university theater as restricting and as the major impediment to the further development of amateur theater. In that year, the last Festival Nacional de Teatro Aficionado e Independiente was held, and the same year the first Festival de Teatro Universitario y Obrero de la Universidad Católica took place under the auspices of the recently created Vicerrectoría de Comunicaciones, among whose functions was that of supporting the organization of the many amateur groups in the country.[37] During this festival a seminar entitled "Realidad Actual y Proyecciones Futuras del Teatro Aficionado" was held and the Asociación Nacional de Teatro Aficionado (ANTACH) was formed to unite and organize amateur groups in the country, to provide training schools, and to guide the groups through "coordinators" and "monitors." Organizational matters were dealt with and new activities planned; again festivals were the centerpiece for the diffusion of popular drama and these were held regularly.[38] With this seminar, the lengthy "analytical study" of the role and proposed development of amateur theater began.

ANTACH proposed the emancipation from university influence, which was seen to thwart the creative capacity of amateur groups, it rejected "imported" works, repudiated a theater for elites that was purely artistic and entertaining, and called for the creation of a theater "for the masses and by the masses." The themes and dramatic forms employed would, in theory, make it possible to make theater into "una herramienta de pedagogía jovial": amateur theater as organized by ANTACH was to be a vehicle for political education. It was not until 1972 that ANTACH finally stepped out of the wing of university sponsorship, when the Universidad Católica withdrew support from a process that was becoming ever more radical. At this point ANTACH entered what was defined as a new and definitive stage of authenticity. But what did this imply?

The answer is graphically illustrated in the only festival to be organized by the "new" ANTACH. This, the first Jornada Nacional de Teatro de Trabajadores y Estudiantes, took place in the province of Coquimbo in the north of the country (held there as a way of decentralizing the organization). Seventeen groups took part in this meeting, and eighty-seven performances were given in total, with an overall audience of around fifteen thousand. The themes treated were primarily those of the class struggle and the contemporary political environment. While prize-giving was frowned upon, a committee judged each group's level of artistic development and political commitment in terms of the level of "reflexión y análisis relacionados con el proceso que vive nuestro país," the use of collective creation, and the presence of a "política teatral."[39] The categories into which groups were classified bears witness to the nature of the assessment: "Advanced Groups" were those that displayed a solid relation between their work and the dynamics of the Popular Unity process; "transitional," those who, as the name suggests, were slowly developing but were still not fully in line; "Grupos Desubicados," those who failed to respond to the objectives of amateur theater as outlined by ANTACH in discussion and training, that is, those who were out of line with the Popular Unity process. Amateur theater as defined by ANTACH was essentially agitprop. Collective creation was regarded as the best form through which to articulate the members' experiences, plays were required to be politically clear, and they were largely based on sketches revolving around shallow social types, presenting black and white renderings of problems and their solutions. The objective was to provide an educational experience for the audience.

An Encuentro Nacional de Directores de Teatro in May 1973 set about the reorganization of the association, primarily in terms of the search for different sources of financial support and the planning of the activities for 1973–74, but this was ANTACH's last activity and the coup saw the complete disarticulation of the organization. By this time there were 350 affiliated groups. There is no doubt that ANTACH's claims of "masificación" were justified.

The nature and growth of ANTACH in the years 1970–73 must be seen in a political light. At the first Convención Nacional de Teatro Aficionado in 1968, Orlando Rodríguez spoke in no vague terms about the development of bourgeois theater:

> Su teatro, el burgués, entretenerá, o a lo más satirizará a la propia burguesía, pero nunca impulsará el reemplazo de esta burguesía por los sectores mayoritarios de la sociedad. Porque si ello ocurriera, el autor y sus intérpretes serán rechazados por el medio social burgués. Entonces, remitiéndose al caso de Chile, no puede haber un teatro popular donde los intereses de las minorías determinan el arte y culturas nacionales."[40]

> [Their theater, bourgeois theater, will entertain, or at most satirize the bourgeoisie, but it will never push for the replacement of this bourgeoisie by the popular sectors of society. Because, if that happens, the author and the actors will be rejected by the bourgeois sectors of society. So, in the case of Chile, there cannot exist a popular theater where the interests of the minorities determine national art and culture.]

Theater, like agriculture and industry, had to be wrested from the hands of the bourgeoisie, and theater was interpreted as part of the "Arte igual herramienta política contingente" equation.[41] At the time of the reorganization of ANTACH in 1972, the boundaries of "correct" amateur theater were being ever more strictly and restrictively defined in accordance with the common perception of a "new spirit," a "new culture," in short with commitment to the Popular Unity process.

The positive side of ANTACH lies in that it gave cohesion to many nonprofessional groups, provided an organization in which to work and an opportunity for amateur groups to present their creations for criticism. But the negative side lies precisely in the nature of the organization. Amateur theater, as we have seen, has developed in a paternalistic structure, guided by other groups or institutions, moving in the period studied here from university to political patronage. Inherent in the growth and organization of ANTACH lay its greatest restrictions: set within the framework of an aligned movement, amateur or student and workers' theater was dependent for support and cohesion on ANTACH. With the coup it could not, by definition, continue to exist, and it suffered the fate of many amateur agitprop experiences before it, disintegrating along with the political organization on which it depended for support.

Independent Theater

Looking at the criticism of Chilean theater in the period 1968–73, it seems to have disappointed anyone who had expectations of radical cultural and artistic change, especially after the election of Popular Unity. The most common complaint was that theater did not reflect on any level the revolutionary changes that were taking place in society. Yet, it would seem that the opposite is the case. The crisis in Chilean theater during this period, if there was a crisis, arose from the fact that it reflected all too accurately the ideological turmoil and political polarization of the moment and, more positively, the diversity of cultural expression.

Latin American eyes were focused on Chile, the testing ground for the "peaceful road to socialism." But hopes for spontaneous cultural renovation were confounded. In 1971, for the first time, there was no Chilean representation at the festival of theater in Manizales, Colombia. Sergio Vodanović explained this as a decision of the director of the festival, Carlos Ariel Betancur: "Y después de una breve permanencia entre nosotros Betancur pensó que, por este año, era mejor no defraudar las expectativas que en toda Latino América había sobre el teatro chileno."[42] Two years later, in 1973, when Chile was represented by Los Mimos de Noisvander, one participant complained that, like Peru, Chile was to all intents and purposes absent because it was badly represented. By this he meant that the groups were not sufficiently committed political agents of their respective countries. Sergio Vodanović answered this by saying, firstly, that Los Mimos, a professional group of mime artists who, during these years moved from classical mime to more contemporary representations, were, in fact, official cultural ambassadors; and, secondly, that in Chile theater expresses "justamente lo que está reprimido." That is, that the space for the freedom of expression in all other areas meant that theater did not play an overtly political role.[43] But how did independent theater really reflect the changes in society?

The best established group in Chile is Ictus, which was founded in 1955 as a breakaway from the Universidad Católica. Ictus began as an amateur group, but by the beginning of the sixties had turned professional and had its own theater, Teatro La Comedia, in the center of Santiago. Some of its most innovative work in the sixties was in collaboration with Jorge Díaz, who presented his first works with them. It was while working with him on *Introducción al elefante y otras zoologías* [An introduction to the elephant and other zoological forms] (1968), a play dealing with dictatorship and the military in Latin America, that the group took the first steps toward a distinctive style of collective creation.[44] It is a series of tenuously related sketches that create opposing images of, on one hand, individual distress and, on the other, unresolved infrastructural social problems. The sketches include an aggressive group therapy and a family dinner with hints of Ionesco, infuriating in its presentation of the members' total inability to communicate. The misery of shanty town life, presented as morbidly compulsive television viewing in one sketch, is juxtaposed with a political debate resembling a boxing match about the provision of a new football pitch in an aristocratic part of the city. And the play ends with the emotional breakdown of a secretary on her retirement, in despair at facing the future emptiness of her life. It is a mosaic of contemporary political, social, and individual preoccupations presented with recourse to humor and the absurd, and it is a denunciation of vacuous political debate.

During this period (1968–73), Ictus produced a weekly television program, "La Manivela," composed of satirical and humorous sketches dealing with topical issues.[45] As a result of this, Ictus did not produce a new play for stage until *Tres noches de un sábado* [Three nights one Saturday] in 1973, a production that drew from the television experience. It approaches the class problem, never far from the stage during this period, in terms of personal and family relationships, not as political conflict. Delfina Guzmán has explained its success in the following terms:

> En ese momento, a nadie le interesaba cómo se iba a hacer el amor en un régimen socialista: a nadie le interesaba cómo se iban a relacionar la gente entre sí. Entonces llega un momento en que el Ictus, en medio de la Unidad Popular, entrega *Tres noches de un sábado* y resulta que esta gente que no habla de la nacionalización del cobre, que no habla de Reforma Agraria ni del desabastecemiento, ni del imperialismo, en plena época de la UP, recoge un rasgo de su tiempo. Y la obra se convirtió en éxito de dos años, lo que revela que era un problema social, que aquello era sentido por la gente como algo muy importante.[46]

> [At that time, nobody was interested in how people were going to make love in a socialist regime; nobody was interested in how people were going to relate to each other. Then there comes a moment when Ictus, right in the middle of Popular Unity, presents *Three Nights on a Saturday* and it turns out that these people are not talking about the nationalization of copper, they are not talking about agrarian reform or shortages, or about imperialism; full in the UP period they take up one relevant aspect of the period. And the play was a success for two years, which means that this was a social problem, that people felt that it was very important.]

It was the only work on stage at the time of the coup that did not have to interrupt performances. On the other hand, "La Manivela" was taken off the air, to reappear for only a short period in 1975.

The café-concert was rising in popularity as an alternative theater for "un público culto y profesional que de alguna manera no encontrara satisfactorio el teatro 'político' directo[47] and the most successful group was El Túnel. Their presentation of Jean Genet's *Las Sirvientas* [The maids] in 1972 aroused a lot of interest; criticism underlined the scandalous nature of the play, principally because of the notorious biography of the author and, secondly, because the maids were played by men. It was also attributed a certain snob value, linked to the supposed desire to "epatar," and the newspaper *Puro Chile* sneered that Genet's work was no more than a conversation piece among "snobs" and those that wanted to be in fashion.[48] It was interpreted as a sensational device for attracting an audience, not as a play worthy of note for its intrinsic dramatic qualities or for the quality of the interpretation. El Túnel then had a great success with the café-concert, *Agamos el amor* [Let's make love] by Edmundo Villaroel, a humorous "report on the Santiago night" that ran for more than a year.

The journalistic vogue of assessing everything according to its political contingency was also applied to Alejandro Sieveking's production of George Bernard Shaw's *Mrs. Warren's Profession*, proclaimed as "a stroke against capitalism." The same company, Teatro El Angel, made up of a group of actors who had reacted against excessive experimentation in the theater of the Universidad de Chile, next produced a highly acclaimed version of *La Celestina* [The Spanish bawd]. El Angel rejected overtly partisan theater as an ineffective means of communication with their still predominantly middle-class audience, and instead they performed works that were, Sieveking has said, "hipócritamente políticas,"[49] that is, they aimed to attack bourgeois values by promoting a gradual transformation in outlook and attitude. Put in cruder terms, they did not underrate the political intelligence of the audience.

Undoubtedly, there were, too, "obras de autor," most of which have been forgotten since and never revived. This is not because of their specific relevance to the period but rather to the Chilean reluctance to embark upon new productions of once-tried plays. This means, for example, that plays by Alejandro Sieveking are all but forgotten. DETUCH produced his excellent *Todo se irá, se fue, se va al diablo* [Everything will go, has gone, is going to the dogs] in 1968 (the same year as *Peligro a 50 metros*), and it has, to my knowledge, never been produced again for the professional stage. It is a complex, psychological piece in three temporal stages, revolving around the memory of a grotesque crime discovered in the protagonist's family's beach house. *La mantis religiosa* [The praying mantis] (1971) was a Kafkesque treatment of the rigidity and innate hypocrisy of social customs and sexual mores set in the home of three spinsters locked in rituals of sexual guilt and destruction. The sisters are exposed as the tyrannical vigilantes of morals while possessing a horribly perverted moral code.

Egon Wolff's greatest achievement in this period was *Flores de papel* (1970), a devastating parable of the paralyzation of the Chilean middle classes in the face of popular revolution. It is portrayed through the experience of Eva, a forty-year-old separated woman whose flat and life are invaded by the tramp, El Merluza. Gradually he takes over, destroying her belongings, filling her home with ugly paper flowers, attacking her values, while she finds herself less and less able to react and finally, numb, is "married" into his life of squalor, dispossessed of everything she had ever owned and valued. *Flores de papel* further develops the study of the inherent middle-class fear of the intrusion of the masses on their territory that Wolff had explored with nightmare clarity in *Los invasores*. In 1970 it was a true expression of the deepest fears of the bourgeoisie, and Egon Wolff was not to write another play for seven years.

The group Aleph, the most successful group to grow from student amateur theater, epitomizes many of the features of theater in the Popular Unity period. Relying on collective creation, Aleph created a distinctive style and a strong following. Their work during this period was almost deliberately naive, with an emphasis on social and political comment, presenting what María de la Luz Hurtado has called "a vision of the world from the point of view of progressive middle class youth".[50]. During the Popular Unity years, the group took on the role of "cultural activists" whose aim was to promote "the struggle and hope."[51]

Había una vez un rey [Once upon a time there was a king] (1972) is undisguised, humorous propaganda. The protagonists are three rubbish collectors: Watusi, fat and exploitative, the decision-maker; Ñafle, skinny, weak and illiterate, the underdog; Sonajeros, the intellectual; and a rich widow, the capitalist. The play begins as the rubbish collectors enter into a business partnership with the widow, who sells them a cart on condition that they share their profits with her. Almost immediately, Watusi invents a new game in which the cart becomes a king's throne. He promises to let Ñafle have a turn as king, but he enjoys power so much that he prolongs his reign, using shabby excuses (such as the need for law and order) to retain power. Sonajeros eventually joins Ñafle in rebellion, but shows his true colors when he uses this as a stepping stone to power, while Ñafle remains at the bottom of the heap until he finally rebels, forcing the others to reflect on the folly of their conduct, the realization of which prompts them to unite with him in renewed solidarity and hope for the future. It is the widow, the personification of capitalism, who is presented as the source of their corruption, and the message is that only by possessing their own means of production can the protagonists avoid the temptations of exploitation and domination inherent in the capitalist model.

Around 1972 audiences began to fall away, the theater-going public still did not excede the 1 percent margin, and part of the traditional middle-class audience rejected what they saw as a theater of indoctrination. Most of the productions in 1972 and 1973 were of foreign or classical origin or, alternatively, comedy and the musical play. The critics were in general agreement that theater had, in the words of one, become an "Antídoto contra la tensa situación política" that, he went on, "tiene en ascuas a moros y cristianos."[52] Some companies saw it as a duty to revindicate noncommitted theater, believing, in the words of Kanda Jaque that "el único compromiso verdadero es con el público para hacer buen teatro."[53] The companies of Lucho Córdoba and Américo Vargas soldiered on, offering the same light comedies and farces, relentlessly and superficially keeping up with the times through low key satire.[54]

In April 1973, among the many comments on the increasing audience for comedies and musicals, one critic stated, "Curiosamente todos los hombres de teatro coinciden en las causas: se le está dando a la gente lo que ésta pedía a gritos" [Curiously, everyone in the theater world agrees about the reasons for this: the public is getting what it is crying out for],[55] that was, entertainment providing escape from the daily drama of a society polarized to an extreme: "It (drama) was found everywhere in daily life: in divided families, in discussion on buses, in union meetings, in factory production committees, at massive street demonstrations pro or against the government."[56] In Manizales, in the discussion quoted above, Sergio Vodánović talked of the social significance of light theater as a fact of life in a society where theater is normally made for the bourgeoisie, which can decide at certain moments to evade the real problems it is actually living from day to day: "y entonces busca la evasión y ésa es una forma también de representar un aspecto social: indicar hasta donde existe la gravedad del problema chileno que fuerza a evadirse de él en un momento determinado" [and then they try to evade this and that is another way of representing an aspect of society: a way of showing how deep and serious the chilean problem is, that it forces people to avoid it at a given moment].[57] Perhaps the middle class did tend to flee dramatic presentations of their hoped for demise, but also, as we have seen, many plays were pitched at the most simplistic level, paternalistically directed at "teaching" the "new" working-class audience. I suspect that a comment like, "se dan puras obras para rotos" should not be taken flippantly in the context, and that it reflects a sense of being insulted not by the overt assaults, but by the cultural and intellectual level of many plays.

For a variety of reasons, no new dramatists of note appeared during this period. Those, such as Miguel Littín and Raúl Ruiz, who had shown promise, turned to the rising film industry as a more effective way of reaching a large audience. Others, like Víctor

Torres, who was for a time regarded as the up-and-coming dramatist of the left, dedicated their energies to political propaganda
(Torres's *Los desterrados* [The exiles], dealing with poverty and
deprivation in a nitrate mine of the north, was presented by DE-
TUCH in 1973. Its crude propagandistic level confounded hopes in
him as a promising new dramatist.). And from 1970 onward the
silence of the university dramatists can be explained in political
terms as part of the conflict between "old" and "new": the majority
of dramatists, by virtue of their social extraction, were "viejos,"
that is, they were "engendrados en el seno de la sociedad bur-
guesa," while the "new man" was, if not a worker, "liberado
material y espiritualmente de la esclavitud capitalista."[58] Of the
"old" dramatists it is Jorge Díaz who most closely identified with
the process of reform (despite having taken up residence in Spain)
and it is he who has best expressed the dilemma of the bourgeois
playwright:

No cabe duda que el movimiento revolucionario, que se está dando en
las fábricas y en el campo, lo está llevando el pueblo y no la gente de
teatro, aunque está alineada en la izquierda. Esta clase media a la que
yo pertenezco, estos dramaturgos e intelectuales de universidad están
siendo rebasados por el fenómeno y se encuentran un poco mudos,
simpatizando con el movimiento pero no siendo ellos los voceros auto-
rizados. La denuncia la ha llevado, en todos los gobiernos del mundo, la
burguesía de formación universitaria. Esa era una misión para nosotros
clarísima ya que el obrero no podía hacerlo por no tener los medios,
lenguaje o lo que sea. En el proceso chileno nuestro papel existe y es
fundamental, pero cuesta mucho adaptarse y descubrirlo. Los dramaturgos chilenos están mudos en estos momentos porque se encuentran
en un período de transición, porque tiene que aparecer gente nueva o
porque la gente antigua tiene que tomar conciencia de una serie de
fenómenos de clases que son inéditos.[59]

[There is no doubt that the revolutionary movement is taking place in
the factories and in the country, that it is in the hands of the people and
not of those who work in the theater, although these may be aligned to
the left. This middle class that I belong to, these dramatists and university intellectuals are being overtaken by the phenomenon and find that
they are dumb, sympathizing with the movement but not its authorized
voice. Denunciation, in every government in the world, has been the
role of the bourgeoisie with a university education. That mission was
absolutely clear to us, since the worker could not do it because he did
not have the means, the language, or whatever. In the Chilean process
our role exists and is fundamental, but it is difficult for us to adapt and
discover it. Chilean dramatists are silent at the moment because they

are in a period of transition, because new people have to appear or
because the people that already exist have to become aware of a series
of class phenomena that were unheard of before.]

In the sixties bourgeois society was under attack from the stage,
both from those who were of bourgeois extraction (Egon Wolff,
Sergio Vodanović, Jorge Díaz), and from artistic sectors politically
committed to socialism. There was a proliferation of plays dealing
with marginal sectors: the works of Luis Alberto Heiremans,
Aguirre's *Los papeleros,* Requena's *Pan caliente,* Díaz's *Topografía
de un desnudo,* among others, reflected the awareness of the changing social and political face of Chile, giving dramatic expression to
the sectors that posed the greatest threat to the bourgeois capitalist
world, and often openly inciting rebellion. The period 1970–73 was
ostensibly the realization of the threat of invasion by these sectors,
the marginals, metaphorically inhabitants of the other side of the
river in Wolff's vivid portrayals of the bourgeois fear of the destruction of their status quo. In theater it was proletarian expression that
flourished in the Popular Unity period, while the middle-class
dramatist, in general sympathetic to reform, if not aligned with
Popular Unity, had nothing to say. But, in society as a whole,
substantial sectors of the middle classes feared the consequences of
the "invasion" of communism and were not struck dumb. Neither
were they paralyzed like Wolff's Eva. They invited and supported
the military coup of September 1973.

After the Coup

The development of theater since 1973 must be studied in the
context of the wider social, economic, and political implications of
the Pinochet regime's policies. Above all, the new regime sought to
"stabilize the country," it "sought to impose a new discipline on
the social body, one . . . supposed to rectify previous trends and
disorders."[60] The sectors that would be worst hit by the measures
for political stabilization and the free market economic policies had
to be controlled adequately so as not to provoke a "premature
reversal of the policies." The previous trends of increased participation by the lower sectors recently incorporated in the political
process were halted through brutal repression. According to the
military discourse, the country was in a state of siege with internal
war being waged against the Marxist enemy. For the new regime
this was a period of purging, cleansing, and healing of society;

institutions were to work in function of national security, and "la tranquilidad pública" became the main justification for repression.

Universities were subjected to a process of counterreform. Rectors, formerly elected by the staff and students, were dismissed and military rectors appointed; university departments were closed down to allow the expulsion of students and staff of dubious loyalties and to eliminate Marxist courses; students' unions and assemblies were banned. All means of communication connected to the previous government were closed and the "normal expression of dissidence as is necessary in a democracy" was annihilated.[61] Suspected left wing books were burnt in an "open, indiscriminate, brutal and often tragic-comic" way.[62] Actors, directors, and dramatists were imprisoned and often later exiled, and blacklists were drawn up to prevent subversive elements from appearing on television.[63] All the above measures were a means of wiping images of the recent past from the collective memory. The journalistic term "apagón cultural" was coined and soon became the most common way of explaining the immediate effects of the coup on the arts.

The university theaters were closed or restructured. The Teatro de la Universidad de Concepción was levelled on the day of the coup and closed in 1976 as a result of its long connections with amateur theater and political organizations in the area. In Santiago DETUCH was closed for a period of six months, the majority of the staff and students were expelled. When it reopened, it was as the Compañía Nacional de Teatro, with a program approved by the supreme authorities of the university and not, as before, by the members of the department. Its very name, changed in 1976 to the Teatro Nacional Chileno, is indicative of the role it was now to play, that of an official organ, producing works with an educational value and providing productions of works on the school curriculum.

In the Universidad Católica the pattern is similar, if somewhat less marked. Again there was a move away from the multidisciplinary approach; EAC was closed in 1976, matriculation for the drama school frozen, and the Escuela de Teatro, Cine y Televisión took its place. This, in its turn, was eventually divided in 1978, one part becoming the school of drama and the other the department for cinema and television. In both universities, a process of self-financing made a big impact on the way the theaters were run and the plays produced, since they could no longer rely on government subsidies, which had formerly guaranteed runs for even the most unsuccessful productions. Now they began to cater for a captive audience of secondary school pupils whose presence was guaranteed on recommendation from the Education Department. The lack of finance meant, furthermore, that the universities were unable to carry on with much of the research they had done before and were equally unable to provide support for festivals of amateur theater. In this way, and with the closure of the majority of provincial university theaters, the role these institutions played in promoting the "ambiente teatral" was sadly diminished.

The university theaters turned to the classics. In 1974 the Universidad Católica offered two Golden Age dramas, Lope de Vega's *El Pastor Lobo* (and Calderón de la Barca's *La vida es sueño* [Life is a dream]. Neither choice was gratuitous. *El Pastor Lobo* [Wolf in sheep's clothing] was described by Juan Andrés Piña as "El encuentro y enfrentamiento del mundo del mal y del bien. El cordero y el lobo. Dios y el Demonio luchando a punta de espada sobre el escenario, en una época o tiempo mítico" [The encounter betwen the world of good and the world of evil. The lamb and the wolf. God and the Devil fighting with swords drawn on stage in a mythic era or time].[64] And *La vida es sueño* was an eloquent call for liberty and justice through Calderón's classic drama of the dilemma of free will and predestination and the illusory qualities of freedom and being.

In the Universidad de Chile the productions included *Orfeo y el desodorante* [Orpheus and the deodorant] by the neglected Chilean dramatist, José R. Morales, Tom Stoppard's *Rosencrantz and Guilderstern Are Dead*, both in 1974, *Buenaventura* by Luis Alberto Heiremans and *Bodas de sangre* [Blood Wedding] by García Lorca in 1975. TEKNOS, before its disappearance in 1976, produced mostly classics (*Bodas de Fígaro* [The Marriage of Figaro] by Beaumarchais, *La viuda astuta* [The Clever Widow] by Goldoni, *The Taming of the Shrew*), with the exception of Fernando Cuadra's *La familia de Marta Mardones* [The family of Marta Mardones].

This "boom de los clásicos"[65] began to cause concern when in 1976 *Don Juan Tenorio* was presented by the Universidad de Chile and Tirso de Molin's version of the Don Juan myth, *El Burlador de Sevilla* was produced by the Universidad Católica. By this time, those who had welcomed the initial proliferation of the classics as a return to the roots of international drama and an attempt to "rescatar los valores permanentes que perviven en ellas"[66] now saw it as a sign of decadence, arising from the fact that, in the circumstances, the performance of accepted foreign drama was the only sure way of financing university theaters as official enterprises. (Lucho Córdoba could not resist making his views on the matter known, for in the "year of the Don Juans" he produced a farce called *Don Juan, el Rasca* [The mangy Don Juan].) Before turning to independent theater, I want to look briefly at the nature of the two original Chilean works produced in university theater between 1973 and 1976.

José R. Morales' *Orfeo y el desodorante o el último viaje a los infiernos* [Orpheus and the deodorant or the last journey to hell], a modern interpretation of the myth of Orpheus and Eurydice, is a fable of the disorientation of modern man, lost in a world of consumer goods, of things that ultimately annihilate the human being, reducing him or her to yet another object. The hell into which Orpheus descends in search of Eurydice, vaporized in an advertisement for a deodorant that would rid her forever of the need to bathe, is an immense factory manufacturing consumer goods for man's every need. When he finds Eurydice, Orpheus forfeits the right to take her out of hell, not by looking back at her, but by reciting the love letters he had written her, thus looking back to a prohibited past filled by the senses, not by things. Eurydice, however, proposes the transference of hell to earth where, she realizes, a far superior infernal kingdom has been created by man, seemingly intent on destroying earth in the quest for a material paradise. Back on earth, Orpheus finds that his exploits in hell have been marketed into a huge musical hit. The myth is distorted as part of the publicity campaign, and Orpheus is murdered by his fans, becoming another victim of the advance of hell on earth, the consumer society.

Morales creates a vision of a world in which there is a double consumerism, "de objetos y de ideologías."[67] Humankind is lost in a world where publicity promotes goods, where propaganda promotes ideas as easily digestible dogmas, and where success and efficiency in promoting this double consumerism override concepts of truth and reality. He created an astute comment on consumerism, one which, written in 1974, anticipated the preoccupation with the consumer boom among other national dramatists of a few years later. But like most of his plays, it neither achieved popularity nor received critical acclaim.

Fernando Cuadra's *La familia de Marta Mardones* has a curiously dated feel about it, reminiscent as it is of the early work of the university dramatists or the radio serials of the fifties. Marta Mardones is the epitome of the strong Chilean lower-middle-class housewife, the benign matriarch, ruling the roost at home, living only for the well-being of her family. Her husband is the extreme of the ineffectual male who generally accompanies such a woman: he

is an invalid, racked with resentment and guilt, who ends his
useless life at her side by committing suicide. Her children look to
the mother for support in all their problems, but nevertheless, they
must leave the roost in order to establish their lives and identities.
Through thick and thin, Marta Mardones never loses her strength,
founded on the force of her female role as the center of *her* family.
The play was made into a television serial and provoked a certain
amount of debate, but essentially it is a return to the living room
melodrama, and a forceful reiteration of traditional Chilean middle-
class values as guarded and transmitted by the mother.

In independent theater the initial period, between 1973 and 1976,
was one of disarticulation, a product of the so-called "apagón
cultural." While there was a great deal of activity, little new drama
of note was produced. The reorganization of the university theaters
prompted many of those expelled to create new groups, most of
which did not survive, but some of which—Imagen, Le Signe, Los
Comediantes—achieved some stability by at first performing works
from the modern international repertoire. With the exception of
Ictus, Chilean drama was represented by the ever-present Córdoba-
Leguía and Vargas-Durante companies, and light comedy by such
as Miguel Frank, Silvia Piñeiro, and Kanda Jaque. There was a
surge in the number of children's plays, in the café-concert, which
evolved toward a more elitist role, and in the number of musicals.
By the mid seventies, international shows were imported, like consumer goods, lock, stock, and barrel from abroad.[68] They responded to a type of spectacular that involved "consumo sin
expresión," and found their audience among the richer sectors of
the community. While musicals had begun to come into their own
during 1973, by the mid seventies, with their identification with the
consumer boom, they were seen as a "símbolo masivo, comercial,
de la cultura oficial."[69] Expensive, foreign and, above all, politically
clean.

Censorship worked during this period on the impetus of fear. Two
groups, the Teatro del Angel and Aleph, tried to adapt to the new
circumstances before their respective exiles. In 1974 Alejandro
Sieveking presented *Cama de batalla* [Bed battleground], which he
later called "the most confused play I've written." It revolved
around "una pareja capitalista que había creado un monstruo, un
hijo imperfecto que había recibido un golpe misterioso."[70] This
crude and somewhat contrived allegorical style, relying on the
evocation of the accepted source of evil, capitalism, and on dubious
puns, is symptomatic of the degree of disorientation experienced
by authors who wished to voice their dissent, but who did not have

sufficient time to develop an adequate language of opposition. While on a tour of Latin America in 1974, the group decided to go into exile in Costa Rica, where they remained until 1984.

A more dramatic example of this initial lack of sophistication was the case of the group Aleph, which, upon returning from a period in France, attempted the first satire on the coup in *Y al principio existía la vida* [And in the beginning was life] (1974). One scene depicts the captain of a sinking ship going down with his crew while declaring that the fight will go on. It was impossible to miss the analogy with Allende's last moments when he broadcast to the nation from the bombarded Moneda palace. The authorities took such violent exception to the play that the theater was raided and the actors imprisoned and then sent into exile.[71] Experiences such as these heightened the degree of self-censorship and warned other groups of the consequences of politically subversive theater.

The experience of Ictus illustrates the apparent inconsistencies in the method of repression. While the group was blacklisted from appearing on television, *Tres noches de un sábado* was the only production to continue uninterrupted throughout the whole period. One reason was its distance from overt political commitment to the "proceso chileno." During the previous period, it had been accused in an article in *La Quinta Rueda* [The fifth wheel], "¿Dónde está la 'cuestión social'?" as showing "una marginación absoluta de lo que importa alucidar en el Chile de hoy" and was chastized as being among those "simpáticos coloraditos" who serve easy works on a plate to their audience.[72] But more important contributory factors to the group's continuing activity were, firstly, the prestige that Ictus had won in Chile and Latin America and, secondly, the strong identification with the social and political preoccupations and aspirations of the Chilean middle classes. Herein lies much of the logic of censorship since 1973. Ictus was banned from television and access to a mass audience with its satirical weekly program, but its middle-class theater-going audience is a tiny minority and deemed to be less of a risk. Furthermore, its productions are, to a large extent, regarded as exhibition pieces by the regime, which can point to them as proof of the freedom of expression in the country.[73] And, to a certain manner of thinking, it acted as an escape valve, used cynically to provide a real space for expression for a middle class with a social conscience, as important economically and politically as other sectors of the middle class. As we shall see, Ictus, using the special space they occupy, has played a vital role in pushing the boundaries of critical theater since 1973.

Given the circumstances of violent repression of political grassroots movements, amateur and workers' theater was silenced immediately after the coup. It began to emerge again, starting in concentration camps[74] all over the country and around solidarity organizations often linked with the Church which, in the vacuum of political activity, became the mouthpiece of the conscience of the country in the face of the repression. Since 1974, student theater could boast strong amateur groups in the Faculty of Medicine in Santiago, where one of the generation's new playwrights, Marco Antonio de la Parra, began his career. In 1978 the Agrupación Cultural Universitaria of the Universidad de Chile[75] held the first of five festivals of university theater, notably with no connections with other amateur theater. The winning work was *Baño a baño* [Bath to bath], a collective creation on the subject of power and domination, relying on the grotesque and the absurd to convey an image of decadence and stagnation in an authoritarian society. It was a work that could not have been performed outside the rarefied atmosphere of a university theater. Indeed, the following year there was an unsuccessful attempt to stop the festival.[76]

In 1981 an Encuentro de Teatro Poblacional, organized by CENECA, brought shanty-town groups together. The themes dealt with in the works presented are ones that have also proven magnetic in professional theater over the last few years:

> Los contenidos de sus creaciones teatrales se centran en las conductas y relaciones humanas que son tratadas a través de la presentación de seres marginales, habitantes de un mundo deshumanizado donde las relaciones sociales se encuentran deterioradas, particularmente aquellas que se refieren al ámbito laboral y familiar como consecuencia de la cesantía, la drogadicción, el machismo y el alcoholismo.[77]

> [The contents of the theater creations concentrate on human relations and behavior, which are treated through the presentation of people belonging to the marginalized sectors, inhabitants of a dehumanized world where social relations have deteriorated, particularly those that have to do with work and the family, as a consequence of unemployment, drug addiction, machismo and alcoholism.]

Until 1976 the "cleansing" of the stage was, on the whole, effective. One of the main impediments to freedom of expression was economic in nature. In November 1974, the 1935 theater law was repealed and in a new law theater became subject to a tax of 22 percent on total box office takings. Companies could gain exemption from paying the tax only if a government commission classified their work as of high cultural value. University theaters, by their very nature as educational institutions, were exempt, and companies that presented works included in the school literature curriculum were also exempted from tax for the duration of the run. Although decisions seemed to be arbitrary (some works have been given exemption for a period only to find that it is refused the next season), they did show a certain logic, and complaints fell on deaf ears:

> . . . una obra para ser auspiciada, debe contener 'valores positivos' y no atacar al régimen: 'Que haya crítica está bien, pero no crítica subvencionada . . . Los teatros no deben creer que la exención del IVA es un derecho; es sólo una concesión de gracia del ministerio para ayudar a financiar espectáculos de calidad.'[78]

> [. . . in order for a work to be subsidized, it must possess "positive values" and not attack the regime: "It's all very well that there is criticism, but not subsidized criticism. . . . Theater groups must not believe that exemption from VAT is a right; it is only a concession granted by the good grace of the ministry to help to finance quality productions."]

The transparent logic of censorship revealed itself again in 1978. The theater of the Universidad Católica had turned once more to national dramatists with two works by Egon Wolff, *Kindergarten* (1977) and *Espejismos* [Mirages] (1978). In June 1978 it was ready to open with *Lo crudo, lo cocido y lo podrido* [The raw, the cooked and the rotten] by Marco Antonio de la Parra. The play takes place in a traditional old Santiago café, El Torres, formerly patronized by the ruling elite but now closed to the public for an unspecified length of time for lack of customers. It is a tale of a dying regime governed by a curious sect to which the waiters belong, and informed by values that are more appropriate to the turn of the century than to the present day. Even from this brief outline, the potential for its interpretation as political satire is evident. The play was banned by the university authorities the day before the premiere. In explaining the decision, the acting rector was adamant that the ban was not political in nature. The reasons given were its "vulgarity" (the censors counted the use of fifty "chilenismos," and claimed inaccurately that one of the characters was a prostitute) and "low cultural level," both of which made the work unsuitable for a student audience.[79] Nevertheless, the play was mounted with only minor changes in the cast when it was taken over by the group Imagen, and it was a huge success.[80]

Around 1976 groups like Imagen, made up of ex-university pro-

fessionals, most of whom had been expelled after the coup, began
to turn to original Chilean drama. When the group was formed in
1974, it found financial support from the Chile-France Institute,
with whom they made an agreement by which they would perform
modern French language drama as a way of introducing it to the
Chilean public, and in return they would have the use of the institute theater.[81] Imagen ran into problems, however, when, in 1977,
an international boycott of the Chilean stage meant that playwrights would not give permission for their work to be performed in
Chile as a protest against the conditions of dictatorship in the
country.[82] Unexpectedly, one of the most direct forms of censorship
had come from dramatists abroad, sympathetic to the cause of
freedom of expression. Faced with this obstacle, the group turned
to original Chilean plays, the first of which was *Te llamabas
Rosicler* [You were called Rosicler] (1976) by Luis Rivano.

Te llamabas Rosicler takes place in 1963 in an old mansion in a
formerly aristocratic area of Santiago. The house is now diminished
in value due to the exodus of the aristocracy and the Military
School to the "barrio alto"; it is now converted into flats, inhabited
by tenants who, like the mansion, have seen better days. Through
the relations of domination, submissiveness, deceit, and pride that
unite the protagonists, we learn of their past glories and aspirations
in contrast with their present demoralized state, which grows as the
play continues until each one loses even the possibility of indulging
in impossible dreams. The central motifs of nostalgia and decaying
ideals are symbolized in the house and in the tango of the title, each
of which represents the hope of renewed purpose in life. Rosicler
(her name is a stage name after the tango of the title) dreams of a
return to her musical career, while her partner, Mario, dreams of
buying the house, thus saving it from demolition. Both fail and
finally each becomes an unbearable mirror of the other's failure.
The house can be read as a metaphor for the impossibility of
recreating a bygone and obsolete age and as a comment on the
perceived aim of the regime to do just that. Since this production,
Imagen has produced mainly original Chilean works.

Sporadic outbursts of violent censorship do occur. One example
was the case of *Hojas de Parra* [Leaves from Parra's book] (1977)
by José Manuel Salcedo and Jaime Vadell, with texts by the poet
Nicanor Parra, presented by La Feria, a group that had formed after
a split with Ictus.[83] The play, performed in a marquee the group
erected in a middle-class district of Santiago, is set in a circus run
by an enterprising empresario who rents it out for different functions. In the course of the play, he rents his circus to a man who

pays to make "Una declaración relámpago del candidato a la Presidencia de la República," Don Nadie [Mr. Nobody], to the "Sociedad de Mantención del Recuerdo Eterno de los Poetas Muertos y Vivos," and he does business with a "Contrabandista" whose merchandise is Chilean goods, which, he warns his customers, are becoming increasingly difficult to buy. From the beginning of the play, the circus is being filled with white crosses as the nearby cemetery encroaches on their space, until audience and performers alike are surrounded by the dead. The empresario, never allowing a business opportunity to pass, rents himself out to perform the funeral services that also take place in his circus.

The succession of scenes forms an easily identifiable parade of the most significant early results of military rule: Don Nadie is a creation of the "receso político"; Chilean goods are interpreted as the contraband of the seventies in the full flush of the boom of imported consumer goods; the repression of the arts is seen as a way of wiping clean the collective memory of potentially subversive expressions; and, most blatantly, the crosses are a veritable invasion of symbols of violent political repression. The advance of the cemetery is an ironic contradiction of the meaning of the circus and, by extension, of the meaning of the very theater, La Feria, since it is a negation of the community act of attending a form of entertainment: " 'Feria' es sinónimo de bullicio, de intercambio, de movilización de gente, y al mismo tiempo se acerca a lo que es el teatro en lo que tiene de transhumante, efímero, cambiante."[84]

There was an outcry in the press among critics who "deplored" the play as a vehicle for an antigovernment message.[85] Neither did the military miss the subversive tone of the play, and it regarded the massive audiences such a production was attracting as a danger to national security. In the week and a half that the *teatro-circo* survived there was an audience of over six thousand. It was closed twice for health inspection (the Old Faithful of guises for politically motivated closures), and after ten days the marquee was burned down by an unidentified group during the curfew.

The incident is relevant on two counts. Firstly, there seems to have been little effort to disguise the critical commentary on contemporary Chile, a measure of the level of disorientation with regard to the boundaries of freedom of expression. Secondly, it underlines the logic of the regime's attitude to freedom of expression: theater is not touched as long the audience is small and politically irrelevant. La Feria took this into account with their next play, *Bienaventurados los pobres* [Blessed are the poor] (1977), a chronicle of the long relationships between the state and various elites, ending with a homage to Padre Hurtado[86] as an obvious comment on the renewed protagonistic role that the Church has played in the protection and succor of the poor. This was mounted under the auspices of two private institutions (CENECA and Fundación Civitas), but the group over-whitewashed their image and publicity was low-key. There was no press coverage, and the result was financial failure. La Feria were still to find a good balance.

Despite these setbacks, and because of the regime's view of theater as an art for an elite, circumstances contrived to make theater a major form of comment on the dictatorship. Its very immediacy makes it more powerful than poetry or the novel, and the only art with comparable qualities is song. Also, censorship is enforced with far greater rigor in the press and the media. Therefore, for example, in 1985, when there was a prolonged state of siege, opposition newspapers and magazines were either silenced or had to submit every edition for prior censorship, but in the theaters of Santiago the majority of the successes on stage were of an overtly political nature and attracted fairly large audiences during long runs.

Since 1941 the theater in Chile has been a constantly developing art. Yet, the specter of a "crisis" is periodically evoked by critics who complain of the irrelevance to contemporary Chile, the small numbers of dramatists and the small audience. But theater is dynamic and versatile, the proof being that one of the richest periods since the late fifties has been 1976–80. It would seem that this has a lot to do with the rearticulation of the role of the dramatist. In 1976, when new works began to appear, Ramón Núñez saw it as the awakening from a ten-year siesta.[87] Some, using a purely political frame of referene, would call this view suspect: didn't the big sleep begin in 1973 with the overthrow of democracy? The fact remains, however, that, while previous years had yielded a great deal of activity and theorizing, no new dramatists came forth. The bourgeois playwright, mostly of the university generation, was on his or her way out, and collective creation was on its way in. If ever there was a "crisis" in Chilean theater, it was during those years: theater needs the triangle of the author, the actor, and the audience to survive, but by the early seventies there were few dramatists and audiences were diminishing; only actors could be found in abundant supply. In these terms 1973 served to deepen the "crisis," which was exacerbated by the conscientious evasion of all things Chilean.

Another reason for the vitality of the late seventies is the degree of agreement between audience and group about the role theater should play. This was seen as one of exploiting the relative freedom from censorship and theater's potential as the most immediate form of communication, in order to unveil the effects, both sociological and psychological, of the dictatorship. New drama responded to what the public "was shouting for." That was, information in the vacuum created by the regime. By 1980, however, groups that had provided this type of theater began to look for new themes, new approaches and an innovative "lenguaje teatral" that would free them from the impositions of being social commentators. While they do constantly search for new forms of expression, the continuing similarity and transparency of the codes used and of the theatrical language employed suggests a basic sharing of perceptions of the development of society. These are also shared by the audience, and a complicity is evident: the audience is rarely shocked, and it ultimately forms a whole with the group against the antagonist outside, beyond the confines of the theater.

Constantly we shall see that the meanings of words are turned on their heads, as the manicheistic view represented in many of the plays in the 1968 to 1973 period finds a perfect counterpoint in the regime's interpretation of who is the enemy within. Black became white and white became black. Complicity with a well-defined audience (middle class in search of politically dissident views) creates a none-too-subtle coded language: references to falls ("caídas") alert the audience to the collective hope for the fall of the regime; the seasons rotate as symbols of death and renewal; dialogues are littered with swift allusions to taboo subjects and often to a "war"; doors remain closed; houses fall to rack and ruin; rituals take over from normal social intercourse; and few plays are free from references to the consumer society. Yet the best theater of the period has transcended simplistic codes: symbols, words, meanings are constantly shifting, invested as they are with multiple levels of interpretation. The rest of this book will explore this world of words, symbols, codes.

2
Facing the Issues: The Themes of Work and Marginalization

1976: Socioeconomic Factors

From 1976 there was a definite revitalization in theater, and the homogeneity of theme in the plays prompted some critics to talk of a movement. It is always problematic to talk of movements, but it is clear that a major preoccupation in the new plays produced was the impact of the regime's economic policies on the lower sectors. Groups that had long responded in their works to social change now responded to what they saw as the need to confront their audiences with the reality experienced by many sectors of the community in the aftermath of the coup. The misery of these sectors was obscured by the continuing prosperity of the middle and upper classes, by propaganda and by the difficulties involved in journalistic reporting of the same issues, which would be censored as subversive and a danger to national security. *Pedro, Juan y Diego* [Tom, Dick and Harry] (1976), by Ictus and David Benavente; *Los payasos de la esperanza* [Clowns in waiting] (1977), by the group Taller de Investigación Teatral; *Tres Marías y una Rosa* [Three Marías and one Rosa] (1979), also by the Taller de Investigación Teatral in conjunction with David Benavente, were conceived and produced against this background.[1]

By 1975 the official rate of unemployment had reached 15 percent.[2] The most obvious social indicators of the recession involved people employing different "survival strategies," indicated primarily by the huge growth of the informal sector; there were higher rates of drug abuse; an increase in prostitution and alcoholism, migration, the break-up of families. A growing number of communal dining rooms and community organizations, many of these connected with the Church,[3] provided as best they could for the worst hit.

In April 1975 the regime set up a scheme called the *Programa de*

Empleo Mínimo (PEM), the aim of which was to absorb 35,460 unemployed workers.[4] It is in this scheme that the characters in *Pedro, Juan y Diego* are employed. Throughout *Pedro, Juan y Diego,* the dialogue echoes the testimonies of people who experience in real life the vagaries of the minimal employment scheme, a scheme that was no more than an extreme form of exploitation, recognized as a government ploy to doctor the unemployment figures. The play graphically portrays the characters' loss of dignity and the demoralization that they try to numb through alcohol.

Los Payasos de la Esperanza introduces another aspect of the search for the opportunity to work: the role of unofficial aid organizations, especially the Church, to which the clowns of the title turn.[5] Through the Church organization, the unemployed clowns gain access to a potential new audience: the most deprived people in society. The clowns' project is an attempt to provide educational entertainment for the children who attend the soup kitchens, but this opportunity to use their talents proves to be illusory, for the clowns' educational and cultural grounding is inadequate to enable them to provide the type of entertainment they intended.[6]

Tres Marías y una Rosa deals with the experience of *arpilleristas,* women who support their families by making *arpilleras,* tapestries made from old bits of cloth and wool depicting their experience of life in present day Chile. The play takes place in a workshop, and as the women discuss and carry out their work a whole array of problems they have to deal with is presented to the audience. In many respects *Tres Marías y una Rosa* complements the other two plays, by giving a vision of how unemployment has affected the family structure, of how women see the changing role they have to play in families where the traditional head has had to migrate, has disappeared, or can offer no support at all to the household because of the total demoralization caused by long-term unemployment.

Both productions of the Taller de Investigatión Teatral were the result of participant observation. Working in close conjunction with the people who would later be represented on stage, the cast set about observing them, their every move, gesture, and unspoken thought, thus creating what some critics refer to as a less literary type of theater in which the barely articulated impression is the means for communication of the central themes and preoccupations. The text is elaborated at the end, when the actors involved feel they have reached a stage of identification with the characters, aware of how they would act within the dramatic situation presented. The style is less explicative than that of traditional Chilean drama, and the spectator is left to create a personal picture of the lives of the protagonists outside the space on stage by piecing together the almost incidental allusions to the everyday problems they face.

Pedro, Juan y Diego: The Loss of the Male Discourse

Pedro, a builder by trade; Juan, an ex-fruit and vegetable seller; and Diego, an ex–civil servant, are all employed on the PEM on a housing estate in the construction of a wall. Their work is badly supervized by an inspector who knows little of the trade, and it is hampered by the scarcity and bad quality of the materials with which they have to work. Only Pedro, a "Maestro Albañil Primero" and proud of the tradition he belongs to, has the ability to carry out the work, but, for this very reason, he is frustrated by the blatant bad management of the construction and by his sure knowledge that the wall is being built in the wrong position. The three men are accompanied by a dumb woman, María, who, they are told, lost her power of speech as a result of a fright she suffered two years previously. In the first part they are digging a hole in preparation for the construction of the wall, which does not progress. At this stage the characters' communication is based on "pura palabrería,"[7] story-telling, fantasizing. In the second part, with the construction under way, they begin to grow together as a team, and as the wall nears completion their fantasizing gives way to concrete memories of past achievements. But this is ultimately destroyed when, in conclusive proof of the worthlessness of their labor, the wall is demolished.

According to Benavente, the theme of *Pedro, Juan y Diego* is not work in itself, but "the dignity of work."[8] At the heart of the preoccupations gnawing away in the protagonists' minds is the fear of the loss of their identity in society, an identity lent them by the male role they traditionally play, founded on the ability to care for wife and family as provider and protector. Unemployment has pulled from under their feet the dignity they had found in their role and the very legitimacy of their claim to it. Throughout the play, the men demand to be accorded the recognition they deserve as workers and to be given a chance to regain the dignity, self-respect, and respect of others that full-time employment had formerly meant to them, while, in contrast, their bosses remain stubbornly blind to what is essentially a moral and existential problem.

The central theme is developed as part of an ongoing, overtly antagonistic dialogue between the men and the bosses, based on the social truism that a man without a job has forfeited his claim to manhood. On one level this forms part of commonplace macho discourse, whereby every sign of weakness or lack of manliness is scoffed at through gibes at gender and sexuality. These exchanges often mean very little, set as they are within an accepted code of macho banter, in which the protagonists verbally parade their virility and establish superiority. But on every level this seemingly superficial male discourse provides insights into how the characters interpret the male role in society and how they see it threatened.

Juan explains his present plight as the consequence of the death of his horse and working companion, Arturo, and the subsequent loss of his fruit cart. The horse's death he attributes to the loss of its virility and therefore of its will to live:

> Se le jodió una bola y hubo que caparlo. Pa qué le digo lo que sufrió; si era muy hombre en los puros huesos quedó. Claro que me hechó la culpa a mí; por los malos tratos, la falta de mastique y la quiebra, decía. ¡Puras mentiras! Se jodió de puro afligido que estaba donde le cortara las bolas." (p. 13)

> [He had a problem with one of his balls, and I had to have him gelded. I don't have to tell you how much he suffered; he was a real man and now he's like a skeleton. Of course he blamed me; because I had treated him badly, because there wasn't enough to eat, because I went bust, he said. That's all lies! He was screwed up because he was so upset after they'd cut off his balls.]

That tragedy was to foreshadow his own, and he is constantly asserting himself to protect his threatened manhood. On the one hand, he is always to the fore in man's talk, ever ready to boast of his vast sexual experience and to cap one tall story with another. On the other, it is he who manifests the greatest truculence in his dealings with the bosses, challenging them with open displays of disrespect, demanding proper equipment, and accusing them of dishonesty.

For Diego unemployment is a great blow to his self-esteem, and he betrays the greatest insecurity with respect to the performance of the workingman's role when he reveals that for the sake of his wife's peace of mind and his own credibility he has not told her about the loss of his job and, instead, has invented an office five-a-side football tournament to explain away his timetable and his aches and pains. For him, the PEM is a way of surviving until he sets up in the booming import business. He is an unusual candidate for this scheme, well educated, formerly a white-collar worker and briefly a university student, and for this reason he inspires a certain suspicion in the others, who at one point believe he may be a newspaper reporter. In fact, he represents the depths of the recession in so far as he, who has far greater access to the modern job market, also finds himself excluded. Yet, he shows the greatest, perhaps desperate, belief in the possibility of escape from the present situation. His constant companion is a suitcase full of books and Topogigio puppets for sale, and it is he who presents wild but seemingly well-researched projects into the possibilities for informal business.

Because of the ineptitude of the management, it is Pedro who effectively directs the building of the wall. For him, the fact of working on an ill-managed scheme in a menial job is an insult to his professional pride, since it throws contempt on the tradition he belongs to and completely disregards the value of his trade, inherited from his father and grandfather. However, he puts all his professional pride into the work, and as the wall progresses he regains a sense of the dignity of the trade and tradition, which he now wishes to pass on to his unlikely apprentices. For this reason, he is the most closely affected by the inconsistent handling of the building of the wall, is in closest harmony with the very idea of the realization of the project and has the most to lose in terms of dignity and self-respect by the threatened destruction of his work.

It is no idle coincidence that the object of their labor is a wall. It is the unifying metaphor of the play. In one sense it is growing visual evidence of the great divide between the men's interpretation of their work and that of the employers. Related more widely to Chilean literature, it has connotations of a prison, of enclosure, ultimately of the protection of the rich from the lower classes.[9] As the wall grows, the men's attachment to it grows accordingly while, in equal measure, their employers' attention to the quality of the work diminishes. The single most important fact about the wall is that it is always destined to be bulldozed down. In this respect, the builders' affinity with the wall is total. The audience is never allowed to doubt the ultimate fate of the wall: from the very first scene, when Pedro threatens to leave the site on seeing the unintelligible plans, it is doomed to failure, and as Pedro, Juan, and Diego toil, they are made all too aware that only orders from above have any importance. That the very idea of the wall is a mockery of the men's time and effort is amply illustrated in the following exchange when Diego, after being challenged about his right to work on the site, threatens to resign and prompts both Pedro's fierce pride in the quality of his skills and their boss's determination that only the "orden del día" has any validity:

JUAN: Apuesto que este viejo se portó mal con Ud.

DIEGO: No, se portó muy bien. Me refiero a otras personitas que no, que no se dan el lujo de comprender razones. Que les importa poco la dedicación que uno le pone al trabajo, por humilde que éste sea.

PEDRO: Eso está muy bien pero aguántese un segundito! Nosotros nos comprometimos a levantar esta pirca para mañana, ¿sí o no?

DIEGO: La pista se puso demasiado pesada aquí. Ud. vio lo que pasó.

PEDRO: Con mayor razón tenemos que construir la mejor pirca del mundo para demostrarles lo que somos capaces de hacer; pa mandar a los inspectores de espalda el loro cuando la vean.

D. CARLOS: No, no. no. Yo no estoy de acuerdo con eso.

PEDRO: ¿Cómo no va estar de acuerdo?

D. CARLOS: ¡Qué tanta bolina con la mejor pirca del mundo! Lo único que necesitamos es que haya algo parado pa arriba el día de la inauguración y punto final. (p. 34)

[JUAN: I bet that old guy treated you badly.

DIEGO: No, he treated me very well. No, I'm talking about certain other people that don't bother themselves to listen to reasons. They're not worried about the dedication we put into our work, no matter how humble it is.

PEDRO: That's all very well, but wait a minute! We agreed that we would build this wall for tomorrow, didn't we?

DIEGO: Things are getting a bit too heavy around here. You saw what happened.

PEDRO: All the more reason for building the best wall in the world to show them what we can do; so that the inspectors fall back in amazement when they see it.

D. CARLOS: No, no, no. I don't agree with that.

PEDRO: What do you mean you don't agree?

D. CARLOS: What's all this about the best wall in the world! The only thing we need is for something to be standing on the day of the opening, full stop.]

This exchange illustrates both the essence of the divide the wall represents and how the building of the wall is synonymous with the rebuilding of the men's identity as workers. In the first act, when this identity was feeble and battered, the protagonists were to be seen digging a hole, a blatant symbol of futility and of their essential invisibility. The hole had no purpose other than filling the time, as Pedro indicates when he reproaches Diego: "Lo dejan sólo y es capaz de hacer un hoyo hasta la China" (p. 13). This symbolism is made more explicit later when Diego, proposing one of his money-making schemes, tells the others that "La única solución es inventar algo para ganar más plata y salir de este hoyo" (p. 17): the hole, clearly, is both metaphorical and physical. And later, as they act out the adventures of "El Zorro," while Pedro childishly refuses to accept "death," Juan is irredeemably "killed" when he falls into the hole: "¡Este sí que está muerto!" (p. 26). In this light the fine wall they build stands as a true monument to the renewed visibility they have gained as workers. Pedro has made sure that the hole has been transformed into strong foundations so that the wall will stand as high as they can possibly make it:

> PEDRO: No, no, no. Sígale edificando pa arriba Ud. no más, mientras más altura agarra la pirca, mejor
> D. CARLOS: No se vaya a mandar guardabajo no más.
> PEDRO: Pa eso la construí entrabá. (p. 37)

> [PEDRO: No, no, no. Just keep on building, the higher the wall, the better.
> D. CARLOS: It better not fall down on us.
> PEDRO: That's why I've built it with good deep foundations.]

The wall is built into the symbolic and physical structure of the play. When he tells Diego to build it as high as possible, Pedro is determining that its height will be the measure of their achievement and the proof of the impossibility of any dialogue between them and those on the other side, those who are blind to its significance in human terms.

As the object of their labor, the wall means different things for each of the protagonists, for each character relates to the work in different ways. Their individual identities emerge from the attitude they have to the task and not from the relationships they create with each other. Thus Pedro emerges as an artisan, Diego as the dispossessed lower-middle classes and Juan as the uneducated lumpen proletariat. Until a very late stage, they remain as three totally different social types who fill the working hours with parallel monologues and very little genuine interest in the others.

By the end of the play the wall has been transformed in the men's imaginations into the Esmeralda, the warship the national hero Arturo Prat died defending during the War of the Pacific. Entering wholeheartedly into the fantasy, they launch the ship, determined, like the real crew, to stay with it until the bitter end. The metaphor of the wall is thus doubled in strength, for like the Esmeralda it becomes a symbol of pride in their identity, and like the warship, it is doomed to destruction. With the launch, the men claim their momentary right to their creation: "Nosotros la levantamos, nosotros la inauguramos. Que la demuelan es cosa de ellos" (p. 43). The bosses in this line of thought are as much their enemies as the Peruvians had been Arturo Prat's, and the men are united at last in the recognition of their shared common circumstances.

If, on the whole, the relationship between the men is one of evasion, then their relationship with the dumb woman, María, shows some degree of concern and a large degree of self interest, the latter dictated by the fact that it is she who sells them their main means of evasion, wine. Their concern for her is informed by curiosity and by the challenge of finding a cure for her dumbness: having found out that she lost her power of speech "por un susto regrande que tuvo," the characters propose remedies, usually of a violent nature—at one point Juan suggests a beating, but this is rejected by Pedro on the grounds that it is unmanly to beat any woman other than his wife—but these only succeed in making her retreat even further into her protective shell.

The inability of Pedro and Juan to understand her silence other than as "logical" or "natural" leads Diego to pose the question, "¿Así es que para Ud. es lógico que estemos trabajando los tres aquí en las piedras?" (p. 6). He compares her dumbness with their work, a natural function that has been deprived her. María, in this sense, is representative of another social type, of those who have been shocked out of their power of self expression. Since she cannot speak for herself, the play provides María with a voice in the shape of La Mujer Evangélica who declares that María will regain her speech only when the wrongs of the world that caused such a fate have been put to rights: "Entonces nosotros aquí reunidos en este escenario te pedimos que le devuelvas la salud porque ella no es culpable. Todos somos culpables porque miramos sin ver, oímos sin escuchar, tocamos sin sentir" (p. 18) [So we on this stage ask you to return her to full health, because she is not guilty. We are all guilty, because we look without seeing, we hear without listening, we touch without feeling]. The message is too obvious to examine any closer, and it moves out of the illusion of theater to speak directly to the audience. María does, in fact, undergo a change in the course of the play. From apprehension at the beginning, when she tries to establish a purely business relationship with the workers, she begins to approach them, to feel at ease with them and to seek their company, little by little gaining the confidence and belief in herself that will lead her to utter a few sounds and, finally, to sing. The fear that had paralyzed her disintegrates as the wall becomes reality, and the men form a working team.

This development is captured in two photographs taken by María. The first is taken in the first act when the men, after having found an old camera, imagine wild schemes for exploiting it commercially and decide that dressing up as El Zorro would attract most customers. This photograph is blurred and unclear: "Estos no somos nosotros" (p. 24), says Juan when he sees it, as if he is looking at a reflection of his present state that he does not associate with the mental image he has of himself. But the second photograph, this time including their boss, Don Carlos, is a success: "Esta sí salió clarita, no como la otra que salió toda borrosa" (p. 45) [This one is clear, not all out of focus like the last one]. The second, clear photograph is testimony to a rekindled sense of identity.

Los payasos de la esperanza: A Drama of Impasse

Los payasos de la esperanza takes place as three unemployed clowns, or tonis, José, Jorge, and Manuel, await the verdict on a project they have proposed to the Church solidarity organization, La Vicaría de la Solidaridad, entailing entertainment for the children who are fed in the Vicaría's soup kitchens. In a disused room they spend a whole afternoon waiting for the woman who will tell them if their proposal has been accepted, but she never turns up. Meanwhile, as they talk and explore the objects in the room, they provide testimony of a life of abject poverty and abandonment, of the mysterious disappearance of a fourth clown, Iván, of the demeaning jobs they have to do to survive and which they experience as an attack on their dignity, for the most important thing in their lives is to work once again as professional tonis. In the end, after a long and fruitless wait they are forced to abandon the room, but in the final scene they seem unable to sum up the courage to leave and face the harsh, hopeless reality outside.

The first impression of Los payasos de la esperanza is of isolation: isolation as a result of abandonment in the outside world, reinforced by distance from one another. Each character arrives alone and enters into exchanges in which conversation does not flow but occurs in fits and bursts, following the soaring and plummeting spirits of the tonis. They are young (all between nineteen and twenty-three), but their appearance is of old, weary men, miserably dressed in clothes that add an absurd air to their appearance. Their state and that of the room show an intrinsic affinity from the very beginning: both are abandoned, derelict—products of lost time, lack of care, and the redundancy of the role they have played. The room is, ultimately, a mirror image of their moral state. It is described at the beginning in the following terms:

> Una pieza. Vieja. Llena de polvo. Las paredes, de color indefinido. Obra del tiempo y de la falta de cuidado . . . La atmósfera es de abandono. Da la impresión de que la pieza no ha sido habitada, ni ocupada para ningún fin práctico, desde hace largo tiempo. . . . La luz es pobre, amarillenta, a tono con el lugar. (p. 28)

> [A room. Old. Dusty. The walls are of an indeterminate color. This is a product of time and the lack of care. . . . The atmosphere is one of abandonment. The impression is that the room has not been lived in or used for any particular purpose for a long time. . . . The light is poor, yellowish, in tune with the place.]

Nothing happens in the course of the afternoon, but the clowns, prompted by the unusual and unfamiliar objects they find in a room that echoes their dejection, voice opinions and worries about their social and moral condition that would otherwise remain unsaid, and their almost unintentional thoughts give life to an unused room. Among the objects are an old trunk, in which they find abandoned prayer books, Bibles, an intimidating life-size statue of a saint with one hand missing—symbols of a religious faith they only obliquely share, but which influences their worldview—and a bench.

The saint is introduced in the first notes: "Fondo izquierda espectador, un bulto cubierto por un paño. Luego sabremos que es un santo. De tamaño natural" (p. 28) [Backstage, left, a shape covered by a cloth. Later we'll find that it is a saint. Life-size]. Their attention is drawn to the statue during a rehearsal of the ritual, buttock-slapping routines to which they introduce the novice, Manuel. These routines, however, are old and worn, and the clowns find it difficult to concentrate on them, turning their attention instead to the statue. By means of the saint, a set of vague religious values are brought to life, often through an unlikely process of association. For example, the clowns imagine themselves as having followed the saints into the circus ring as latter-day victims of a cruel world, but equally redeemable by virtue of their moral integrity and their belief in their vocation: like the saints, they imagine, they will endure anything rather than surrender to superior forces.

As the clowns reflect on injustice in this world and Catholic promises of the salvation of the poor in the next, they consider questions of life and death with a deep skepticism, peppered with the satisfying prospect of revenge to be relished in the next life. They home in on the promise of the poor being the inheritors of the kingdom of heaven, and in this scheme of things their human role is passive, they are acted upon by circumstances beyond their control and, they themselves are incapable of changing a predetermined course. In many senses this attitude is an indication of overall social underdevelopment, for it distances the blow of the economic hardships they suffer by shifting the emphasis away from wordly comforts to heavenly promises. Responsibility for their fate can ultimately be transferred to a heavenly body that may work in mysterious ways, but that has only their best spiritual interests at heart. This is expressed in its most literal sense as the future recognition of their professional worth:

JORGE: . . . Oye, ¿los santos resucitan?
MANUEL: Claro, pus.
JORGE: ¿Y nosotros?
MANUAL: También, pos.
JORGE: (A JOSE) ¿Te cachái, güaso?
JOSE: ¿Qué?
JORGE: Que resucitáramos.
JOSE: [*Poniendose una peluca de toni que ha sacado de su maletin*] ¿Y pa qué vamos a resucitar?
JORGE: Pa ser tonis.
JOSE: Si, pero con fama. No toos cagaos.
MANUEL: Tonis con casa. (p. 65)

[JORGE: . . . Listen, do saints come back to life?
MANUEL: Of course they do.
JORGE: And what about us?
MANUEL: We do as well.
JORGE: *(To José)* Did you hear that?
JOSE: What?
JORGE: We come back to life.
JOSE: *(Putting on a clown's wig that he has taken out of his bag.)* And what are we going to come back for?
JORGE: To be clowns.
JOSE: Yes, but famous ones. Not all screwed up.
MANUEL: Clowns with a house.]

This notion of the hereafter as a brighter version of the here and now is expressed in a clowns' poem that describes the fate of the professional clown in a melodramatically pessimistic way, in terms of the ruthlessly transitory nature of their performing life and of their fate to be immediately forgotten by an ungrateful public. This is finally an integral part of their identity: "Tal vez cuando el payaso se muera, / de aquel que se han reído / ni siquiera se acordarán. / Cual música pasajera que lentamente se va, / ni el recuerdo se quedará. / ¡Oh! ingratitud de la vida, / así como de todos se olvidan / de estos payasos se olvidarán" [Perhaps when the clown dies, / the people he made laugh / will not even remember him. / Like passing music that slowly fades away, / not even his memory will remain. / Oh ungrateful life, / just as everyone is forgotten, / these clowns also will be forgotten] (p. 71). The poem engages the same suggestion of the essential cruelty of this world and adds a dose of sincerely felt self-pity: the archetypal clown in tears behind his painted mask.

The bench is the central prop. Throughout the long wait they sit on the bench as if in a rota, never sharing it, as they each vie for a place and inevitably fall off in typical slapstick routines. It becomes finally a symbol of hoping and waiting, when, at the end, it serves as the prop for the relentless religious imagery as they all share Jorge's stolen bread in a scene aping the last supper:

Es la repartición del pan. Jorge parte la hallulla en dos y cada parte en tres y reparte. Manuel corre el baúl hasta ubicarlo entre el santo y el banco. Comen con deleite. Como si fuera un banquete. Tiempo. (p. 74)

[This is the sharing of the bread. Jorge breaks the bun in two and then each part in three and shares it out. Manuel slides the trunk along until it is between the saint and the bench. They eat the food with pleasure. As if it were a banquet. Time passes.]

The sharing of the bread unites them in a grave ceremony in a way they had consciously or unconsciously avoided beforehand:

Manuel mira el techo. Mira a José y a Jorge. Hay algo nuevo en esa relación. José le hace un lugar a Manuel en el banco. Manuel va y se sienta entre Jorge y José. Jorge casi cae del banco. Empuja del otro lado. Hasta que apenas se acomodan los tres en el banco. Muy juntos. (p. 79)

[Manuel looks at the roof. He looks at José and Jorge. There is something new in this relationship. José makes space for Manuel on the bench. Manuel goes and sits between Jorge and José. Jorge almost falls

off the bench. He pushes from the other side. Until all three can just fit
on to the bench. Very close together.]

At this stage they seem to be at one with each other and with their
immediate environment. What is the new element in their relationship? Only that they have accepted the fact that they are all in
the same situation, for, by introducing Manuel to the profession, the
tonis have made one significant step during the wait, they have
decided that they must offer some hope to those who have no straw
to cling to. Once part of the "army" of waiting or hopeful clowns,
Manuel has an equal right to a place on the bench. His "puras ganas
de ser toni" (p. 54) have been replaced by the wait for the opportunity to work in his new profession.

   Jorge dreams of another life in the south where his fears and
problems would be washed away: ". . . La lluvia parece que te
lavara por dentro y por juera" ("It's as if rain washes you inside and
out", p. 55). Outside it is raining, but the rain of Jorge's imagination
has nothing to do with the rain battering against the window panes
and only drives home the reality of their isolation from an alien
outside. Jorge relates to the positive elements in rain, he makes a
big raindrop prop from a piece of wire he finds, but he is aware that
this water also has a negative side. He likens their wait to that of a
castaway who, after an interminable wait and countless SOS signals, is eventually discovered as a heap of bones, still in an attitude
of hopeful waiting: "Así vamos a estar nosotros con la esperanza"
("That's how we're going to end up waiting", p. 57). For this reason
he convinces himself that the saint (really St. John) is Peter, a
double symbol, both doorman to heaven and vigilant fisherman,
"the one that's always looking out to sea."

   The dynamics of the wait are given their rhythm by the contrasts
forced on the protagonists as their dreams and illusions provide a
stark contrast to the dinginess of the room. Jorge's elated dreams
are followed by dives into the depths of despair, as is the case when,
for the first time, the abandoned state of the room is explicitly
recognized:

JORGE: . . . A veces creo que estamos cagaos de aentro. Que no tenimos güelta. Parece que hubiéramos estao siempre así. Que nunca
   hubiera habío nadie.
JOSE: ¿Cómo?
JORGE: Así, pus.

Jorge y José recorren con la mirada toda la habitación. Como si la vieran por primera vez. Descubren lo vieja, sucia y polvorienta que es. Jorge mira lentamente a José.

JORGE: Así como too muerto . . .

JOSE: [*luego de una pausa*] Fin de mundo. (p. 55)

[JORGE: . . . At times I think that we must be totally screwed up inside. That there's no way out. It's as if we've always been like this. As if nobody's ever been here.

JOSE: What do you mean?

JORGE: Just look.

Jorge and José look around the room. As if they were seeing it for the first time. They realize how old, dirty and dusty it is. Jorge looks slowly at José.

JORGE: As if everything's dead . . .

JOSE: (*After a pause*) The end of the world.]

The geographical end of the world that would mean escape, rain, and renewal is far removed from this crude and cruel reality. Almost imperceptibly at first, the room is set up as a metaphor for Chile, a name that is said to mean "donde acaba la tierra," the end of the earth.[10] In other passages the *tonis* are depicted as being lost in the reality of present Chile where a limbolike state reigns, and where they cannot legitimately hope for an escape. This is brought home again by Jorge in an unusually long and lyrical passage when he relates the essence of being Chilean to the only time he has seen a condor, preying on a flock of sheep:

Y yo miro . . . y ahí lo veo que viène por el aire. Chis, las medias garras que tiene. Son así como el brazo de uno. Si es cierto. Y entronces se va tirando en pica . . . y nosotros dale con esparramar a las ovejas. Y agarra a una y se la lleva volando. A mí me dio susto. Y me dio pena también por la ovejita. (p. 77)

[And I look around . . . and then I see it flying through the air. Jeez, the size of its claws. The size of an arm, I swear. Then it comes swooping down . . . and we're trying to scatter the sheep. And it grabs one and flies away with it. I got a fright. And I felt sorry for the poor sheep.]

It is at moments such as this that the primary symbols of the play come together. The memory of the natural power and energy of the great bird of prey brings him back sharply from what had been "a sensual and emotional memory" to the harshness of daily life in which they, too, are governed by such powerful and undiscriminating forces:

> JORGE: Como al Iván.
> MANUEL: ¿Ah?
> JORGE: Se lo llevó el condor. (p. 77)
>
> [JORGE: Like Iván.
> MANUEL: Eh?
> JORGE: The condor flew off with him.]

So Iván is represented as one of the flock unable to defend himself from the clutches of an unfathomable force with the power to eliminate without rhyme or reason. The condor and the sheep are part of the natural struggle for survival, while Iván has become the victim of a new way of life for them, where, as the weakest, there can be no certainty against falling prey to circumstances, that is, the arbitrariness of the system. This is reflected in the dramatic structure of the play in which the conflict is provided by an absent power.

In one description of the play, it is stated that, along with José, Jorge, Manuel and the absent Iván, "Quizás sí los acompaña un quinto personaje: inmóvil, ciego, mudo, mutilado. Es la figura del santo" [Perhaps a fifth person is with them: motionless, blind, dumb, mutilated. The figure of the saint].[11] Yet, there is a sixth character, Señorita Sonia. She represents the (albeit here benevolent) machinery grinding behind the scenes, dealing in names and figures, but not in faces and lives. The fact that they can put a name to this machinery lifts their hopes, sets success within reach, and conditions their willingness to wait. However, this name will become synonymous with rejection and despair.

Los payasos de la esperanza is based on observation, on a kind of man watching through which every action of the characters speaks for their whole being and for a vision of the world. As they work on the material, the actors look for what they call "la columna vertebral" that is, the central preoccupation of the protagonists at that specific moment. This is what the company say about the "situación madre" that required the central idea to be that of the wait, held together by unity of time and space:

> . . . el antagonista estaba fuera del escenario. No pensamos nunca en una situación de conflicto que se dijera entre los personajes, sino que la situación de conflicto era el "impasse" que vivían ellos.[12]

[. . . the antagonist was outside the space on stage. We never thought of a conflictive situation between the characters, but that the conflict was the "impasse" that they were living.]

It is for this reason that Señorita Sonia becomes another character, part of the machinery that regulates their experience, that condemns them to wait and condemns them to act in the typical manner of those trapped in impasse situations, reduced to making ineffectual moves. One such is the letter about their dilemma, which they write with great difficulty and finally fold up and guard in José's pocket. This brings us to the crux of the matter: the permanent cultural nature of their predicament, for the actual writing of a letter demonstrates their hopeless lack of education. Although the *tonis* themselves do not possess the means to escape from their position, this is not exclusively a result of the new circumstances, but of a social and educational background that has dictated their place in society and, in the reigning social and economic atmosphere, leaves them standing at a great distance even from the starting post.

The greatest dilemma of the *tonis* is that of their complete marginalization, for they cannot even be fully incorporated into the only organization that can offer them a possible way out. Before his disappearance, Iván had given up all hope of being a *toni* in the future; José, on the other hand, clings to the positive side of waiting, of being what Jorge's father had called a "soldadito de la esperanza." Despite the fact that he remembers his father's words that "lo más bonito es la esperanza," even Jorge must call on all his moral resources to turn waiting into hope: "Es como si me hubieran matado otro soldadito más. Yo no sé si voy a ganar esta guerra, pero yo sigo igual no más" (p. 56). And Manuel's initiation into the group is initiation into a state of permanent waiting.

An integral part of this play is the use of moments of suspended action when the *tonis'* attitudes suggest camera stills. They usually occur when the clowns are looking toward the outside in the vain hope that someone has eventually arrived to provide a solution (pp. 33, 43, 73, 77, 79). The photos are of three "payasos de la esperanza," looking to where they imagine their hope lies. Only the last photograph, which catches them huddled together on the bench, does not show them looking out, for now they are merely listening to the rain and nervously and reluctantly contemplating departure. The room offers them a certain freedom, for there they can act as they wish, suspended in time and sheltered by their distance from crude reality. And they are kept hanging on, too, by a desperate hope and a fear that someone might turn up if they abandon the room.

Toward the end of the play, the moral disintegration becomes complete. The dialogue takes on features of the absurd, as the exchanges break down into unfinished sentences, disconnected in composition and only completed through a strained common effort. The whole atmosphere is one of resignation: "Total que no hicimos ná" (p. 78). Time is the essence of this play; its passing without event adds a circular quality brought out in the plays of light that suggest an ever-repeated pattern. At the beginning the light is "Pobre, amarillenta, a tono con el lugar"; by the end, "La luz ha disminuído más todavía. Es la misma o menor que la del comienzo, cuando entró Jose" [The light is dimmer. It is the same or less than at the beginning, when José came in] (p. 79). It is a return to the opening situation, to the long pauses and inarticulate exchanges, suggesting that the clowns lack the energy to make sense of their situation and are united by their total inability to provide any way forward, at one with the fading light and the abandoned room. It is finally not belief in their future as *tonis* that provides the hint of a hope, but the dream of the impossible cleansing journey south. Meanwhile they are trapped in the room, unwilling to leave and face the real rain outside. They may even take the absurdity of the wait outside with them when they eventually do decide to leave:

JORGE: [*a Manuel*] Ponéte los zapatos de toni.
MANUEL: ¿Pa qué?
JORGE: Así llegái más rápido. (p. 78)

[JORGE: *(To Manuel)* Put on the clown shoes.
MANUEL: What for?
JORGE: You'll get there quicker.]

· *Tres Marías y una Rosa:* Female Labor as Testimony

Tres Marías y una Rosa is set in two acts, each divided into three scenes, or *cuadros,* each one devoted to the presentation and the subsequent resolution of specific problems affecting the pro- tagonists. In the first *cuadro* a new member, Rosita, is introduced to a workshop where *arpilleras* are made, causing conflicts for the existing members, Maruja, María Ester, and María Luisa; by the second scene she has been accepted, and the members set about teaching her the trade. The first act closes in the third scene at a moment of crisis when they find out there exists a glut of *arpilleras*, as a result of which the central controlling body has decided that work must be suspended until further notice. Two of the members, María Luisa and María Ester, decide that survival must come before loyalty and offer their services to a "butic" in the commercial sector where *arpilleras* are sold as fashionable art to the rich.[13] The second act sees the resolution of this problem when, after discovering that they cannot accept the restrictions imposed on their compositions by the management of the *butic*, who object to their portrayal of working-class themes, the two wayward members ask to be accepted back. With the workshop reestablished, the members then set about the creation of a giant *arpillera* commissioned by a foreign priest in the nearby parish. The measure of their unity is put to the test in the hurried completion of the giant creation, "La Cueca del Juicio Final."

Tres Marías is a work that echoes the vivid realism of the *arpilleras. Arpilleras* are wholly documentary, and in the years since 1973 have taken on a real social and political value. The tapestries emerged as the testimonies of the wives of political prisoners, of victims of the repression and of the unemployed.[14] The play acts as a valuable counterpart to the other works studied here since it provides insights into the broader implications of male unemployment on the family and the changing, more openly protagonistic, role of the women. At the heart of the play lies the question of dignity and a sense of identity, both severely undermined in the present circumstances. As the family suffers through the demoralization of the former breadwinner, the destruction of a whole way of living becomes imminent, and part of the women's role is to fend off its total disappearance.

The clearest statement of the man's present role in the family is his absence from the stage. A recent study into the impact of unemployment on the family sums up male marginalization in the following way: "Ha perdido su identidad, y su discurso de hombre trabajador a quien hay que servir y atender después de la jornada, se ve debilitado. Ello se expresa, según la mujer, en el mal genio, intolerancia, agresividad, insomnio, aislamiento, angustia, evasión en el alcohol" [He has lost his identity, and the discourse of the working man who has to be served and attended to after a day's work has been weakened. That is expressed, according to the woman, in bad temper, intolerance, aggressiveness, insomnia, isolation, anguish, evasion through alcohol].[15] All these products of long term unemployment felt at first hand in the home become, as María Luisa bitterly comments, "otra condición 'básica' para entrar al

taller" (p. 202). In effect, the real basic requirement for entrance to
the workshop is that the partner is unemployed and that there is no
other source of income into the household.

The only man whose existence is physically acknowledged is
Negro, Maruja's husband, and that only because the workshop is
held in his house. His bicycle is alternately present and absent in
each scene, indicating his intermittent outings to look for work.
Negro's spoken role is limited to the "voice en off," only ever
shouting abuse at the women, angry at the fact of his house being
occupied by a bunch of "viejas de mierda" (p. 198), and frustrated
by his own marginality. As a trade union leader, he had a reputation
in the shanty town of activeness and involvement, but as a result of
his activities he lost his job and was a victim of severe political
repression that, according to María Luisa, left him "medio raro."
Now his place in Maruja's *arpilleras* is of a man standing at a
window, looking out at a world of which he has ceased to be a
useful part. His ability or willingness to support his wife is nil, the
only time he does offer encouragement being when he thinks that
the *taller* is on the brink of disintegration.

The marginalization of the other husbands becomes manifest in
different ways. In broad terms each of the three women has been
failed in her marriage: María Ester has to live with the humiliating
knowledge that her husband's only source of income comes from
sleeping with the shopkeeper and her daughter; María Luisa's
husband has gone abroad to look for work but has sent home
nothing but postcards; Rosita's husband works in a factory where
his grotesque pay is Donald Duck and Mickey Mouse toys, which
she is then forced to try to sell. These absent men are the protagonists in other plays, those who can come to terms neither with
the fact that their historic role has been taken out of their hands nor
with the growing suspicion of the permanent nature of their present
weakened state.

To some extent, the women are living a reverse situation to the
men. Woman has always been on the very margins of society, where
traditionally her man wanted her to be, doing the job he believes
she is cut out for and supporting him in the accomplishment of his
role: "Resulta que ya saliendo la mujer a trabajar ya el hombre
como que se ata más a la casa. Yo tengo este concepto, que la mujer
lo esté alimentando a uno, le digo sinceramente, no me gusta. Como
debe ser: el marido trae plata y la mujer en la casa" [The fact is that
when the woman goes out to work, the man seems to get more tied
to the house. Quite frankly, I don't like the woman to be the bread
winner. Things as they should be: the husband brings in the money

and the wife stays at home].[16] The women know they must tread lightly as they fill the gap left by the inability of the male member of the household to support the family. Behind their determination to support their families is the constant awareness that they must not damage the men's pride. Before entering the *taller*, Rosita has her eyes opened to the fact that she is encroaching on male territory:

MARUJA: ¿Usted ha hablado esto con su marido?

ROSITA: No he hablado nada.

MARUJA: Tendría que hablarle primero después se molestan donde una trabaja.

ROSITA: ¡Qué tiene que venir a decir! ¡Si no tiene plata no tiene que venir a decir, po!

MARUJA: Se molestan donde es una la que pone la plata pa'la casa, Rosita.

ROSITA: Ah . . . (p. 203)

[MARUJA: Have you talked about this to your husband?

ROSITA: I haven't said a thing.

MARUJA: You should talk to him first, because then they get angry when you go out to work.

ROSITA: What can he have to say! If he doesn't bring in any money he can't say a thing, can he!

MARUJA: They get upset when it's the woman who's bringing the money home, Rosita.

ROSITA: Ah . . .]

Despite their new role, the women are still caught in the macho mold of their society. Maruja, the head of the *taller*, is told: "Hay que saber ponerse los pantalones pa'ser Jefa y tomar decisiones" (p. 203). Only at certain moments, when they are alone and know that there are no men eavesdropping, do the four *arpilleristas* openly voice their discontent with the traditional role imposed on them, a role characterized by violent treatment, disregard for the vital part they play in the family and disrespect for their individual needs and rights. It is only among "puras mujeres" that the freedom to assert their personal identity exists. In a mock wedding ceremony Rosita is initiated into a revised institution of marriage:

M. ESTER: ¿Señora Rosa Martínez acepta usted seguir a este hombre en el dolor, la adversidad, la desgracia, la miseria, el hambre y los terremotos?

ROSITA: No.

M. ESTER: ¿Acepta que la cachetee, que le ponga el gorro, que la llene de chiquillos, que no traiga plata pa'la casa, que llegue curao?

ROSITA: No.

M. LUISA: Así me gusta.

M. ESTER: Y usted, don Rafael, promete solemnemente ante este altar sagrado no cachetearla, no ponerle el gorro, no llenarla de chiquillos, no llegar curao y traer plata pa'la casa?

MARUJA: ¡Bravo, señor cura! ¡Otra vez, señor! ¡Otra vez! [de pie.]

M. ESTER: ¿Promete que no le va a dar todas las noches con la cuestión porque aburre también?

M. LUISA: ¡Que prometa! ¡Que prometa!

M. ESTER: ¿Promete pedir el favor solamente cuando ella tenga ganas?

TODAS: ¡Prometido!

M. ESTER: ¿Promete que después de occurrido el hecho, hacer por lo menos un cariñito? (pp. 233–34)

[M. ESTER: Señora Rosa Martínez, are you willing to follow this man through suffering, adversity, misfortune, poverty, hunger and earthquakes?

ROSITA: No.

M. ESTER: Are you willing to accept that he beats you, goes with other women, gives you loads of children, doesn't bring any money home, and is always drunk?

ROSITA: No.

M. LUISA: That's what I like to hear.

M. ESTER: And you, don Rafael. Do you solemnly promise before this sacred altar not to beat her up, not to go with other women, not to give her loads of children, not to come home drunk and to bring money home?

MARUJA: Well said, Father! Say it again! Let's hear it again! (*Standing up.*)

M. ESTER: Do you promise not to bother her every night for you-know-what, because that gets a bit boring?

M. LUISA: Yes, make him promise!

M. ESTER: Do you promise only to ask for her favours when she feels like it?

ALL: Promised!

M. ESTER: And do you promise that once you've finished, you'll at least give her a little cuddle?]

Yet, the mere voice of Negro reduces their fantasies to follies. An ideal world may consist of a life without the various painful conditions of marriage, but the reality of their role as wives and mothers means that they will never abandon the family in which their role, now more than ever, is to provide support, economic as well as moral. This common experience is given expression in the *arpilleras*. For, although the women may often talk of their husbands as if they were irresponsible, uncontrollable adolescents whose immature images of themselves are a cause for exasperation, nevertheless, in the tapestries they are usually portrayed with dignity.

The *arpilleras* provide a very personal view of contemporary Chile and are an insight into the dreams and aspirations of their creators. These dreams may, on one hand, relate to better treatment and more respect from the men, but, on the other, they relate to visions of a better and more just life altogether. María Luisa, for example, does not depict soup kitchens and shanty town life, instead she creates "un mural de vida" (p. 213) into which she pours all her anger and hunger for justice. She portrays her need for a promise of salvation which, by definition, must come from another world since this one has proved such a dismal failure in that respect. In her interpretation of the Last Judgment, God descends from a UFO to judge the rich and pardon the poor, a view of divine retribution born of the ingrained bitterness and disillusion that characterize her *arpilleras,* all a variation on the search for a spark of hope.

As an essential requirement for the market abroad, the scenes must be shown to be explicitly Chilean, and the most prominent sign of this is the *cordillera* which, as Marjorie Agosín demonstrates, becomes a symbol both of Chileanness and of a different world: "El intenso colorido, los personjaes en movimiento, los árboles verdes, el anhelo de agua fresca y la cordillera de los Andes enmarcando todas las arpilleras, transmiten una esperanza de vida distinta. Una arpillera sin la cordillera de los Andes no sería real" [The intense color, the people in motion, the green trees, the longing for clean water and the Andes mountains, transmit a hope for a different life. An *arpillera* without the Andes would not be real].[17] Yet, as Rosita points out toward the end of the play, the value of these symbols is relative, for an image that may be the sign of all things Chilean to a foreigner may not hold any bearing on those Chileans whose experience of their country is limited to their shanty town and who can only dream of access to the picture-postcard style environment that provides the most blatant symbols of the country's identity.

This is borne out by their final interpretation of the Last Judgment, the subject of the giant *arpillera* commissioned by the foreign priest. Here, heaven is populated by very bored people sitting on clouds, while hell is a *caracol*,[18] where the devils are having a wonderful time around a *parrillada,* a barbecue. For the priest this is an engima, for it is a very personal vision of the Day of Judgment, rooted in the image of contemporary Chile as a consumer heaven for those that can have access to the *caracoles,* and hell for those who do not. The priest's reaction to the giant *arpillera* shows him to be in search of a simpler, more positive image, less sad and despondent, and more Chilean, for even the presence of the Cordillera de los Andes does not convince him in this case.

Finally, they do as the priest requests and change María's Luisa's stern, apocalyptic interpretation of the Day of Judgment with God as a policeman catching everyone in his net, into a happier, folkloric account, in which signs of Chileanness are provided by the *cueca,* the Chilean national dance, and "unas fondas bien endieciochás."[19] The result is a vision of the fulfillment of the promise of the salvation of the good, that is, the poor. But even then, María Luisa must be persuaded to take her wayward husband out of the flames of hell—in case he turns up and demands an explanation! This *arpillera* finally becomes a fusion of María Luisa's great obsession and their interpretation of contemporary Chile.

Tres Marías bears witness to the drastic changes in the hitherto well defined role played by each member of a family unit. It is a play that provides an insight into the multiple role played by the *talleres* and the work carried out in them. For women who have had to adapt their lifestyles to fast diminishing resources, who often cannot count on the support of men demoralized by the loss of their traditional identity, who have been absolutely abandoned or who, in many cases, have considered that the only escape is through suicide, the *talleres* provide a mechanism of moral support as well as of financial subsistence.

By its very nature, *Tres Marías* is an eloquent symbol for the marginalization of those who become the subjects of the *arpilleras.* The *arpilleristas* use a formerly unpaid traditional female skill to provide the only source of income in the family, thereby introducing it to the, albeit marginal, labor market. Despite the fact that these women are now the principal support for their families, the income is precarious, and they and the work they produce remain invisible in the wider public sphere. Finally, as the men struggle to retain some vestige of dignity or, alternatively, retreat into anonymous shells, women like the *arpilleristas* become custodians of an identity and artists of human dignity. Scenes of hope and solidarity allow glimpses of a spirit that still exists, if somewhat cowed by circumstances.

Testimonies of Marginalization

A sense of double marginalization lies at the heart of *Pedro, Juan y Diego, Los payasos de la esperanza* and *Tres Marías y una Rosa:* one the concrete marginalization through a lack of access to help and support mechanisms, the other the growing sense of exclusion from a society that is undergoing many changes to which the protagonists have no access. From a sense of temporary exclusion, this gradually develops into one of permanent exclusion, and the means of escape gradually diminish, becoming restricted to short-term strategies to survive. The long-term future bears no meaning for these characters, and the men especially fill their limbo with often unrealistic schemes or fantasy escapes based on far-off nostalgic notions of happiness and success. Alternatively, work or its rehearsal becomes an obsessive ritual. In *Los payasos de la esperanza,* the *tonis* endlessly use the objects they find in the room to create new numbers for their act, and imagine their success in the circus ring. In *Pedro, Juan y Diego,* work is rendered a ritual in which the men do not believe, but which allows for a recollection of self-respect. It is only in *Tres Marías y una Rosa* that the work the women are involved in is a source of fulfillment; here rituals relate to the unchanging aspects of their domestic lives.

Each of these plays portrays the deterioration of human relationships. Juan complains of the lack of companionship he encounters in his job, where the relationship with his workmates is superficial, normally distant, but charged with underlying conflicts that are never faced up to, evaded in childish games, wishful thinking, or pure nostalgia. Rosita, like so many other characters, has considered that suicide is an alternative that would demand less strength than to stand up to things, as it is her role to do. José, on the verge of defeat, explains the lack of solidarity they experience by the fact that they are not the worst off—". . . la solidaridad empieza por los más cagaos" (p. 48)—and by the far more cynical, "Deben pensar que andamos cagaos de la risa" (p. 56). In both *Tres Marías* and *Los payasos de la esperanza,* solidarity has become synonymous with help from abroad, it is something the characters no longer associate with their immediate environment.

Dialogues are littered with nostalgic recollections of times past. They relate to a time of relative strength, of a well-established identity, of participation in making decisions about their own lives. They take the shape of childhood memories, of times of security in a safe family unity when there was hope in the future. They are evoked now as a way of passing idle moments or as indirect ways of lamenting the present atmosphere, the antithesis of all that is care-free and open. In this atmosphere, the characters cannot even provide their own children with an illusion of security, for the family has begun to disintegrate: Negro's belief in himself is so utterly destroyed that he has given up responsibility for his daughter by sending her to live with her grandparents until he can play the role of father again. Time and again characters or relatives alluded to shrink back from the present reality, the men in alcohol, María in her dumbness, and one character's mother in a strange condition that stops her from expressing herself fully. All speak for the general growing marginality of their class, their lack of access to the means of communication; but the *arpilleras* provide testimony to continuing existence and resistance.

There is also evidence of a much more sinister reality which, unlike the physical hardships that cause desperation, causes terror. When the women in *Tres Marías* describe the constant circling of helicopters over their shanty town and mention how they must sleep with identification close at hand; these are asides that report their loss of any peace of mind, disturbed by the constant sub-conscious memory of the Ivéns and the Negros of their world—those who have disappeared mysteriously and without trace and those who have been victims of political repression so fierce that it has destroyed their former selves. Sudden evidence of this reality terrifies them, as is demonstrated in *Los payasos de la esperanza:*

> Se escucha una sirena. Primero como de un carro de bomberos. Luego se le unen otras. Se van acercando. Sensación de un gran accidente. Se debe crear una amósfera de estado de emergencia. José y Manuel se paran. Están como paralogizados por el sonido. (pp. 58–59)

> [A siren is heard. At first like the siren of a fire engine. Then others are heard joining it. They are getting closer. There is an sensation of a big accident. An atmosphere of a state of emergency should be created. Jorge and Manuel stand up. It is as if they are paralyzed by the noise.]

These indications of the concrete reality against which the plays are set, in the form of unexplained sirens or voices that strike fear into the characters, are a fundamental part of the drama, for without them the picture of the protagonists' lives would be incomplete. Indeed, the drama itself would be void of conflict if they were absent, for they are the voice of the antagonist. On a wider social scale they are constant reminders of the forces that govern them and that wage a war against potential insurrection in the shanty towns. As they eat Jorge's stolen bread, the *tonis* confess different petty crimes they have committed, but their reaction to the signs of power described above indicates that somehow they always feel hunted, guilty of some undefined crime.

These themes are dealt with in other plays where the major effects of unemployment are exposed as a loss of identity, of the means of expression and of a wealth of cultural history founded on common aims and needs. *El último tren* [The last train][20] by Gustavo Meza and Imagen, addresses all these themes. It takes place in a small railway station that has been run for generations by the Maragaño family and is now in the hands of Ismael Maragaño. The branch is under threat of closure, a move that is wholeheartedly supported by Marcial Contreras,[21] the local supervisor, and opposed by Ismael, who fights the closure, sure of his good record and convinced that his name and history of good work in the community will ensure the support of the locals. The play begins with the arrival of Ismael's sister, Mercedes, from Venezuela, freshly divorced and looking to start anew in the heart of the family. But she is horrified when she finds that her niece, Violeta, has turned to prostitution in order to pay off her father's debts after being forced to sleep with Contreras to save her father his job—while he lives under the illusion that it is his good name that has won him time and money. The climax comes when the order for the closure of the station arrives and Violeta, having lost her local employment, decides she must go to work in the city in order to save her family. But it is too late, for Ismael has already taken refuge in madness and the memory of happier times.

The fate of Ismael and the railway, both representative of an old stable tradition, demonstrates the ruthless disregard for this past. As the railway becomes redundant in the new way of things, it is made clear that the characters are in the process of losing more than their livelihood, for the railway had also been a place for cultural expression and artistic gatherings. Ismael preempts this by retreating into a world of madness, irresponsibility and aimless remembering. Violeta, on the other hand, responds to the dictates of the fight for survival according to the new rules, realizing that the former values of unity, solidarity and care for the weakest are no longer valid. The rules for the fight for survival are dictated by Marcial Contreras, the personification of the economy which he himself describes as "dura, fría . . . hasta implacable" (p. 131). It is this anonymous force, The Economy, that has been the cause of their incipient exclusion from society. The Economy and its offspring "el milagro económico," which the characters constantly refer to in amazed wonderment, for they can see no evidence of a miracle, is another constant in these testimonial works.

The treatment of the themes of work, unemployment and marginality on the professional stage serves several purposes. It counterbalances the general silence about these sectors and the repression of their freedom of expression, which is seen to be intrinsically subversive of the new order. By looking beyond the superficial "tranquilidad pública," possible only through the repression of these sectors, groups reach the "temática entregada" that the *arpilleristas* rely on. By dealing with chronic unemployment and the marginalization of such great numbers of people from active participation in society, the groups aim to confront the relatively cushioned middle classes with a bitter reality, to prompt reflection on a state of "adormecimiento que se nos ha afectado a todos"[22] and to transform the public's perception of what is happening around them. At the same time they introduce new stage metaphors for the new overall atomized state of society, which we will see echoed as we turn to questions of power, seen in terms of stagnation and renewal.

3
Questions of Power: Stagnation and Renewal

1978: Questions of Power

By 1978 the Pinochet regime was firmly in power, the economy was looking up after a severe recession, and the free market economy was in full swing, with the ensuing influx of luxury consumer goods. Prosperity was in the air for the better off. Marxist "contamination" was at bay, and while opposition was finding a limited voice, it was nothing that could not be coped with, and repression was more selective. "La tranquilidad pública" was reigning. Pinochet, who seemed to have little to fear, was already making plans for at least sixteen years of military rule. Nineteen seventy-eight saw the first performances of three plays, *Una pena y un cariño* [Sadness and joy] by Teatro la Feria: *Baño a baño* (Bath to bath), a collective creation by Jorge Vega, Jorge Pardo, and Guillermo de la Parra; *Lo crudo, lo cocido y lo podrido* by Marco Antonio de la Parra[1] that explore the image painted above and the grim truth of the way it is achieved and maintained, and have at their center a preoccupation with the manipulation of power.

With *Hojas de Parra*, Teatro la Feria had first hand experience of the means by which public order is achieved; with their second production, *Bienaventurados los pobres*, they still could not find a balance, alienating a potential audience and losing financially. With *Una pena y un cariño*, performed in a disused hall far from the center of Santiago, they began to achieve some artistic and economic balance. The work had a run of fourteen weeks, and while it was not a financial success story, neither was it a financial disaster.[2]

Using the device of a play within a play, *Una pena y un cariño* presents a microcosm of society and introduces some of the themes and symbols we will see repeated in other plays. The form is that of a rehearsal for a touristic spectacular called "The Roots of Chile," designed to give an account of Chile's history, music, and people,

89

and which will, above all, allow the audience to appreciate their own proverbial warmth and hospitality. The rehearsal takes place in an old hall far removed from the picture-postcard version of Chile, and the company is composed of struggling actors and desperate extras, enticed by the promise of a tour of North America.

The trite message of the propaganda is of a country growing stronger and stronger in the face of great adversity: "Después de cada desastre este país sale más fortalecido. Eso es muy importante. O sea el Ave fénix renace de sus cenizas" (p. 328) [This country emerges stronger from each disaster. That is very important. The phoenix rises from the ashes].

Yet, this image of disasters is wrought with problems of interpretation and is rid of any dangerous implications by making reference only to natural disasters, such as earthquakes. By contrast, the increasingly demoralizing effect of the social disasters faced by the actors every day must be hidden from sight, avoided at all costs. The objective is an image of tranquil unity in an atmosphere of quiet progress, in reality created artificially by silencing dissident sectors and superimposing an official cultural and political norm: "En Orden y Paz Chile Avanza."[3]

The difficulties involved in providing the required image of Chile form an analogy between the creative and political processes. Because materials are scarce and resources limited, many scenes must be reduced or scrapped altogether, so inevitably the end result will be imperfect. Those at the top of the hierarchy, while demanding very specific results, do not provide the means by which to achieve them. While making ample use of the promise of a tour, of amounts of money that will solve immediate economic problems and that encourage endurance of immediate hardship, the actual rewards are nowhere to be seen, and there is the possibility that the employees, unpaid and with no stated rights, may inevitably tend toward an option that will be far more rewarding morally, if not financially. If the only reward the promoters offer is monetary and the money is not forthcoming, the actors may well be tempted away by groups who do not pretend to pay, but who satisfy the need to express grievances and achieve artistic fulfillment.

Una pena y un cariño gives a clear, if over simplistic, idea of the propagandistic creation of a "decontaminated" society in which real social problems become unclean and untouchable. The sequence of scenes serves to reveal the divide between propaganda and reality. This is reminiscent of José Ricardo Morales's idea of "double consumerism": Chile is a product to be sold by means of publicity, and the publicity, in the form of the "Roots of Chile" spectacular, is propaganda, aimed at an audience eager to consume pretty images of a Chilean paradise. In this sense, the actors are pawns in the building of the consumer society. Yet, on stage a tableau of the rural idyll of a benevolent and just management of paternalistic power is consistently intruded upon by the real misery of the marginal urban poor. This device will be repeated in *Baño a baño* when the quintessential decontaminating agent, the Turkish bath, becomes the backdrop against which those in power parade their grotesque methods of cleansing society.

Baño a baño: Baths and Barracks

Baño a baño, in one act, is a crude, unsophisticated, gut criticism of the regime, surprising in its blatant allegorical style and in the grossness of its representation. It uses such unmistakable signs for a Chilean audience as presenting four characters (the constant number in the Pinochet *junta*) who are totally obsessed with the power they wield and with what they believe is their ingenuity in creating new laws designed to keep them in power and strengthen the divide between them and the evil-smelling masses, a cause for which they will stop at nothing.

Into a dark auditorium enter Jorge Juan and Ramón Raúl, "prepotentes y agresivos," dressed in bath robes and rubber sandals, their faces expressionistic white masks with red lips and carefully combed hair. They are carrying spotlights with which they hunt out a man, El Perseguido, who is hiding among the seats. On being spotted, El Perseguido flees to the stage where Juan Ramón, dressed like the other two, is waiting with the Angel. The latter—"hermoso, saludable," and dressed in white—hands Juan Ramón a revolver with which to execute El Perseguido. As the lights come up the setting on stage is revealed as a Turkish bath, from whose impeccable surrounds these three guardians of the status quo, watched over by the ambiguous figure of the Angel, preen themselves meticulously and facetiously create new laws governing "la tranquilidad pública." Their outstanding characteristic is the belief in the inviolability of their state, a belief that is nurtured by total seclusion from the outside, but which is seen to crumble as their perfect surroundings begin to show signs of disintegration. The end, the destruction of the Turkish bath, is heralded on three occasions by the Angel, who sights the masses, approaching the sanctuary, bent on revenge. *Baño a baño* is a play that juxtaposes a veneer of tranquility with perpetual undercurrents of imminent violent conflict.

As their overlapping names imply, the three characters—Jorge Juan, Juan Ramón, and Ramón Raúl—form links of a common identity. They live in an atmosphere of orchestrated serenity and calm, but that calm is periodically violated by their shows of megalomaniac aggression:

> Miran al público desafiantes. Silencio.
> [*al público*]
> J. R.: Este es el lugar donde TODO es siempre tibio.
> J. J.: Donde no hacen falta las estridencias del sol.
> R. R.: Aquí no hay posibilidad de muerte.
> J. R.: Aquí no hay desesperación, NUNCA habrá un desastre.
> J. J.: ¡Permaneceremos con vida joven, hermosos, inagotables!
> R. R.: ¡Aquí no hay lugar para ojos hundidos, para pellejos pálidos ni cuerpos huesosos!
> J. R.: ¡Nuestro destino es retorcernos en deleites, con dientes limpios, dedos y sexos aseados!
> J. J.: ¡Seremos íntimos, inviolables . . .!
> TODOS: ¡¡¡Definitivos!!! (p. 288)

> [They look defiantly at the audience. Silence.
> [*To the audience.*]
> J. R.: This is the place where EVERYTHING is always lukewarm.
> J. J.: Where the harshness of the sun is not necessary.
> R. R.: Here there is no possibility of death.
> J. R.: Here there is no such thing as desperation, there will NEVER be a disaster.
> J. J.: We will always be young, beautiful, inexhaustible!
> R. R.: Here there is no place for baggy eyes, pale skins or bony bodies!
> J. R.: Our destiny is to revel in delights, with clean teeth, clean fingers and well washed sexes!
> J. J.: We will be intimate, inviolable . . .!
> ALL: DEFINITIVE!!!]

This strident, almost hysterical, declaration is repeated at various points throughout the play, each time with a different emphasis, but with the same basic function of counteracting incidents that are perceived as disruptive. It is first heard in the opening moments of the play, as the first words uttered by the protagonists after the elimination of the hunted man, El Perseguido, when it is used as a sign of their imperturbability while executing the forms of repression that they regard it their legitimate right to employ. On the next three occasions it is pronounced following the Angel's sightings of the groups of the working class making their way to the Turkish bath, and with each pronouncement the conviction with which the protagonists voice the words diminishes. Hints of their dwindling inner tranquility are crudely evoked when the protagonists, after the second sighting, "make an effort" to seem certain and then, after the third sighting, pronounce the declaration "con visible temor" (p. 301).

The dominant attitude of the protagonists is one of detachment from anything but their own bodies; their behavior is that of children with a new toy, the management of power, which they pick up, play around with by making a few preposterous laws, and then put down again, forever squabbling over whose turn it is to dominate, to be in control of repression or abuse. The constant sexual allusions involved in these games evoke the altogether more sinister specter of the sexual gratification derived from violent repression. As they make the laws, they emerge as power-crazed imbeciles, forever jockeying for power and favor, forever fearful of being left isolated on the wrong side of the fence.

The laws they create by word of mouth alone bear no apparent relation to reality, and words are used detached from their meaning. In one scene, "Power and the law," they create new laws, the first of which has to do with lunatic asylums. Initially the law seems to be based on bureaucratic considerations about who should be allowed to enter asylums. They easily agree that only those with the due authorization and medical certificates may do so. Secondly, families with authorization and medical proof may commit a mad member to an asylum. Thirdly, any destitute madman or one whose attitude damages "la tranquilidad pública, también deberá colocársele en una casa de locos" [public tranquility will also be put in a madhouse]. (p. 289). The fourth point seems to break off at a tangent: ". . . si el preso enjuiciado criminalmente perdiere el juicio, también deberá ser colocado en una casa de locos" [. . . if the criminally condemned prisoner loses his reason, he should also be put in a madhouse.] (p. 289). At this stage the making of new laws enters the murky realms of the definition of "loco" and "preso," now the key words in their "debate": " 'Loco' es el que no porta, el que no usa, el que no posee o al que le han quitado las facultades mentales normales," [A madman is he who does not have, does not use, does not possess normal mental faculties, or else has these taken from him] and ". . . un preso es el que está detrás de una

reja" [. . . a prisoner is a person who is behind bars.] (p. 290). Little
by little and through an inane association of words and ideas, the
two types are merging. A madman is someone who *is* mad or who
has gone mad, for example, a prisoner. Their satisfaction is complete when they finally arrive at the correct conclusion:

> J. J.: Ramón Raúl, ¿por qué no nos hace un preso?
> R. R.: [*payasea un preso detrás de las rejas.*]
> J. J.: Eso es un preso, Juan Ramón, dígame, ¿estaría preso?
> J. R.: Yo, ni loco.
> J. J.: [*a R.R.*]: Y usted, ¿Estaría loco?
> J. J.: Yo, ni preso. Diez minutos loco y me vuelvo preso. Empero, lo que
>   presos y locos tienen en común es que ambos . . .
> Todos: [*histéricos*]: ¡¡Perjudican-la-tranquilidad!! (p. 290)

> [J. J.: Ramón Raúl, why don't you pretend to be a prisoner?
> R. R.: [*He plays being a prisoner behind bars.*]
> J. J.: That's a prisoner, Juan Ramón. Tell me, would you want to be a
>   prisoner?
> J. R.: Not me, not even if I was mad.
> J. J.: [*To R. R.*]: And you, would you want to be mad?
> J. R.: Not me, not even if I was a prisoner. Ten minutes of being mad
>   and I would turn into a prisoner. Thus, what prisoners and mad men
>   have in common is that both . . .
> ALL: [*Hysterical*] Disturb the peace!]

The value of this scene is the emerging vision of a state in which
words and concepts have no value unless they have been contorted
and convoluted until they are worthy props of the central aim, the
notorious "tranquilidad pública." On this level, the play illustrates
the appropriation of language as a propaganda weapon through
which no word can be taken to have one definite meaning. In one
scene during which the audience is goaded into singing an infantile
song, "La mar estaba serena," the word "primavera," the strongest
single symbol of resistance and hope for renewal, is appropriated by
the protagonists and hurled at the public:

> A medida que avanza la canción, J. J., J. R. y R. R. se ponen cada vez
> más agresivos.
> J. J.: ¡Eso es, chilenos! ¡Alegría! [*para avanzar a*]: ¡Alegría, mierda!
> R. R.: ¡VIVA LA FELICIDAD DE ESTE PUEBLO! ¡PRIMAVERA!
> J. R.: ¡Viva esta eterna primavera! (p. 297)

[As the song goes on, J. J., J. R. and R. R. become more and more aggressive.

J. J.: That's it, Chileans! Happiness! [*Then they go on to shout*]: Happiness, fuck it!

R. R.: Long live the happiness of this country! Springtime!

J. R.: Long live this eternal springtime!]

Words cannot be trusted in this environment, and those that seemingly belong to the vocabulary of freedom are vulgarized and shown to be essentially empty and, therefore, capable of meaning different things according to the context. The most obvious example is the use of "la tranquilidad pública," which really means the creation of a silent mass of conforming individuals by means of massive propaganda and brutal repression.

There can be no question in the audience's mind that the emerging picture is of an environment in which the "beautiful" people are being pandered to unashamedly, at extreme cost to the welfare of the lower sectors and the destitute; where the physical divide between the rich neighborhoods and the poor ones is more and more manifest, and where, above all, this glorious playground is protected by an institution that finds no contradiction between this tranquil society and the violence used to create and preserve it— amid great hilarity another law is created to control the growing numbers of beggars, who would need authorization and would have to bear a badge ("una huevadita de lata en el pecho") denoting the local authority to which they belong. In this context the masked faces, white and red, perfect and anonymous, are functional as the passport into the physically perfect society the protagonists purport to represent.

In contrast to the three main protagonists, who emerge as boorish individuals whose physical and verbal abuse is a matter of course, the Angel remains aloof. The character is ostensibly a physically and morally immaculate figure who assumes the role of announcing coming events using two distinct codes, one to be deciphered by the audience, the other by the protagonists. The Angel announces the sight of people getting on a bus in a shanty town, an everyday event except that now they are making their way to the Turkish bath; the second and third announcements of "un movimiento inhabitual" provoke growing uneasiness, especially when this becomes a huge procession of jubilant masses through the main avenues of Santiago. The audience cannot fail to recognize the allusion to Salvador Allende's last words when he imagined the return of democracy symbolized by mass popular expression and the return of the masses in procession to the "grandes alamedas."[4]

The message to the other protagonists is couched in the only terms they understand, those of the decay of the Turkish bath and the objects that support their superficial state: the soap runs out; likewise the steam and then the central heating breaks down and the water is cut off. They are, in fact, besieged, helping to engineer their own destruction by their total refusal to act with anything but the worn-out propaganda of perfection. In effect, it is not only the Angel who recognizes the signs, for they have all experienced some deterioration in their physical state, suggesting that something is in the process of happening, but they do not have the will or capacity to act effectively. The final scene, "Sangre," follows revelations about murderous crimes they had committed, all as a result of their innate intolerance of anything less than their definition of perfection. It is a scene of retribution for their bloody crimes of repression, the blood on their hands being transformed into the blood raining on them through the walls of the Turkish bath.

The Angel is an ironic figure. He cannot be seen as uncontaminated by the ugliness of obsession with power, for he guards the sanctuary, he provides the revolver for the execution of El Perseguido, and his announcements are made dispassionately. As the Turkish bath is plunged into darkness and chaos, it seems that the Angel escapes untouched, suggesting that he may be distinct from the evil around him. But what are the implications of his detached, cleaner-than-thou nature? Beneath the surface lurk the true motives of this character, whose aloofness from the violent execution of power relieves him from all blame. He watches over the boorish squabbling for power between the three characters, and he turns a blind eye to the grotesque methods of repression and enforcement of public order, allowing the immediate enforcers to pay the price.

In this respect the Angel is a satire on the figure of Pinochet, a leader whose image was founded on illusions of fatherhood and moral superiority.[5] Distancing himself from the vile crimes of repression executed by his security forces, Pinochet managed, to all intents and purposes, to survive the knowledge that he was at the head of the operations. Other members of the *junta* or heads of the secret police took the blame, they became the scapegoats facing public outrage. The Angel produces the revolver that kills El Perseguido, but while someone else is pulling the trigger, he is merely preparing his next moves. Just like Pinochet, the Angel, detached from the brutality, manages to keep a clean image.[6]

But how does he get away with it? *Baño a baño* suggests one of the more obvious interpretations, that of the value of material enticements to the military as a means of ensuring loyalty. For what is the Turkish bath if it is not a barracks? The characteristics most commonly associated with barracks behavior, such as crudity, infighting, proofs of manliness, go hand in hand in the Turkish bath with the exquisite surroundings, the superior equipment, the carefully maintained conditions.

Throughout the play the audience is systematically insulted and subjected to the grossness of the protagonists. The reactions of the audience are scripted into the notes: "J. J., R. R., y J. R. continúan insultando agresivamente al público que antes los seguía bovinamente" (p. 297). The spectators are being asked to play a role that would expose the extent to which they have internalized the behavior imposed in a violently repressive atmosphere, and their reaction to the play is intended to create an awareness of the complete lack of expression they experience in everyday life. An atmosphere of guilt, uncertainty and fear is established from the opening scene when the public is included in the search for El Perseguido. Subsequently, it becomes clear that the protagonists are aware of the public's presence but do not feel that it warrants any consideration other than heavy-handed manipulation. The audience will, in the eyes of the creators of this play, assume its role admirably, for the assimilation of traditional responses of silence in the theater is complete. This state, however, has its counterpart in the sightings of the uprising crowds, the object of whose role is to demonstrate that a general silence masks serious discontent and the threat of effective opposition. The imminent revenge of the repressed is a distant echo of the fear of the impoverished intruder into bourgeois society that was so prominent in the theater of the sixties.

The superficial impression of the play is one of stalemate, of the juxtaposition of two seemingly immutable limbos. Yet the Turkish bath is in a gradual, relentless process of decay as the protagonists' hold on the instruments of power weakens and fear creeps in. The real state of limbo is in the audience, whose initiative has been numbed through submission and who are paralyzed through inactivity, yet this is contradicted by the advance of the "numerous groups of people, of different ages, sexes and social extraction" making their way to the Turkish bath (p. 304). This image of a limbo precariously balanced on the edge of inevitable disaster is evoked again in *Lo crudo, lo cocido y lo podrido.*

Lo crudo, lo cocido y lo podrido

Aquí transcurren los años,
Con mucho acudir de gente.
Ya la Alameda ha cambiado,
Y el Torres sigue vigente.[7]

[The years pass by, / and the people come and go. / The Alameda has changed, / And the café Torres goes on just the same.]

In El Restorán de los Inmortales, a typical old restaurant of Santiago, in former days the meeting place for the oligarchy, three waiters (Elías Reyes, Efraín Rojas and Evaristo Romero), members of the mysterious sect *la garzonería secreta,* the secret brotherhood of waiters, and Eliana Riquelme, the daughter of the founder of the sect, await the arrival of Don Estanislao Ossa Moya, the last surviving member of the oligarchy they had formerly served. The length of the wait is unspecified, time is occupied in ritually repeated games and rehearsals through which the waiters strive to retain perfection. When Estanislao Ossa Moya eventually appears in the doorway, he is an unrecognizable drunken wreck bearing no resemblance to the leading citizen he may have been before. Like the rest of his class, he has come to die in this, the last bastion of their golden age, and to be placed in one of the niches reserved for him. But the nature of his demise is indicative of fundamental changes taking place and heralds the end of an era. Nevertheless, while the possibility of perpetuating the old system still exists, Elías, the *maître,* is bound by duty to go through the ritual of initiating his successor, Efraín, to his new post. But Efraín, aware that their role is now redundant, refuses to accept the name, age, and identity he has been destined to inherit as the *maître.* As Elías drinks the "suicide wine" as his master did before him when he, in his turn, saw new codes of behavior that he regarded as assaults on decency and order, Efraín, in his real identity, abandons the restaurant, followed by the bewildered Evaristo.

The professional world of the waiter has been described as being a "tribal" one of "rites and rituals, of status passages, of minutely divided hierarchies and secret knowledge that can never be understood from the customers' side of the green baize door".[8] Here is a "tribe" of waiters vying in never-ending power games for superiority over their colleagues and control of their customers. They belong to an international community bearing essentially similar characteristics, all divided into small groups, resistant to change or to ideas of collectivity, each one working within a specific area in an enclosed space, the restaurant. In this way, a closed institution is created, one which, while it is in interaction with the outside world, is separate on account of its internal composition.

The waiters in *Lo crudo, lo cocido y lo podrido* belong to a familiar tradition in Chilean literature, that of the serving classes, be they domestic or military, who protect, manage, and emulate their masters; these waiters are examples of the *siútico*, "a middle-class individual who emulates the aristocracy and its usage," but they do not, as a real *siútico* would, "hope to be taken for one of its members."[9] The waiters, the members of *la garzonería secreta*, have long ago mastered the habits and usages of the upper classes, and furthermore they create the conditions in which these habits can be practiced. With their detailed knowledge of the best kept secrets, they have acquired the ability to make and break any upstarts who threaten to intrude upon the premises of the aristocracy, and this power is guarded by *la garzonería secreta*, to which they adhere with mason-like loyalty. *La garzonería secreta* is a covert institution of control. Behind masks that denote humility, servility, self abnegation, lurk experts in the manipulation of power relationships:

> ELIAS: ¿Se dan cuenta? Se trata de parecer vulgares . . . nadie debe saber que sabemos.
>
> EVARISTO: Es un disfraz.
>
> ELIAS: Eso, somos máscaras.
>
> EFRAIN: Por eso no debemos mirarnos al espejo.
>
> ELIAS: Por eso. Por eso no tenemos rostros . . . ni nombres . . . borrosos . . . solo servimos. . . . No podemos aplastar al cliente con una pronunciación académica. . . . Debemos darle la oportunidad de sentirse rodeado de inferiores. . . . Cierto que a algunos clientes los aplastamos premeditadamente. . . . A esos arribistas, advenedizos, nuevos ricos. . . . Por eso la garzonería secreta es secreta. . . . A pesar de nuestra influencia.
>
> EVARISTO: ¿Nuestra influencia?
>
> ELIAS: ¿Cuántos crímenes? ¿Cuántos amores? ¿Cuántas glorias y pasiones guiamos en nuestro restorán? . . . Que ellos se sientan controlándolo todo . . . pero basta un gesto nuestro y podemos quitar un candidato a la historia. (p. 262)

> [ELIAS: Don't you realize. It's all about seeming vulgar . . . nobody should know that we know.
>
> EVARISO: It's a disguise.
>
> ELIAS: That's it, we're masks.

EFRAIN: That's why we should never look at ourselves in the mirror.

ELIAS: Exactly. That's why we don't have faces . . . or names . . . we're shadows . . . we only serve . . . We cannot overwhelm the customer with perfect pronunciation. . . . We must give him the opportunity of feeling that he is surrounded by inferiors. Of course we squash some customers deliberately. . . . Those social-climbing upstarts, nouveaux riches. That is why the secret brotherhood of waiters is secret. In spite of our great influence.

EVARISTO: Our influence?

ELIAS: How many crimes? How many love affairs? How many glories and passions do we guide in our restaurant? . . . Let them think that they control everything . . . but it just takes one act by us to remove a candidate from history.]

The play works on two levels of power relations: firstly, on the level of the waiters themselves as they guard the strict hierarchy of the trade and, secondly, on that of the manipulation of the customers, a level which, in effect, no longer exists, but which they keep alive through ritual. The door to the restaurant has been closed for an unspecified length of time, but it has been noted as open in the meticulous inventory kept by Eliana. It is, therefore, a double metaphor, both of the closed nature of the institution and of the ritual nature of the belief in the continuing relevance of their role. It is the recording of facts (that the door is open) not the truth of facts (that the door is closed) that is most important. The inventory is the gospel by which they must abide, regardless of the fact that it is blatantly false.

The opening scene has Efraín and Evaristo playing make-believe, acting out the roles of fictitious customers who praise the commendable work of the waiters. As the perfect imitation degenerates into childish insults, however, it is clear that, while they may be connoisseurs of the behavior of their erstwhile clients and they are able to emulate perfectly their social graces, the waiters can never fully shake off the tell-tale signs of their real identity, betrayed here by their rivalry in inventing the most glowing terms of praise for themselves. In this scene Efraín and Evaristo act out an important part of the daily ritual, in which they conjure up the ghosts of the elite and populate the derelict restaurant with such names as Carlos Gardel, Clark Gable, Arturo Alessandri. But as the waiters' proud mime degenerates into a childish squabble, the first cracks in the impeccable facade are revealed. Evaristo and Efraín betray the individual behind the mask, and the waiters are revealed as part of a transparently flawed regime.

Efraín is the living embodiment of the threat inherent in their present condition, for his need to play his role in reality prompts him to question the value of waiting. On one hand his ideal is to serve as he had done before, but on the other hand, and in contradiction to this, he contemplates the treacherous idea of opening the doors to the general public. He recognizes the need to modernize and adapt to changing circumstances to survive. On that level he represents a serious threat, for he is willing to invite unpredictability and ambiguity into their midst. Efraín deviates from the libretto; he mocks, ridicules, and tries to escape the ritual exchanges; he fantasizes to Evaristo about a new-look café-bar complete with juke box, sandwiches, paper glasses, "just like everywhere else." Evaristo is horrified:

> EVARISTO: ¿Te estás trastornando? . . . ¿Y la garzonería secreta? . . . ¿Y el juramento?
> EFRAIN: Sí, sí, sí sé . . . pero ahí volvería la gente. . . . No tendríamos que tener la puerta cerrada . . . a lo mejor.
> EVARISTO: La puerta está cerrada para que no entre nadie.
> EFRAIN: ¡No! Está cerrada porque no entra nadie. En serio . . . Si a lo mejor volviéramos a estar de moda. . . . otra vez veríamos crímenes políticos. [*En su entusiasmo se ha encaramado a una silla.*] . . . Esos nobles adulterios de la gente culpable. . . . Esas borracheras de las autoridades. . . . Esos ministros maricas. . . . Esos guardaespaldas vulgares, esos hoyos en el espejo. . . . Volver a recoger esos secretos . . . Evaristo. . . . Otra vez, como antes. . . . Llenos de secretos. (pp. 259–60)

> [EVARISTO: Are you going mad? . . . What about the secret brotherhood of waiters? And our oath?
> EFRAIN: Yes, yes, yes, I know about all of that . . . but people would start coming back. . . . We wouldn't have to keep the door closed . . . perhaps.
> EVARISTO: The door is closed so that nobody comes in.
> EFRAIN: No! The door is closed because nobody comes in. Seriously. . . . If, perhaps, we could be fashionable again . . . then we'd see other political crimes. [*In his enthusiasm he has jumped up on to a chair.*] Those noble adulteries of guilty people. Those official drunken brawls. Those queer ministers. . . . Those vulgar bodyguards, those holes in the mirror. . . . We'd start keeping all those secrets again . . . Evaristo. . . . Again, like before. . . . We'd be full of secrets.]

Efraín quite clearly sees that closing the doors bars desirables as well as undesirables, that behind closed doors they can never hope

to be real functionaries of "la garzonería secreta," to possess the
power they formerly held. While he remembers all too well the past
feats of manipulation, recalls the scandals created, and still guards
old secrets, he sees that the intrigues and scandals they rehearse
are no more than a ritual rendering of a by-now mythical state.
Efraín's desire for change does not imply a coherent moral acceptance or condemnation of the order to which he belongs—merely a
desire to play a role again, to act on his own initiative, and to shed
the destructive identity of a person who is merely waiting.

Efraín suffers for his doubts and ideas. Not only as a result of
mental torture or even physical repression, but as a scapegoat
character. In his room leaflets for modern gadgets are found, leaflets
that could adversely influence the less experienced, impressionable
Evaristo. Elías, fully aware of the course things will take, finds
Efraín's doubts a useful decoy to distract attention from the blatant
signs of decay. Efraín is accused of being a bad omen, a contaminating force, and it is he who is blamed for the death of Adolfo, their
pet rat and a favorite of Don Estanislao Ossa Moya: "Por culpa de
Efraín se murió, se está haciendo contagiosa tu enfermedad . . ."
(p. 273). He is a sickly person in the midst of their supposedly
healthy regime, his advocacy of modern machines a sign of foreign
contamination, of outside subversive ideas, of rebellion, and his
plans and pamphlets seditious propaganda. Efraín is the democratic option, he seeks an alternative, but any alternative is, for a
member of *la garzonería secreta,* unacceptable, for the illusion that
the only alternatives are the old regime or chaos must be maintained at all costs.

Evaristo, on the other hand, is the equivalent of the "distressed
adult citizen"[10] who has found certain refuge in regression to an
infantile state of mind, to a childlike dependency on a set of imposed patterns of behavior. He adopts a child's "proclivity for
feeling powerless, ashamed, deserted, and guilty before the elders
who command his submission."[11] He can never pose a threat to the
order, for he does not make decisions and is devoid of personal
initiative. Efraín's sacrilegious utterings about serving fast food
inspire great concern in Evaristo, since they openly take him out of
the realms of safe ritual into the realms of thought and subversion.
His own deviations from the norm are the mischievious actions of a
child—he chews gum and sticks it under a table that is in Efraín's
patch, terrified at the thought of being found out. His is the position
of one who has assumed the infantile identity provided him in a
paternalistic hierarchy and his acceptance of his role makes him the
perfect waiter, the perfect nonperson. Without clients they will

always be nothing: "Por favor . . . un garzón no siente . . . un buen garzón jamás siente ni piensa . . . no tiene más vida que la que le dé el cliente, su nombre, su apodo, su propina" [I beg your pardon, a waiter does not feel, a good waiter never feels or thinks . . . the only life he has is the life the customer gives him, his name, his nickname, his tip] (p. 264).

According to the definition of their role, the waiters, as nonpersons, should have little trouble accommodating the wait, since all that is asked of them is absolute loyalty and faithfulness to the cause. The language used to evoke this ideal and the model for behavior is relentlessly evocative of a military establishment: the waiters are drilled in their profession; awful threats hover over the heads of dissidents or—in the word of Elías, whose arrival on stage is that of a general inspecting his troops—"desertors." As Number One, Elías defines reality, he decides what does and what does not exist and uses Eliana's inventory to legitimize this with the authority of the written word. The subordinates, by accepting the legitimacy of the inventory, accept that of the wait, and conversely the inventory, in the hands of Eliana, can have comforting properties for the tormented mind:

EFRAIN: A veces tengo tantas dudas; antes era más fácil, pero ahora veo las puras telarañas, siento la humedad, me crujen las tablas del piso . . .

ELIANA: No existen estas cosas, Efraín. No están anotadas en mis libros. . . . Así que no existen.

EFRAIN: Tiene razón. . . . Si no están ahí, es que no existieron nunca. (p. 269)

[EFRAIN: Sometimes I have so many doubts; before everything was easier, now all I see are the cobwebs, I feel the dampness, the floorboards creak under my feet . . .

ELIANA: These things do not exist, Efraín. They are not noted down in my books. . . . So they do not exist.

EFRAIN: You are right. . . . If they are not there it is because they never existed.]

The existence of Eliana, cashier and accountant, is nothing more than an obsessive counting of the objects in the restaurant, her inheritance from a father who bequeathed her a petrified identity: ". . . tu pobre hija ridícula . . . tu poca cosa . . . tu accidente de maricón que se mete con la pastelera y me cría entre las mesas . . . tú me hiciste cajera . . . tú me hiciste víctima de ilustres agarrones

. . . tú me pegaste la afición a contar y recontar . . . no sé cómo me llamo ni cuál fue mi nombre si es que lo tuve . . ." [. . . your poor ridiculous daughter . . . your nothing . . . your mistake, the homosexual who gets involved with the baker and brings me up among tables . . . you made me into a cashier . . . you made me the victim of those illustrious men who always grabbed at me . . . it was you who addicted me to counting and counting over . . . I don't know what I'm called, nor what my name was if I ever had one.] (p. 282).[12] It is her father's memory that she now evokes as a means of making the waiters listen to her narration of an ominous dream: "Es que quiero contarlo. . . . No sé cómo anotarlo en mi inventario. . . . Es confuso" [It's just that I want to tell you about it. . . . I don't know how to write it down in my inventory. . . . It's confused] (p. 269). The dream will only become reality when it has been interpreted by Elías, exorcized of all evil before being registered in the book where everything that is to be believed is written.

The narration of the dream is a catalyst to the action. Hers is a premonitory dream of the total destruction of the restaurant, heralded by a number of signs: among them the death of Adolfo, the pet rat, the breaking of crockery, the wailing of cats, the arrival of Ossa Moya, her own death, and the shattering of the mirror into thousands of pieces. The fulfillment of the signs begins immediately, and from this point on until the arrival of Ossa Moya, an oppressive sense of finality pervades the stage.

At the beginning of the narration, she wonders if it might not be true that it was dreamt by "la otra . . . la del espejo . . . la que me mira fijo cuando recorro las grietas del espejo. . . . Esa mujer vieja rodeada de fantasmas" [the other woman . . . the one in the mirror . . . the one who stares at me when I count the cracks in the mirror. . . . That old woman surrounded by ghosts] (p. 269). This would have a double advantage, since it would release her from the blame for the crime of dreaming unintelligible dreams and would erase the need to note it down. But on stage Eliana becomes the other, her voice changes, she acquires authority of her own and demonstrates that "the one in the mirror," the "other," the real identity she has been denied, does indeed exist. Eliana is the essence of ambiguity in their midst.

The mirror, a central image in the play, and the identities of the waiters are inextricably linked and are gradually transformed into mutually reflecting signs of the decay and demise of an old regime and the birth of a new order. The restaurant has no windows, the door is boarded up; the only relief in this tomb-like atmosphere are the reflections in the mirror. In this context, the mirror is the epitome of a totally self-referring institution, reflecting endless images of decay in a self-perpetuating limbo. The mirror had been a tool of the trade, a way of keeping a watchful eye on the customers without their knowledge. The normal purpose of a mirror has slowly been obscured; like the waiters, its role has been defined solely by the existence of the clients. Their prolonged absence naturally forces a redefinition of both mirror and waiters. The mirror, in the course of the endless wait, begins to assume its more normal function of reflecting the waiters whose individual identities, in turn, begin to surface. Elías accuses his colleagues of signs of individuality: "Los he visto mirándose al espejo, han empezado a mirarse la cara, sobre todo tú, Efraín; ya ni siquiera te tiñes bien las canas" [I've seen you looking at yourselves in the mirror. You've begun to look at yourselves very closely, you especially, Efraín; now you don't even dye your gray hairs] (p. 274). The reestablishment of the roles marks the beginning of the end of the regime.

Evaristo may ask for an unambiguously positive interpretation of Eliana's dream in terms of the rebirth of the old regime, but the evidence of change can no longer be denied and the illusion of a united group living only to perpetuate the myth of an ideal system is shattered along with the mirror. It is Elías's role as the signs in Eliana's dream come true to expose the general nature of decay, to admit that, indeed, time has been wasted. Yet he will never admit to his successor, Efraín, that he knew they were the only ones left, "que sólo gracias a nosotros la civilización se mantuvo de pie" [that it is only thanks to us that civilization is still on its feet] (p. 284).

The "banquet" that follows the arrival of Ossa Moya is a morbid parody of a party to celebrate political victory, perfect in its ritual evocation of the correct menu, the appropriate guests, the standard jokes, the toasting of "el candidato de la decencia y el respeto" (p. 277). However, Ossa Moya's "speech" combines the faulty repetition of set campaign phrases with gross language, indecent behavior, immoral demands. Evaristo, dismayed by the humiliating spectacle before his eyes, constantly asks for reassurance that the client is really an old tramp who slipped the net, but no such easy solution is at hand: "Quien más voy a ser, Evaristo . . . quien más . . . si lo conozco . . . yo los recuerdo y los distingo . . . y ustedes me confunden . . . antes era al revés . . . pero ahora se les nota . . . igual que a mí, somos transparentes" [Who else could I be, Evaristo . . . who else . . . I know you . . . I recognize you and can distinguish between you . . . and you're not sure who I am . . . before it was the other way round . . . but now I can see the differences between you . . . now you're like me, transparent] (p. 281). Ossa

Moya's vulgar rantings, his detestation of democracy, his longing
for the scandals and intrigue of campaigning, seen once as the
glorious actions of the great leaders, are no more than vulgarities in
the mouth of a tramp. The facade of decency and respect has gone.
Ossa Moya becomes incorporated into the reflecting images of
decay, the now transparently rotten face of the old order. The
waiters reluctantly perform the final ritual burial in the knowledge
that they cannot escape the force of predestination.

This is the demise of a whole institution intrinsically linked to the
cultural act of eating. Part of the waiters' role is defined by political
intrigues elaborated around food and drink; for those of Ossa
Moya's tradition, politics without food is unthinkable: "Un partido
que come bien merece ser elegido" [A party that eats well deserves
to be elected] (p. 277). Now the societal conventions that had
turned the raw, or natural, into the cooked, or cultural (through its
contact with man), have been transformed into the rotten, here the
disintegration of the framework that sustained this form of power
relations. And according to Elías in his mock version of the truth,
"la decadencia es general, . . . el mejor signo de esto es la desapari-
ción de los garzones". (p. 284)

Their long distancing from playing a real role has rid the waiters
of the ability to act other than symbolically. They have become
people who are acted on, ordered, provided to react to authority
according to strict codes, and who have begun to look to another
power, that of Ossa Moya, for a solution to the stalemate that traps
them. Elías's comforting interpretation of the dream, that the cries
and moans are from outside, not from inside is proven to be false
when Ossa Moya arrives, bringing with him, not the ingredients for
a farewell banquet, but the cries from outside, invading the place
with the misery of decadence. And in her dream Eliana sees that
hidden behind the mirror are "ladrillos demolidos, la ciudad ensangrentada" (p. 271). As the cries from outside become those
inside the restaurant, power shifts and the waiters, thrust by the
evidence of decay into a world of uninvited ambiguity, reassert their
protagonistic role. Elías, knowing that an era has ended, rejects
Efraín's proposal of survival through adaptation and drinks the
suicide wine. Efraín and Evaristo act according to form: Evaristo
remains the distressed being whose world has been turned upside
down, for he had truly associated prosperity with former times, and
had accepted that, only with the reestablishment of the old order
could prosperity return. Efraín, on the other hand, rejects the
myths of past glory and the promise of power for an uncertain

future in a changing world. Again, his actions analogize with the democratic option.

Lo crudo is a massive metaphor for a society that is seen to be in an ideal state if it achieves the all-encompassing aim of perpetuating an image of a mythical past, of stopping time at a moment when the most powerful were favored by specific circumstances of under-development among large sectors of the community. Yet the final image is one of renewal, for the final scene reasserts the right to take active part in a culture of which the waiters, after all, are founder members, and they return to the set of social rituals defined by the fundamental act of eating. As Agustín Letelier has indicated, when Efraín, using his real name, leaves, the audience will breath a sigh of relief: "Su decisión de no aceptar convertirse en el sucesor del gran maestro de la garzonería secreta nos alivia tanto en lo emotivo como en el plano de las ideas" [This decision not to accept becoming the great leader of the secret brotherhood of waiters is a relief to the audience, both at an emotional level and on an ideolog-ical level].[13]

No +

No + (No more) was produced in 1983, when the regime had celebrated ten years in power, and it was in 1983, with the deterio-rating economic situation, that the first major opposition rallies were held. *No +*, set in the archetypal dominator-dominated situa-tion, that of the classroom, proposes that liberating actions are natural, but equally, are responded to by renewed methods of domination. At a forum in Concepción in 1985, one participant expressed the opinion that *No +* was the most effective drama of recent years. In the midst of the very verbal tradition in Chilean drama and the volumes of words spoken and written about Chile since 1973, this was regarded as the utmost irony, for *No +* is a mime based on a play by the German, Peter Handke.[14] Yet this irony is belied by the strength of the two words that form the title of the play. "No +" (No more) has been common graffiti in Chile, usually followed by words like death, violence, or even Pincohet.[15] These words are the first sign the audience will see on the stage set, which is a chess board floor with a wall surrounding it on two sides on which is written "No +" [. . . and, a little lower a blurred word, where one can just make out DEATH] (p. 172).

In this way, the play is invested with a specific significance that will dictate how the audience will interpret the sequence of scenes, using the teacher-pupil relationship that forms the central conflict to concentrate on immediate symbols of the use and abuse of power. The initial impact is all important: in everyday life, graffiti may only be registered subconsciously, but the fact that it is used on stage imbues it with a special symbolic quality. It is real in terms of being graffiti and, in its symbolic role, representative of a whole set of more general concerns.

No + revolves around the conflictive and mutually dependent relationship between the characters, a tutor and his three pupils. As the chess-board setting suggests, *No +* depicts their power struggles as a game in which participants maneuver into positions of advantage and confrontation, and which holds within it the necessity of checkmate for the game to end. The alternative is stalemate. The pupils, in an inherently weaker position, subordinate by virtue of their identity, seek ways throughout the fifteen scenes of the play of freeing themselves from the master's domination, forever forcing the tutor to respond with new ways of maintaining his superiority. Each scene is a completed action in itself—of initial state, confrontation, resolution, punishment, or stalemate—and each scene is a response to events that have taken place previously. As the mime continues, the images grow increasingly violent, culminating in a state of war and bloodshed with, first, the disappearance of one pupil and, finally, four limp bodies strewn on the floor.

The pupils' every action is dictated by their natural desire for freedom from rigid domination, and although the play consists of very ordinary, everyday actions, each of these is loaded with the preoccupation of what is permissable. The central relationship is developed so as to suggest that the most important element is the precarious balance of power as the tutor's acts of domination generate among the pupils responses that arise from a natural desire for freedom. Yet, the pupils have only one model for freedom, that is the tutor: freedom of movement and expression are only within the possibilities of the master. The central argument is made explicit in the title of the original play: the pupil wants to be master.

In the first scene, "Comer manzanas es una acción muy simple" [Eating apples is a very simple act], the three pupils, dressed in black suits, shirts, and ties, are purely and simply engaged in the act of eating apples in absolute peace. But the appearance of the tutor, dressed like the pupils, disturbs the action, imperceptibly at first as the eating becomes slower and more difficult, until each pupil in turn has stopped and the Tutor exercises his implicit right to the last apple. In this initial scene, the central pivot of the tension becomes clear: the mere presence of the tutor destroys the simplicity of the action, which is repressed for no other motive than submission before menacing authority.

In scene six, ironically entitled "La comida, plato común olla común," [Food, communal plate, communal pot] the tutor ostentatiously eats in front of the hungry pupils. One pupil dares to approach only when the tutor has finished. Then he guzzles the leftovers directly from the bowl. The others follow suit until, degraded and animal-like, they clean the bowl. While they eat "con ganas," the tutor had eaten "con fruición." While the tutor's position affords him dignity and plenty, that of the pupils leaves them at the mercy of the tutor's whims, and they have no dignity to call upon when they finally have access to the food. While for the tutor the satisfaction of basic needs is enjoyable, and accompanied by the ritual of good manners [He cleans himself with a napkin], for the pupils this satisfaction is desperate, and manners are an empty consideration [Their faces are covered in food]. And like the graffiti, the "olla comun", the "common pot," or soup kitchen, brings closer the reference to real existing poverty, part of the audience's consciousness, if not experience.

A similar device is used in the third scene, "Todo lo que tienes no te pertenece y tampoco puedes rayar cuando se te occurra" [Everything you have does not belong to you and you cannot scribble whenever you like]. When the tutor drops off to sleep, the pupils march in single file to pick up a newspaper, which they then lay on the table next to the tutor, who reads it while the pupils are looking at "libritos pequeños." Given the tutor's apparent absorption in reading, the pupils begin to take liberties, they draw on their books, on themselves, on the floor, and finally one prepares to write on the wall, unaware that the tutor, who is watching every action, has begun to crumble up his newspaper. In the course of this action, the newspaper becomes transformed into something far more sinister, a ball, a bullet, a noisy, crunching object of repression. When the pupil finally realizes that he is being watched, he performs an immediate act of self-censorship, for he not only hands over the chalk, but he and the other pupils give up their pencils, books and all their possessions from their pockets. As they do so they seek anonymity, oblivion, kneeling down until finally they are under the table, invisible to the eyes of the tutor.

In the wake of these aborted acts of defiance, the tutor reasserts his right both to act as he pleases and to impose his discipline. The wall, out of bounds to the pupils for writing and the limit of their freedom of movement is, in all ways, within the access of the tutor, for writing on the wall is an action the tutor carries out in broad daylight, while the pupils' "rayados," scribblings, are clandestine and subversive. In scene eight, "Rayado de muralla," the tutor begins to paint over "No + muerte" and replaces it with "Viva," evoking the fascist salute, "Viva la muerte." As the tutor executes the change, one of the pupils begins a game of throwing little white balls at him. Since the latter does not acknowledge the fact that his back is slowly being covered with these little white balls, the pupil becomes more enthusiastic in his game. When the tutor finishes his writing on the wall, he calmly takes a pair of scissors and begins to back into the pupil. Just before they bump into each other, the tutor swings round, still with the scissors in his hand, but the pupil commits a final, almost comic, act of defiance, he sticks the little white ball onto the tutor's hat (p. 192). The tutor's right to express his thoughts on the wall is openly, albeit, ineffectively challenged. The scene that follows is one of punishment, centered on the bloody image of the scissors, which are the only objects moving on a silent stage, and while the scissors whirl around, a new image appears: "Un borbotón de agua. Casi un chorro. Después menos. Hasta convertirse en un delgado hilo de ¿sangre?, ¿agua?" [A burst of water. Almost a stream. Then there is less. Until it becomes a thin trickle of blood? Water?] (p. 192).

Throughout the play, actions that form unexceptional parts of life are displaced so that they take on a shock value. Eating, in other frames of reference a social activity, is performed as a selfish act of indulgence on the part of the tutor and a fight for survival on that of the pupils; cutting toe nails, not a social activity, becomes an action born of the tutor's domination over the use of the space, his right to define socially acceptable acts, and the scissors he uses to cut his toe nails, bring underlying violent currents to the surface: "Escuchamos el peligroso sonido de las tijeras cortando uñas" [We hear the dangerous sound of scissors cutting nails] (p. 189). When the tutor writes "Viva," he has the scissors to hand as a weapon whose mere presence is threatening, and they eventually take on a life of their own, twirling—". . . las tijeras dan vueltas vertiginosamente a sus pies"—gathering momentum in the increasingly violent atmosphere. The scissors embody an image of severing, by implication of blood and death, an image that soon becomes reality.

Scene twelve is "La guerra" [War]. The three pupils are very close, seeking one another's comfort and protection. Their silence is broken by the sound of someone digging a hole in the ground, a sound that causes them to retreat until they reach the wall. The tutor comes in, calm and apparently or deliberately unaware of the pupils, and he then leaves, heading in the direction of a sound of hammering that slowly blends into the sound of machine guns, bombs, fleeing people, war. The hole is a distant reminder of the grave, the dead; the hammering, a sound related to the finishing of coffins; and the sounds of war, the cause of death. In scene thirteen, "Recado. La camisa ensangrentada" [Message. The bloody shirt], only two pupils are present. Then a message arrives, a packet containing a bloody shirt. The other pupil is missing.

The stage is then set for the final scene of confrontation, which takes place in relation to the only space for expression possible, the wall. A barely visible figure is heard spraying paint, and in the light between blackouts the wall appears with numbers, parts of words, signs, the disjointed beginnings of expression. Now the presence of the tutor implies imminent confrontation, for in the endgame, the pupils advance toward their master, apparently now without fear. The final scene is one of catastrophe: the stage is divided into two parts, there are four bodies strewn on the floor, each covered by a newspaper. The wall continues to play a role and to imply resistance: "La pared al fondo, completamente rayada. Por sobre todo lo demás, un enorme manchón en el cual se logra leer: 'No +'" [The wall at the back. Completely covered in scribbling. Above everything else, a huge stain in which can just be made out: "No +"] (p. 204). The graffiti is a faded protest: "No more" announces the death of the four protagonists.

No + relies purely on mime. According to the group, interpretations are implied in the execution of the actions, and it is up to the spectator to add the finishing touches that will transform the mime into a recognizable whole.[16] This design embodies a definite construction of a set of codes (at the heart of which are the wall and the chess board) insinuating the intended meaning, despite the stated aim of giving the audience freedom for interpretation. Nothing the tutor does is excessively violent or bad, he is part of a cycle of rebellion and response, and within the context of the pupil-teacher relationship, he has a legitimate, accepted right to authority to which the pupils must respond and bow. The situation is one familiar to every spectator, it is even benevolent in many ways, until the end when the war takes over, and the tutor is undoubtedly on the side of the violent oppressor. In the final scenes, the specific roles of master and pupil give way to the symbolic representation of oppressor and oppressed.

Noise, music, sounds play an important role in *No +*. Sounds are alternatively intrusive and complementary, alienating and shocking. Intrusive sound is associated with the role played by the tutor. Disembodied loud breathing invades the scene as he appears, it hints at abnormality, at distress; likewise other noises, like a metronome nervously ticking at "prestíssimo," the newspaper being crunched up, or the toe nails falling, all suggest unwanted intrusions, violent affronts on the privacy of others. Music, on the other hand, is complementary—happy at the beginning as the pupils simply eat apples, sad when they grovel in the bowl, bitter and nostalgic at the outbreak of war, childish and sad in the final scene. Both the music and the noises uphold the identity of the respective characters, adding further shades of meaning to their acts, intrusive and oppressive on the part of the tutor, nostalgic and melancholic on that of the pupils. Against the otherwise silent background all the noises are heard in isolation, always separated from the action on stage. Where do they originate? They are external signals of the roles played, functions of natural urges for freedom on one hand and ostentatious security of position on the other.

The central issue in this play is that of the freedom to move and act within a certain space. The pupils, all too aware of the confines of their position, search for new ways of using the space to their advantage, but there is a doubly negative outcome built into this system. Firstly, they will always be punished for signs of individuality and, secondly, the only model of freedom they have is that of the tutor. There is very little difference between the four, for the notes say of the Tutor: "No hay nada especial que lo identifique. Quizás el terno más nuevo y mejor planchado, y los zapatos lustrados y de mejor calidad" [There is nothing special by which to identify him. Perhaps his suit is a bit newer and in better condition and his shoes polished, and of a better quality] (p. 174). In other words, he is a more perfect version of the pupils. Equally, they are imperfect versions of their master. He is described as calm, he contemplates situations, momentarily founders, and is defeated; but does not hesitate to punish and reimpose his authority, leaving him "fuerte," "entero." The pupils are often seen to be imitating him and although in one military style scene the situation is reversed and he imitates them, finally being defeated on account of their greater agility, this merely serves to prove that they cannot all do the same things in the same space. In the final analysis, only the tutor has the means to assert his right to do as he pleases. And the pupil wants to be master.

No + says that it is natural to fight against repression. The characters form part of the set: they maneuver and outmaneuver one another in calculated moves, in a game in which access to the wall, to the right to expression, is paramount. There is a feeling of a closed situation, of well defined boundaries and perfectly defined roles. But by the final scenes, the roles are more loosely interpreted, the pupil-tutor identities less marked, as the pupils perfect their methods of resistance. The war is a measure of the threat that they begin to constitute as their ultimate goal, that of emulating the practices of their master, comes within reach. But how will it end? In bloody confrontation. Does it always have to end like that? The faded writing on the wall pleads that it will not, that there will be no more cycles of violent oppression. But the fact of the four dead bodies on the floor declares that, for the moment, the cycle continues. Like a game of chess, it can be endlessly repeated.

Stagnation and Renewal

Una pena y un cariño, Baño a baño, Lo crudo, lo cocido y lo podrido, and *No +* all take place in confined spaces, governed by strict hierarchies of power. In the theater, the restaurant, the Turkish bath, and the school that are their settings, the audience is faced with familiar places that are part of normal experience, but are removed from their everyday lives. In this way an atmosphere of blame or complicity and release from it is created, the audience becomes conspirator and innocent bystander and is integrated into the gray, limbolike area portrayed on stage, which in turn becomes a grotesque mirror of lived experience. The pervasive vision that emerges from these dramas in the period in which they were first performed is one of a society in a state of siege, one where sets of cliques gather together to conspire, manipulate, and protect certain rigid values or sets of rules.

These are places in which language, words, communication is either meaningless, unnecessary, or prohibited. *Una pena y un cariño,* where dialogue seems to run normally, gives a poignant example of the deception involved in the manipulation of linguistic symbols. Words are used to provoke, to threaten, sometimes to explain and even negotiate, but they have no value as a means of communication or resolution of the problems, for it is fear, threats, and repression that really do the talking. In *Baño a baño,* we witness language reduced to dissociated noises. The laws the protagonists create by word of mouth have no semblance of connection with reality, they are merely symbols of the arbitrary nature of decisions of power, founded on nothing more than lust for greater power. Their language and actions are vulgar and grotesque, they seem inappropriate for the impeccable environment of the Turkish bath, but their crudity prepares the stage for the final scene in which their masks, their perfect facades, disintegrate. Again, when language seems to be normal and straightforward in the appearances of the Angel, his words are so designed as to evoke a whole new register of implications and of warnings. And the protagonists' confessions of crimes do not signify remorse: they are merely pleas for mercy.

In *Lo crudo, lo cocido y lo podrido,* communication is actively discouraged, for it would pose a threat to the continuation of the already dubious wait. Even when they are alone, Efraín and Evaristo avoid real communication, only once touching on a question of real importance to their lives, that of the door that bars their access to the outside and a revitalized identity. Communication becomes subversive, a threat; words, in their perfect state, are empty objects, at the service of the perpetuation of the myth, and accountable in Eliana's book: "Llevo contadas 12616 palabras y aún no se repiten los menús . . ." (p. 252), and her dream will only be significant when the words used to narrate it are divorced from their real meaning and given an official interpretation.

All these plays, by making use of various levels of disintegration of communication and the duplicity of language, expose the inherent ambiguity of words. *No +* abandons unreliable words, relying on the gesture instead. Yet, the only two words, "No more," speak volumes. Silence is the background for sequences of carefully orchestrated actions that, ideally, the spectator should have the scope to interpret. But actions are also wrought with duplicity, and an imposed or desired interpretation is all but inevitable, for the author is one more interpreter of the signs he creates.

When plays present a generalized social paralysis of the ability to react or voice dissent, this is often accompanied by the implication that the audience, representative in the theater of the public at large, aids and abets the perpetuation of tyranny through timidity and acquiescence. In *Baño a baño* the protagonists abuse the passivity of the audience, juxtaposed with the sighting of activity that poses a potential threat to the status quo, which the audience is written into the play as supporting. If those in the auditorium were to react, the central metaphor of the play would be immediately destroyed.

Ictus, in their play *La mar estaba serena* [The sea was calm] (1981), tackled similar themes of the passivity of the majority.[17] The first sketch, "Atención Barra," revolves around the experience of a family at a football match in which the rules are grotesquely distorted. Before the game begins, a communal humming noise invades the stadium, replacing the normal shouting and cheering, and as the players come on to the pitch, the spectators are provided with whisky, pom-poms, and hats. The game is being played with two balls, there is no referee and there are unequal numbers in the two teams, the cynical philosophy behind which is a parody of free market policy: "Todos son buenos jugadores. Tienen derecho a jugar. Así los malos se van eliminando solitos" (p. 4). When a penalty is to be taken, the spectators are ordered to put on the hats, which cover their eyes, and they are provided a running commentary, according to which the penalty was missed. The father, however, looks, only to find out that a goal was scored. When one of the players protests he is beaten to death and is later announced as having "recientemente fallecido en digna y leal justa deportiva" (p. 7) [recently deceased in a worthy and loyal sporting battle]. It is only the father who protests at the outrages, while the general public seems willing to accept the mockery. "Todo el mundo parece conforme, papá" [Everyone seems to agree, dad], his daughter tells him, and she had begun to harbor the doubt that maybe the loud-speaker version is correct, that two balls are used in football, that teams do have unequal numbers. No matter what, it is better not to become involved. Truth is what is officially recorded, not what is witnessed. Compare this with Eliana's comforting assurance in *Lo crudo, lo cocido y lo podrido,* "Lo importante es cómo lo anote yo en mis crónicas, no se preocupen" [Don't worry, the important thing is how I note it down] (p. 275).

Throughout we have seen that the language used to instill the correct values into the characters is one of unity of purpose, of loyalty to a mission, of faithfulness to truth sacrificed to efficacy of the image of perfection. It relies on images of undiminishing strength, as in the anthem of the Turkish bath, in which the inmates declare they will be "íntimos, inviolables, definitivos," like "espigas." This is echoed in Elías's inspection of the waiters when he urges them to be "constantes, incondicionales, dispuestos," and in the description of the tutor as "entero" when he is truly in command. All these images imply immutability, resistance to change, defensive strength, and it is to this that authors turn once and again to provide allusions to the underlying currents of insecurity or weakness in the various bastions.

But what of those in subordinate positions? The father in "Atención Barra" is an anomaly, for it is not safe to voice dissident opinions in the environment to which he now belongs, where the way of surviving is through blending in with the background, seeking anonymity as the pupils in *No +* do when they have overstepped the bounds of their freedom, and as the waiters are forced to do throughout their long wait. This "afán de anonimidad,"[18] is in keeping with the limbolike situations in which characters are imprisoned. Time has lost its meaning, individual development with it; nothing happens. In the most realist of all the plays, *Una pena y un cariño,* the actors are willing to conform because of the distant reward, and because there is an army of faceless individuals equally willing to take their place. The rehearsal is frustratingly unproductive, there is a sense that they are playing at being actors, and while the spectacular purports to be about "The Roots of Chile," the roles they are asked to play are of the timeless and effectively fictional products of a dead patriarchy.

These plays share the common perception that the main objective of those in power is to halt the progress of history. There is a common vision of a forced detention of the historical process for the imposition of a model of society advantageous to a tiny minority important among whom are the manipulators of power themselves, who have an ever-increasing interest in maintaining the status quo. This new state can be maintained only through force and repression. Very few don the wooly hats unwillingly. The images of war, of imminent rebellion, of serious threat evoked as the alternative to the present state would seem to exist only in the confines of the dramatic space. Perhaps this is an indication of the efficiency of the halting of time, but such stagnation is unveiled in these plays as artificial and sterile.

A measure of this sterility is the place of ritual existence in plays where games and reality become suspiciously confused. Cocooned within the protective walls of the Turkish bath, suspended in the illusion of their perfect moment, the protagonists of *Baño a baño* play. Do they merely play at making laws, secure in the knowledge that the subjugation of the people is so complete that they need not impose them? Perhaps. But these games are manifestations of a grotesque cynicism, the laws are parodies of those actually designed to impose public order, to control social pests, like tramps, lunatics. Law-making is a dangerous game when left to the imbecile mentality. The protagonists childishly and narcissistically play games of power that hold within them the seeds of destruction, for while they play, others act.

In *Lo crudo, lo cocido y lo podrido,* games have another significance. The games the waiters play tirelessly to fill the time before the arrival of Ossa Moya are doubly important. On one level they are infantile, the pastimes of those who have no contribution to make to society. But, on another level, and deriving from this, games are the last remaining vestige of their role: "Play is order; it creates order. Into an imperfect world it brings a temporary, a limited perfection."[19] They are a means of reinventing the order of the restaurant, of reinforcing the hierarchy of power to which the waiters still adhere, and they degenerate into petty violence when they deviate from this function, when the waiters step beyond the closely monitored, superbly organized game of being waiters. Like the set pieces of *No +*, the games in *Lo crudo, lo cocido y lo podrido* can also be construed as training, training in the first instance, for the correct delivery of the subordinate role, and secondly for the proper assumption of the dominant role. The pupil is destined to be master, and the waiter is destined to be maitre. Elías is adamant that games are forbidden while rehearsals are mandatory, Evaristo can no longer distinguish which is which, and Efraín knows that they ultimately mean the same thing. For the waiters, games are reality.

Games, finally, are signs of expression for those marking time in this limbo of inactivity (remember that the protagonists in *Pedro, Juan y Diego, Los payasos de la esperanza,* and *Tres Marías y una Rosa* also invent games). They belong to a children's world, to the world of those who neither do nor speak. Games are part of a ritual existence, but none of these plays accepts this ritual existence as permanent. For games can also be unreliable: although they can be endlessly repeated, they contain the inherent possibility of a different outcome, and through games individuals learn. In the destruction of the Turkish bath, the sporadic signs of solidarity among the actors, Efraín's exit into an unknown future, the pupils' growing defiance, each one of these plays has the suggestion of renewal, of the hoped-for alternative. They unveil discontent and they search for optimism.

In these plays, the illusion of access to and understanding of the mental machinery of power is created. Somehow, perhaps through identification with the settings, accessibility to this machinery of power is a feasible illusion. In the next chapter we move to the other extreme as we explore the world of Juan Radrigán, populated by the dirty, smelly sectors who live on the margins of "decontaminated" society, where the exercise of power is remote and arbitrary, and where no illusion of access to its internal machinery can exist.

4
Worlds of Marginality: The Ubiquitous "El"

1979: A New Dramatist, Juan Radrigán

Since the performance of his first play in 1979, Juan Radrigán has been one of Chile's most prolific dramatists. He has written and produced thirteen plays, and in 1982 he was awarded the prize for the Best Dramatist of the Year by the Círculo de Críticos del Arte.[1] By then it was generally agreed that "Radrigán es a los pobres lo que Egon Wolff, Vodanović, Cuadra, son a la burguesía y clase media chilenas en la dramaturgia nacional. Todos ellos son fieles a sus clases" [Radrigán is to the poor what Egon Wolff, Vodanović, Cuadra, are to the Chilean bourgeoisie and middle class in our national drama. They are all loyal to their classes].[2] Juan Radrigán's characters are the most extreme examples of the dispossessed; they are down-and-outs, prostitutes, tramps; they belong to the lumpen proletariat; and they live on the margins of society. The problems that afflict them are those of survival, and they fight fiercely to protect the last vestiges of human dignity that remain to them.

On first sight these protagonists are close relatives of the marginal sectors we saw in the works of sixties in Heiremans, Díaz, Aguirre and, to a lesser extent, on the other side of the river in Wolff's work. Yet Radrigán's world is far removed from that one. Firstly, one of the most significant contributions to theater that Radrigán has made is in the realm of the authenticity of his language, for whereas the lumpen of the dramatists mentioned above spoke a form of correct Chilean Spanish, Radrigán's characters speak lumpen Chilean—a closed slang, crude, funny, vivid, and often incomprehensible to the outsider. At the same time it is lyrical, poetic, evocative of a whole inner world of nuances of despair and optimism, cynicism, and faith. Agustín Letelier, talking about *Borrachos de luna* [Moondrunk] (1986), underlines the poetic elements in the language: "Pero es una poesía suave o que detenga

en imágenes en busca de la belleza. Es una poesía que busca elevar
el tono del lenguaje para darle dignidad y para mostrar con mayor
fuerza la causa del dolor o de la soledad" [But it is a gentle poetry
or one that halts at certain images in search of beauty. It is a poetry
that seeks to highlight the tone of the language to give it dignity and
to show with greater force the cause of the pain or the loneliness].[3]
The coarse and graphic slang is interspersed with unexpected poetic elements that lead ultimately to the discovery of the innermost
fears and worries of the protagonists. Radrigán's is a dramatic
language born of belief in people, a language intended to paint the
inner landscapes of emotion, "Porque hay gente que es buena. Que
adentro tienen paisajes, tienen colores" [Because there are people
who are good. Who have landscapes, colors inside them].[4]

Critics in search of conventional dramatic conflict, development
and resolution, are constantly disappointed by their absence from
Radrigán's sparse plays. One critic complained that his first play,
Testimonio de las muertes de Sabina [Testimonies of Sabina's
deaths] (1979), had "escasos elementos dramáticos" [very few dramatic elements], that the play lacked "caracterización de personajes" and that it was "casi un reportaje periodístico actuado."[5] As
his work has developed, these dramatic elements do not appear; the
stage remains bare and inhospitable, the dialogues still bear the
mark of reports of the protagonists' lives and are still performed in
apparent voids. Herein lies the second and more significant difference in Radrigán's drama. Other dramas dealing with topics of
marginality have been set within an oppressor—oppressed antagonism. In Radrigán's work, however, the marginals are the central
and only characters, they inhabit an isolated world, petty recrimina-
tions substitute for dramatic conflict, and conflict in the sense of the
development of the action toward crisis and resolution is insignificant. Yet there is a tension, an awareness of antagonism bearing
down from beyond the space the protagonists occupy on stage—a
bench, a room, a hut, a clearing by the river. The major conflicts are
to be found within the protagonists, often in the form of a continual
grating of past and present, of the loneliness they experience in the
present compared with the memory of a fuller past of by now
unfulfilled dreams. They fight against physical and moral disintegration, against the loss of human dignity.

Because of his background and the themes and protagonists of
his works, Radrigán has been consistently and mistakenly compared with the only other dramatist of working-class extraction that
Chile can boast, Antonio Acevedo Hernández. A number of obser-
vations should be made. Firstly, Acevedo Hernández's work was

normally set within a tight melodramatic structure, a mixture of tragedy and sure redemption, usually linked with a political solution. His works were part of a drama growing from the workers' movement, and the characters belonged to a well-defined social structure. The same can be said of the work of other dramatists with whom Radrigán's work has been compared—for example, Aguirre, Requena, and the earlier socially committed works of Díaz—in which the situation of the protagonists was seen to be hopeful as long as they remained capable of taking up consciousness of their socially and economically deprived state and seeking a way forward through organization and political struggle against the ruling classes.

In Radrigán we find no such clarity of interpretation and no offering of solutions. There is no political way out, and while his social commentary is always painfully explicit and ultra realistic, it is rarely linked to the possibility of redemption through political awareness or consciousness-raising:

> Yo no creo que sacar a un hombre de la pobreza consista en hacerlo rico. . . . Un tipo es absolutamente feliz con 20 mil pesos. Porque después empieza a buscar más y buscar más. . . . Y cada uno es culpable de que no seamos felices así. Por eso yo no busco la revolución en masa. No me gusta tirar piedras, sino que cada uno se intranquilice, que cada uno medite.[6]

> [I do not believe that you make a man rich by taking him out of material poverty. A person can be absolutely happy with twenty thousand pesos. Because then he begins to look for more and more. . . . And each one of us is guilty of not being happy with what we have. That is why I do not call for mass revolution. I do not like to throw stones, instead I want each individual to worry, each one to think].

The essence of Radrigán's work is that he redefines marginality. Here marginality is not purely economic; it is emotional, physical, human, and its roots are to be found in the question of human dignity, which, the author feels, "en el pobre está más pura y más pristina. Pristina en el sentido de primitivo y claro. Ellos no tienen los problemas de la incomunicación. . . . Ellos todavía no. Ellos tienen el problema del hambre" [in the poor [human dignity] is purer, more pristine. Pristine in the sense of primitive, clear. They do not have problems of incommunication. . . . They do not have those problems yet. They have the problem of hunger].[7] This is the world that Radrigán explores, a world of moral marginality, a world where little happens, where theater does not mean dramatic conflict, but where there is an oppressive tension nevertheless:

> Porque el teatro de Juan Radrigán sigue siendo poco teatro. Hay poesía, monólogos, historias intercaladas, conversaciones que casi no integran una acción integral, muchas observaciones y frases que se captan mejor al leerlas que en la apretada exposición teatral. Un teatro muy poco teatro, pero de pronto . . . un gran golpe al alma y lo dramático se viene encima. Nos demoramos en un andar lento, muy estático, pero cuando aparece lo que estuvo preparando en medio de entrecortados silencios, duele y tendemos a pensar que eso no puede ser, pero sabemos que es.[8]

> [Because the theater of Juan Ragrigán has still very little to do with theater. There is poetry, there are monologues, interspersed with stories, conversations that almost do not make up a whole piece of action, many observations and phrases that are understood better from the page than in the concentrated theater representation. It is a theater that is not really theater, but all of a sudden . . . there is a great blow to the soul and the drama hits you. We linger at a slow pace, almost motionless, but when what had been on the point of happening does happen, in the midst of faltering silences, it hurts and we tend to think that this cannot be so, but we know that it is.]

Radrigán's work has been regarded as one continuous play, for characters from one play turn up in another in later stages of degeneration; there are references to incidents from other plays and the dramatic community seems to transcend the barriers of the stage. This is a central aspect of Radrigán's theater, for the characters share life experiences governed by broad social circumstances. These are comparable to the social indicators of deprivation studied in the plays about work: problems of alcoholism, dejection, the loss of dignity, all linked to the effect of economic and political changes—called with cruel irony "miracles"—on the protagonists' lives. For Radrigán's characters, with very few exceptions, the events dictating changes in society are far removed from them, and it is this distance that defines their experience. The existence of a remote power, usually referred to as "El," is an integral part of this world.

"El" is never given a proper title, but he is wholly accessible to the imagination of the audience. He is always a male figure, known to represent power or to be all powerful; he is mysterious or remains a mystery to at least one of the characters or one sector of the dramatic community; he is normally at the root of some evil or at the roots of a definite period of hardship, and as such he is an intimidating figure with, for some, unfathomable powers. One of the major consequences of his existence is a sense of alienation. "El" is not a character exclusive to Radrigán's work. In many of the plays of this period, allusions are made to a remote figure with power over the dramatic community or to a figure in whom the characters invest their hope for survival, but who generally remains invisible and unyielding. In the work of Radrigán, "El" finds his most complete expression as a symbol of the remoteness of power and the extreme polarization between social sectors in Pinochet's Chile.

Testimonio de las muertes de Sabina

In *Testimonio de las muertes de Sabina* (1979), Juan Radrigán's first play, the two protagonists, Sabina and Rafael, are old fruit-sellers. In the first act they recall their life together in what seems like a frequently repeated dialogue, through which we learn about the ups and downs they have suffered over the thirty years they have spent together, and through which we glimpse an enduring, if seldom tender, love. The audience learns that lately things have been going badly for the couple and that they feel as if they are an exception to a general rule of prosperity, since other people seem to be doing well ". . . ahora tiene dos quioscos en la estación central y este año ya ha cambiado de abrigo tres veces. . . . Toos se arreglan y nosotros caa vez vamos más pa'bajo" [now she's got two kiosks in central station and this year she's had three coats already. . . . Everyone's getting on fine and we're worse and worse off] (p. 67). In the final scene of the first act, Sabina suddenly remembers that she must tell Rafael that they have been fined for an unexplained offense. The fine leaves them with a sense of foreboding, which is echoed by the faraway footsteps of someone approaching their room.

In the second act, one month later, they are still trying to make sense of the fine. After being moved around in bureaucratic circles, going from one place to the next, being ignored and badly treated, they are still in the dark, not even aware of what they have done wrong in order to warrant problems with the law. The only advance they have made is to be told the number of the law they have broken, for they were given its number in order to prove its existence, but nobody knows to which law the number belongs. At the end of the second act, with the imminent loss of the stall, their fear is growing, and the steps that had been heard to approach before are now nearer and clearly belong to two or three people.

By the beginning of the third act, Sabina's fears have been confirmed and they have lost the stall. She feels destitute and abandoned. By this time they are both in despair, but are gradually piecing the story together. It is established that their licence was out of date and that a fine should have been paid, but since the ticket was taken from them by one of the bureaucrats, they could never prove that it was issued and could not pay the fine, no matter how much they wanted to, and they lost the stall as a consequence. This brings to the fore their quarrels of mutual recrimination, and Sabina above all feels that nothing worthwhile is left in her life, the loss of the stall having killed even her ability to create dreams that she knows will never be fulfilled. Someone has destroyed her life for her, but she does not know who, and by the end of the third act the steps that are approaching are loud and menacing.

Testimonio de las muertes de Sabina introduces the sense of the remoteness of power that will pervade the rest of the dramas to be studied in this chapter. Whereas in other Radrigán plays this idea finds personification in a distant and seemingly omnipotent character, "El," the most frightening aspect of the story of Sabina and Rafael is the fact that they are totally in the dark as to who is persecuting them in such a way. The fear they experience is set in perspective when it is made clear that for them it has always been perfectly normal to be summoned by the law to account for minor offenses, but that this time something has changed: "Los han sacao partes por tener la pesa arreglá, por no barrer o por ocupar mucha verea; pero siempre los han entregao un papel donde dice porqué los sacan el parte y lo vamos a pagar y too quea arreglao, pero ahora no sabimo qué pasa; no sabimos qué's lo que hicimos" [They've fined us for fixing the weight, for not sweeping up, or for taking up a lot of space; but they've always given us a piece of paper where they tell us why we've been fined and we go and pay, and everything's okay, but now we don't know what's happening; we don't know what it is we've done] (p. 85). Everything about this most recent encounter with the law is sinister, inexplicable, and Sabina suspects that they are being cruelly mocked.

Rafael is frustrated by the abstract nature of the power that now governs them. Who can they turn to? Who can explain the problem?

. . . No viste como los jueron apretando dia'poco, sin dar nunca la cara. En la comisaría, en la municipaliá, en el jugao; toos decían lo mismo,

"Es la ley, no poímos hacer na." Y la ley no está por ninguna parte, no tiene cara, no tiene ojos, no tiene cuerpo. ¡Así no se puee peliar! ¿Cómo crestas te vai a agarrar con alguién que no veí, que no'stá en ninguna parte? ¡Entiéndame, po! (p. 97)

[. . . Didn't you see how they kept on getting at us, without ever showing the face. At the police station, the town hall, the courts; they all said the same thing, "It's the law, we can't do anything." And the law's not to be seen anywhere, it hasn't got a face, or eyes, or a body. You can't fight against something like that! How the hell are you supposed to fight against something you can't see, that's nowhere? Listen to me, for God's sake!]

The law becomes the instrument of the cowardly, personified as a bully persecuting the weakest without ever having to explain or face up to the victim. This is the dilemma that affects to a greater or lesser extent most of Radrigán's characters. They find themselves in dead-end situations, and the only way out seems to be in the hands of a character they cannot see, of whom they have no immediate knowledge, and who is cruelly unjust and uncaring. The constant insinuation that the gravity of the situation is a recent develop-ment—that some time in the past, power and its executors were not so remote, so totally faceless, so cowardly—pervades Radrigán's work. Now Sabina feels as if she is being treated like an animal, that she is no longer respected as a human being.

Sabina has lived a poor life, surviving from her stall, which is her economic security for the future and through which she can create some illusion of hope in her life. Although she knows deep down that she will never have all the things that dreams are made of, she needs the illusion of a better future: "Yo sabía que no las iba a tener, que no eran para mí, pero siempre me hacía ilusiones. . . . Ahora si los quitan el puesto nunca más voy a tener esperanzas. ¡No puen robar eso, no pueen!" [I knew that I wasn't going to have these things, that they weren't for me, but I always had my dreams. . . . Now if they take away the stall, I'm never going to have hope again. They can't take that away from me! They can't rob that!] (p. 85). She feels desperately alone, next to but unaccom-panied by a drunken husband and forgotten by her children, she feels that the foundations of her life, the respect for her work and her modest dreams, are about to be taken away from her. If the stall goes she will face the same fate as the fruit she sells, she will be trodden underfoot.

Sabina is haunted by the prospect of death, but death for her is not a simple notion, it is a constant creeping part of life. On one level, the simple awareness of death is an inevitable result of old age, for all around them their friends are dying, generally of alcohol-related diseases. Rafael is struck by the thought that death is closing in, he is shocked by the fact that he will inevitably die, and death conjures up notions of loneliness, of losing Sabina. Sabina's fear is not of death itself, but of an unpeaceful death. She tells Rafael the story of a death she witnessed as a young girl, when a dying woman was tormented by the women who had come to help her to "die well." Yet, as she pleads to Rafael that he should never let her suffer the same fate, she is struck by the sure memory of having told him the story many times before. Can it be true that Rafael does not remember having heard it, that she had been talking to herself? Can it be true that he will remember nothing of her worries, her life, her memories when she dies?

RAFAEL: (Perdiendo la paciencia) Güeno vos sabís que siempre he tenío mala memoria, qué querís que liá'ga . . .

SABINA: Si vos te muriera y alguien me preguntara alguna vez como erai, yo me acordaría de too lo que te gustaba, de lo que hablábai, de lo que queríai; me acordaría hasta de la manera de andar que tenís, pero voh . . .

RAFAEL: Yo también, po, yo también.

SABINA: ¡No de mí no se va'cordar nadie. Nadie me va'ir a ver o va'hablar de mí; yo me voy a morir más que toda la gente! ¡Yo me voy a morir tanto cuando me muera!

RAFAEL: ¿Cómo te vai a morir tanto? Ya no te pongai lesa. Toos los morimos una vez nomás. (p. 90)

[RAFAEL: (*Losing patience*) Well, you know I've always had a bad memory, what do you expect . . .

SABINA: If you died and somebody asked me what you were like, I would remember everything you liked, everything you talked about, what you wanted; I would even remember how you walked, but you . . .

RAFAEL: I would too, for God's sake, I would too.

SABINA: No, nobody's going to remember me. Nobody's going to go and see me or talk about me; I'm going to die more than anyone else! I'm going to die so much when I die!

RAFAEL: What do you mean you're going to die so much? Don't be stupid. We all just die, for once and for all.]

If death for Rafael means loneliness, then for Sabina dying with no trace in the memory of the person with whom she has shared thirty years is the ultimate sign of the utter futility of her life. A life of talking alone, like a mad woman, followed by a death of incomparable abandonment.

Sabina tries again to make Rafael aware of the meaning of death when, in a graphic example of his inability to respond to her and change her monologues into dialogues, she tries to describe a dream. In it she comes to visit herself:

> Vine a verme, era joven. . . . De repente me vi pará ahí. [*señala algún lugar en la pieza*] Yo taba ahí (señala), parchándote el chaquetón. . . . Vine y me queé mirando un güen rato. . . . Claro, yo misma. Pero mucho más joven. [*pausa*] Como era antes de conocerte a voh. . . . Y de repente los pusimos a llorar las dos. . . . De lástima, de vergüenza. . . . Si hubiera tenío un revólver me habría matao"

> [I came to see myself, I was young. . . . Suddenly I saw myself over there. [*She points to another part of the room.*] I was there [*pointing*], patching your jacket. . . . I came over and stood watching myself for a good while. Yes, it was me. But much younger. [*Pause*] The way I was before I met you. And suddenly we both started crying. . . . Out of pity, shame. . . . If I had had a revolver I would have killed myself.]

In her dream Sabina divides herself into parts, stages of her disillusion with life. She sees the long-dead younger self visiting the present dying self, and both are tempted to provide the *coup de grâce*. Rafael cannot comprehend Sabina's attention to a dream; he does not believe that in a similar dream he would have any reason to cry, but then the very fact that it is Sabina who dreams is indicative of their different experience of life. He has a life outside the home, friends, drinking partners with whom he conscientiously evades thinking about the nature of his existence, and at home he answers Sabina's fears with anger, impatience, or jokes. Perhaps he does remember Sabina's childhood experience of death, but he has so practiced the art of evasion that he need make no effort to erase it from his mind. Sabina, alone, with no means of evasion has discovered that thoughts and memories are autonomous from her desire to control them. As memories of her optimistic youth intrude even on her sleeping moments, the truth of her eroded life invades her peace of mind, and the prospect of a peaceful end grows dimmer. Death looms as a constant erosion of life.

The steps that end each scene, growing more and more menacing each time, are the steps of those who will execute the dictates of the law; they are the steps of those who will finally rob Sabina of her stall and the last illusion of life; they are the steps of death closing in. Radrigán's language leaves no doubt as to the criminal undertones in the imposition of the law, a law that will "rob" the protagonists of their right to earn a living and will "kill" their reasons for living. At the root of all these plays is a deep preoccupation with questions of justice. The law is seen to be faceless when the characters have to fight for justice, but, as the steps indicate, all too real and tangible when it comes to putting the finishing touches to the couple's destruction, their deaths.

Radrigán's plays hinge on the study of questions of dignity and respect, the durability of love in poverty, justice and injustice. In all the plays it is continually stated that the period of injustice is in contrast to a past period of respect and care. While it is rarely stated when this period existed and there is always the hint that it is nostalgia for a not-so-perfect past, it is clear that the period of the remote power of "him" and "them" is the period since the coup. Characters fear the power wielded, yet whoever wields it is deemed nevertheless to have the means to extract them from the deathlike limbo they inhabit or, alternatively, to put an end to all hope. This is stated in its more explicit form in *El invitado*.

El invitado: He Came to Stay

El invitado [The guest] is the third part of a larger piece called *Redoble fúnebre para lobos y corderos* [Funeral knell for lambs and wolves], made up of two monologues and a dialogue.[9] On a stage decorated only by a black bench, the play takes the form of a dialogue between a couple, Sara and Pedro, in which they describe how they live in a room occupied by a mysterious guest, El invitado, whom neither is aware of having invited into their home. They cannot adequately explain how he arrived, only that he slipped through an open door and is now comfortably settled in their home, where the level of coexistence is claustrophobic in the extreme— "Aquí en este lao tenimos la cama de nosotros, la del invitao ta allá en esa otra punta" (p. 258)—and where their every move is made in the knowledge of his presence. The dialogue is, in effect, a diversion from the main purpose of their presence, which is to challenge the audience to show some sign of life by answering the question that haunts their every living minute: "Querimos que los digan cómo se acostumbraron a vivir con el Invitao: querimos ser como ustedes" [We want you to tell us how you got used to living with the guest: we want to be like you] (p. 274).

Sara and Pedro have always been poor, but now they live in misery. We learn of the gradual economic and moral deterioration

in their lives through flashbacks to the various strategies they have
adopted to survive: they walk the streets day after day looking for
work, Sara appears in television quiz shows that ridicule the extremely poor, and Pedro acts as a sparring partner to up-and-
coming boxing stars, who, in their turn, are exploited by un-
scrupulous managers. Their reduction to demeaning jobs and begging is, Sara says, the result of a miracle: ". . . milagro económico
he oío que le llaman" (p. 257). Their experience of the miracle is
sharply contrasted with that of the tranquil people sitting in the
audience, tranquil because they do not share the same misery, and
therefore must have experienced another side of the "economic
miracle."

On one level, the arrival of El invitado remains a mystery that is
never fully explained but which, taken in the wider context the play
is written in, will be all too obvious for the audience. The home of
Pedro and Sara is a metaphor for the state of the country, the
intruder analogizing with the intruder of recent Chilean history and
the whole situation analogizing with the postcoup period. The most
important point about this "El" is the extent of his control over the
dramatic community and, by extension, over the community at
large. At various points during their dialogue, the question of his
arrival is raised, somehow against their wills, as if they are com-
pelled to talk about something they really would rather forget. They
try to hide behind ways of avoiding responsibility for the disaster,
or, like Sara, they try to forget, ". . . hablando d'eso las palabras
sólo sirven de cuchillos nomá. Lo que tenimos que hacer es olviar;
olviar pa poder empezar a vivir" [. . . if we talk about it, the words
are just like knives. What we have to do is forget, forget, to go on
living.] (p. 255). Yet they cannot be free of the awareness of his
presence or of the need to explain it away, to locate the beginnings
of their present misery at the moment he arrived. But did he arrive
or was he invited?

> PEDRO: Antes no éramos así: too empezó cuando llegó el Invitao.
> SARA: Invitao no; invitao es cuando uno convía a alguien: y a ése yo no
>   lo invité.
> PEDRO: Yo tampoco: llegó solo.
> SARA: Ni el viento llega solo, pero pongámole que sí. (p. 258)

> [PEDRO: We weren't like this before: everything started when the guest
>   came to stay.
> SARA: No, he's not a guest; a guest is when you invite someone; and I
>   didn't invite him.

PEDRO: Neither did I: he arrived on his own.

SARA: Not even the wind arrives on its own, but let's just say that he did.]

They can never hide from the fact that they are among the totally defeated in the new situation and that somehow they, especially Pedro, could be held responsible for his arrival. They cannot avoid the suspicion that although the guest was not actually invited, his entrance was not foreseen and prevented as it perhaps could have been.

The decay in the speakers' lives is almost complete. Pedro's manhood comes more and more into question as, first, he is unable to ward off their "guest," and then as the degree of his failure to provide for his wife grows. Sara's resentment is rarely far from the surface, and in her desperation she insults Pedro's human dignity: "Al invitao ya le falta poco pa obligarte a andar a cuatro patas" [The guest has almost got you on all fours]; but Pedro only reminds her that they reflect each other's degradation: "A mí nomá no, a voh también" [Not only me, you too] (p. 270). Instead of the togetherness they once felt, and that they now envy in others, Pedro and Sara are torn apart by the degradation they suffer daily. They fight, they blame each other, they try to love, but the presence of El invitado renders this all but impossible: ". . . él no sabe eso. El amor viene y se muere di'hambre nomá" [he doesn't know that love just dies of hunger] (p. 262). Sara blames the fact that they have no children on his presence: "Los quitó la casa y la alegría. No los dejó tener un hijo" [He took our house and our happiness. He stopped our having children.] (p. 266). She says that "el horno no'stá pa bollos" (p. 255) having decided that, even if she could, it would be wrong to bring a child into this world: "Una mujer sin hijos púee ser muy desgraciá, pero una mujer con un hijo muerto o pidiendo comía casa a casa, es cien veces más desgraciá" [A woman without children may be unhappy, but a woman with a dead child or begging from house to house is a hundred times more unhappy] (p. 259). They cannot even make love, for he is constantly present, the diligent voyeur.

The most extreme physical consequence of his arrival is the reduction in their living space. Sara tells how they have "too junto," and Pedro explains that they now live in "una sola pieza." They nostalgically remember the days when they had a home, friends, and a sense of community; when they went to the local theaters and second-hand book shops; but now they are isolated. The move from home to room speaks out as a symbol of their decaying existence and as a symbol of the closing spaces of communication. Communication with other people is seen to be directed through other channels, no longer from person to person. People, it is suggested, live in separate units, ostensibly at peace with each other and the world, rarely involved in community activities that rely on free social interaction.

Radrigán demonstrates graphically the growing propagandistic power of the media. In Sara's description of their room, the symbols of the machinery of propaganda are to the fore: "En la cabecera de la cama d'el hay un poster del Colo Colo, en la de nosotros, uno con tres marraquetas" [On his bedhead there is a poster of Colo Colo, on ours is a poster with three loaves of bread]. To which Pedro replies, "O sea en eso tamos a la moda, pan y circo" [So we're in fashion, bread and circus.] (p. 258). The imagery may be contrived, the dialogue forced, but the intention is clear. The poster of Colo Colo, Chile's most popular football team, functions as an Orwellian screen from behind which El invitado controls the protagonists' existence. El invitado provides "bread and circuses," the classic form of mass culture, the abandonment of "political responsibilities for doles of food and the lures of the racetrack and the arena."[10] In this case, the pseudo-nationalist emotions raised by Colo Colo numb the desire for action while whetting the appetite for a superficial national pride. Propaganda, such as that surrounding Colo Colo, isolates the people politically while creating an impression of community. The manipulation of information keeps the "followers" in ignorance and eradicates the need for autonomous memory. In this way the consumers of the information are alienated from the processes in society that directly affect them; changes like the "economic miracle" that destroyed Sara and Pedro become the work of an obscure force that they cannot attribute in certainty to El invitado, but that definitely coincided with his arrival. The isolation they feel in this void becomes frightening, intimidating, hence the need to be sure that they are not the only ones for whom coexistence with El invitado is intolerable, and that the slow but sure erosion of accepted values is either common to all or reversible.

El invitado is written in the form of a confrontation. And "tranquilidad" is, again, a key concept of the play, subtitled *O la tranquilidad no se paga con nada*. This is inevitably evocative of the crude propagandistic "tranquilidad pública," but more importantly this is a picture of the painful existences hidden behind the tranquil facade, of which the audience is cast as a part. The audience is, in effect, being challenged with the accusation that they are part of this "tranquilidad," living peacefully with the ubiquitous guest because they invited his presence. The implication is that those who are unchanged by his arrival are either cowed into silence by his presence, that they are part of the "economic miracle," ("Entonces tienen qu'estar endeudados hasta las masas, porque la tranquilidá no se paga con na" [They must be in debt to their teeth because tranquility is not free] [p. 255]), or alternatively, that it is they who left the door ajar. This is not the almost obligatory gratuitous dig at the morals of the bourgeois audience, but a grave comment on the nature of the enduring strength of the intruder. For Sara and Pedro the evocation of "tranquilidad" does not harbor any false promise of a peaceful society, but means purely and simply the ruthless creation of a consumer society to which they cannot belong. "Felicidá pa grande ésta / d'estarse muriendo en tranquilidá" [What great happiness to be dying in tranquility] ends the poem that introduces the play.

El toro por las astas: A Parable of Moral Redemption

El toro por las astas [The bull by the horns] (1982) takes place in a "prostíbulo de mala muerte." The characters—Lucía, the madam; Víctor, her pimp; Antonio, the *campanillero* (doorman-cum-lookout); and two decrepit prostitutes, Jaque and Made—live in squalor, surviving from day to day on the pitiful income of the brothel, which has next to no clients. Lucía has heard of the existence of El Milagrero, a man who has become renowned for his miraculous works, and she hopes to bribe him to come to the brothel in order to perform the miracles that will change the course of their lives. While Antonio sets out to find El Milagrero and arrange the meeting, the prostitutes are ordered by Lucía to stop work so as to purify their souls and are set the all but impossible task of cleaning the brothel of years of filth and grime, all in preparation for his arrival. In the course of the first scene, the characters reveal the miracles they want El Milagrero to work: Lucía wants the freedom of her son, a political prisoner whose one wish is to see the light of day; Víctor longs to eat "un tremendo asado," a huge roast, for he is convinced that his years of injustice have their roots in hunger; Jaque, who has lost a breast through cancer, contracted, she believes, as a result of being manhandled by her clients, will ask for a new one; and Made, who was refused a job in a cosmetics factory because she was a prostitute, is making a blue apron in preparation for the miracle of being employed there. Only Antonio has no miracle to request since, he says, he has spent his life from the moment he was born simply passing through every door that has been left open for him.

When El Milagrero arrives, sooner than expected and unannounced, he comes only to return Lucía's bribe. There follows a scene of utter confusion in which the characters fail to recognize their savior in the ordinary man, a potential client, standing before them, and his identity is only revealed when Antonio recognizes him. In a long monologue El Milagrero tells how he was employed by a mysterious, never fully explained figure called El Hombrón for the job of imparting a pseudo-Christian message of love and resignation to the most desperate sectors of society. Yet, the very fact of being in contact with these sectors had opened his eyes to the depths of their misery and the emptiness of the message he was preaching. Having realized that he wasn't equipped to deal seriously with problems of such magnitude, El Milagrero had confronted El Hombrón and had been freed from his role, so that, by the time he arrives at the brothel, he is again an ordinary man.

The only message he can impart is the one he has learned as the miracle-worker, that is, that there are no miracles and that people must find within themselves the strength to free themselves from the wretched circumstances in which they live. For the protagonists this message means the loss of even the illusion of hope of miraculous release from fate. In anger and despair El Milagrero breaks down the door of the brothel for them to leave and start a new life outside, but his final actions bring all the wrath of El Hombrón upon him and he is struck down dead. While the rest fall *en masse* into despair and defeat, Antonio takes the opportunity provided by the newly open door and leaves.

The key to this play lies in the names of the two prostitutes, Jaque and Made: those in the brothel are in checkmate, a position of complete defeat from which there is no way out. It is stated time and again that there is a war going on outside the brothel and that their lives have become unbearable from the time the war started. Jaque's lover went off to the war and never returned, leaving her alone and with nothing to live for, and Lucía's son is in prison as a traitor. All around them the war both reaps and thrives on confusion. Their one certainty is that they are among the defeated, and their one hope is that El Milagrero will save them from this limbo of defeat and isolation.

Jaque and Made have three sources of information: firstly, what are called "las noticias atrasás" of Víctor's old radio, from which all that is heard are the various noises of war, noises that they dread:

"Intempestivo ruido de balazos, ayes, carreras; disparos en ráfaga y tiro a tiro. Se paran asustadas, mirando, escuchando, buscando refugio. El sonido cambia de tono, con algunas variantes, helicópteros, órdenes. Luego, vuelve a cambiar" [An ominous noise of shots, cries, running, machine gun fire and the firing of guns. They stand up frightened, watching, listening, looking for shelter. The tone of the noises changes, there are variations, helicopters, orders. Then it changes again] (p. 319); secondly, what they learn from the newspapers the clients leave behind, where they read that "ahora hay paz y tranquilidá" (p. 326); and thirdly, from Antonio who, Jaque says, has told her that "there are signs everywhere that say we're doing fine." Antonio also reports the vast changes in society and the possibilities they could have outside: "No, si las cosas han cambiado mucho ajuera, Jaque: ahora podís ir a patinar a un bulevar o te pueden dar pega en una casa de masajes, después te metís la torta a una AFP y quedai flor" [No, things have changed a lot outside, Jaque: now you can go and skate in an ice rink, or get a job in a massage parlor, then you put your money in a private savings plan, and you're made] (p. 328).[11] With such limited and contradictory information, the prostitutes cannot form a coherent idea of society. They are never fully convinced by the second-hand propaganda they receive, nor are they convinced that the war is over. While reporting the propaganda, Antonio contradicts it by telling Jaque that outside there is no longer respect for anything, a state she recognizes as characterizing the war, her last experience of the outside. And she herself gives the lie to the news from the clients' newspapers when she remembers how she had suffered before taking refuge in the brothel: "Pero eso dicen los diarios, no la gente; la gente se quea callá cuando una le habla d'eso. . . . Lo único que sé es que allá ajuera hay muchos como yo, o sea que no son viudas, solteras ni casás . . ." [But that's what the newspapers say, not what people say; people keep quiet when you talk about that. . . . All I know is that there are lots of people out there that are just like me, they're not widows, or single, or married] (p. 326).

The war has engendered a whole new subworld of poverty and desperation, providing fertile ground for miracle workers. For El Milagrero is not unique. Before going in search of El Milagrero, Antonio warns Lucía: "¿Sabe, señora? Taba pensando . . . andan hartos vivarachos por allí que se la'stán dando de Milagreros . . ." [Know what? I've been thinking. . . . There's a lot of wise guys around making out that they're miracle workers] (p. 339). And it is he who demonstrates the relative value of miracle working: "Pero cuando la gente empieza a llamar milagro a comer dos días seguíos,

puede llamar milagro a cualquier cosa. . . . Hacer milagros es re
fácil: basta con quitar algo a la gente y después entregárselo de
repente; la receta no falla" [But when people start calling eating
two days in a row a miracle, they can call anything a miracle. . . .
Working miracles is really easy: all you have to do is take something away from someone and then give it back all of a sudden; it
just can't fail] (pp. 328–29). Antonio sees El Milagrero in purely
political terms, he interprets him as a phenomenon produced by the
age, he refers to his miracle-working as a job, and when they find
out at the beginning of the play that El Milgarero has fled to the
hills, Antonio attributes it to an attempt to escape the repression of
what could be interpreted as politically subversive activities:
". . . junta gente, lo siguen: eso es peligroso. . . . Parece que le dio
miedo y se fondió" [He gathers people together, they follow him:
that's dangerous. . . . It looks as if he got scared and disappeared
into thin air] (p. 337). He believes that only the characters themselves can find their escape, and is of the opinion that religion is not
a game the poor should play. He is cynical about "la campaña de la
decencia y la moralidá" promoted by Lucía and Víctor, and about
the sacrifices the prostitutes are being forced to make as proof of
their faith. In many ways, Antonio is a counterpart to El Milagrero
for he too warns of the futility of believing in a miraculous redemption, aware that they are, in effect, digging the grave for any future
hope in life. "El que cava la fosa cae dentro de ella, y el que rueda
una piedra se le viene encima" [He who digs a hole will fall into it,
and he who rolls a stone will fall under it], he tells the prostitutes,
but the moral reaches uncomprehending ears (p. 326).

Death is a central motif of this play, as it is throughout the work
of Radrigán. In the opening scene, only the voices of Jaque and
Made can be heard as they enter the unlit salon of the brothel,
looking for the place of their "death." The immediate impression
that their voices create is of "ánimas en pena," the wandering souls
of the dead in purgatory, who have not yet been cleansed of their
sins and who, in popular belief, roam between heaven and earth
awaiting the moment when their suffering will have made them
ready for the entrance into heaven. Jaque believes that she has been
killed, that she cannot look forward to a natural death, that their
existence is one of severance from real life: ". . . los tironiaron
hasta que nos separaron de la vía" [they shook us until they tore us
apart from life] (p. 317). According to Made, "La muerte es una
sola, Jaque; si la desgracia grande jue que a nosotros los mataron
por dentro, no por juera" [There is only one death, Jaque. Our
problem is that they killed us on the inside, not outside] (p. 317).
Theirs has been a spiritual and moral death: ". . . nadie contó

chistes en tu velorio, ni t'echaron tierra encima, pero'stai muerto. ¿Aónde te moriste?" [. . . nobody told jokes at your funeral, or threw earth on your grave, but you're dead. Where did you die?] (p. 329).

Jaque and Made suspect that they have no future, but their weakness is such that they can find no alternative other than the miracle solution sponsored by the owners of the brothel, their executioners, Los Verdugos. They follow the instructions, and in the process of cleansing themselves, they assume as their own the struggle to build hope out of this one mysterious, miraculous opportunity. But their belief is laced with a fear that Jaque makes explicit: "Puea ser que la cuestión no sea como ir a meterse a un basural más grande nomás. . . . A ratos me da miedo; junté too lo que me quedaba pa poder armar esta esperanza; si la pierdo nunca más voy a poder creer en na" (pp. 327–28). Even La Verduga shares the fear: "Creo que el mieo que tengo, es que si El me falla, ¿a quién voy a recurrir?" [Maybe we're just digging ourselves deeper into the pit. . . . Sometimes I get scared; I gathered together everything I had left in me to make this hope; if I lose it, I'll never be able to believe in anything again. I think I'm scared that if he fails us, who else can I turn to?] (p. 335).

El Milagrero does confirm some of Antonio's intuitions about his role, but not all, and it is in the juxtaposition of mistaken concepts that the meaning of the roles played by El Milagrero and El Hombrón lies. El Milagrero tells his own story:

Era lindo ir diciéndole a la gente que se quisiera y que entonces lo demás venía solo, el pan, la pega, la tranquilidá y too eso. . . . ¡Pero pónganse en mi lugar po! La cuestión ta muy espesa, muy podría; el amor se l'escapa a la gente a chorros por los agujeros que les hizo la guerra, tan queando caa día más vacíos; y tienen razón también po, cuando la muerte o la amenaza de la muerte es cosa de toos los días, de qué se va asombrar uno. (Pausa) Yo no digo que no tengan salvación, no vamos a venir a vivir con el corazón encerrao en el pecho como un animal asustado, no po, el corazón tiene qu'estar siempre abierto como una ventana, esa cuestión la sé. Pero lo que pasa es qu'el Hombrón me dio la pega, pero no me dio las herramientas; no tenía na aquí aentro [*se golpea el pecho*] pa convencerlos, ni aquí en los ojos ni en la garganta ni en las manos: ¡no tenía na aquí en ninguna re crestona parte! . . . Yo no sé por qué la agarró conmigo; nunca he sío na. Nací, crecí, aprendí la pega de la carpintería con el viejo de mi taita, y cuando apareció La Magdalena los juntamos po. ¿Aónde había algo pa que la agarrara conmigo? En ninguna parte po. ¡Por qué tenía que elegirme a mi! (p. 351)

[It was good going around telling people to love each other and everything else would come naturally, bread, work, tranquility and all the rest
of it. . . . But put yourselves in my place, for God's sake! Things are
really heavy, really rotten; love escapes in floods from people through
the holes left in them by the war, they're emptier and emptier every day;
and they're right too, when death or the threat of death is an every day
thing, why are they going to get worked up. [*Pause*] I'm not saying that
there can be no salvation, no, we can't start living with our heart shut in
our breast like frightened animals, no, our heart has always got to be
open like a window, I know all that stuff. But the thing is that the Big
Man gave me the job, but he didn't give me the tools for the job; I didn't
have anything inside here [*he beats his breast*] to be able to convince
anyone, I didn't have anything in my eyes, or my throat or my hands: I
didn't have anything anywhere, damn it! . . . I don't know why he
picked on me; I've never been anything. I was born, I grew up, my old
man taught me carpentry, and when Magdalena came along we got
together. What reason could he have had for picking on me? None, for
God's sake. Why did he have to choose me?]

The story El Milagrero tells of his life is laden with Christian
overtones—he is a carpenter by trade, following in his father's
footsteps; he is called by a superior being; and he comes to the
brothel, ultimately to his death, on a Friday. But he calls Víctor and
Lucía heretics when they confuse him with the person who cured
lepers and walked on water. He confirms Antonio's theory about
the fear of repression: ". . . ni me dio na con qué peliar contra ese
frío que me corría desde los tobillos hasta'l pelo cuando se paraba
un auto sin patente a mi lao" (p. 351). More importantly, he introduces them to the idea of his miracle-working as a job and names
his employer, El Hombrón, a figure whose existence they had not
even suspected. His job, as defined by El Hombrón, is to provide the
desperate with promises of a better life in return for good behavior
and the rejection of hate and desire for revenge. For El Milagrero
preaches to people who are the maimed survivors of war, who have
seen death and destruction all around and whose driving force is
often revenge: ". . . ahora si uno pone la otra mejilla, la gallá llega a
tomar güelo pa mandarle el otro aletazo, y el hombre más manso de
corazón que he encontrao, sueña con abrir a su enemigo de arriba
abajo y tirarlo a los canales donde corra el agua más podría"
[. . . now, if you turn the other cheek, folk are just pleased to hit
you again; the most gentle man I know dreams about opening his
enemy from top to bottom and throwing him in the stinking water of
the dirtiest canal] (p. 352).

El Milagrero now sees himself as a pawn used by El Hombrón, he sees that the message he was to teach was based on words without feeling or meaning. Through him El Hombrón used the endlessly malleable parables of the New Testament to preach a message of abject resignation to the spiritually dead, trusting in their inability to react. Here the Christian message is cynically endowed with a politically advantageous creed of resignation. Yet, El Milagrero is profoundly and essentially alienated from the words he utters and, Christ-like, he is met with "burlas y piedras y golpes" for, like Jaque, people hear the propaganda of peace and tranquility, but find no way to relate it to reality. The message is a tragic and transparent hoax.

Instead of the peace promised by his preaching, El Milagrero himself loses all the peace, love, and dignity he had known before, and as he begins to recognize this, he sees his own image reflected in those to whom he preaches. The language he speaks is their language, and the images he uses are their images: "Pucha, claro, yo caché al tiro; ustedes son los que no tienen velas en ningún entierro; son los cojos del alma, los masacraos a plazo. . . . Claro po, los caché al tiro, así que cómo voy a querer engañarlos, si vamos gritando el mismo grito desde que nacimos" [God, of course, I saw at once; you're the ones that never have candles at your funeral, you're the ones with lame hearts, the ones who've been killed bit by bit. Of course, I spotted you at once. So how can I lie to you, if we've been shouting the same shout since we were born] (p. 350). More than any other, this common image of "death by instalments" both identifies El Milagrero with the poorest in society, and finally sets him apart. It had been the recognition of this sameness and of his message as one to cow the defeated that had caused El Milagrero to renounce it. Freed from the burden of his mission, El Milagrero's message is one of the belief in the strength of the individual: "Escondíos aquí como ratas no tienen salvación, podrían 'tar llorando y esperando cien años, docientos, pero no sacarían na; porque la via'stá aentro de ustedes, así que si no la viven ustedes, quien puee vivirla" [You've got no hope of salvation, hidden away here like rats. You could be crying and waiting here for a hundred years, two hundred years, but you'd still end up with nothing, because life is inside you. If you don't live it, who can?] (p. 360). What hope can Jaque and Made have?

Radrigán is explicit in the notes that with the release from El Hombrón, El Milagrero began a new life: "Es un hombre que se ve pleno, como lleno de esa armonía entre tierna y orgullosa que sigue al acto sexual, cuando no ha mediado otro compromiso que el del amor. (Es un símil que tomo por la tranquila sensación de bienestar que conlleva.)" [He is a man who seems satisfied, as if full of the harmony, between tender and proud, that follows the sexual act when only love is involved. (I use this simile for the sense of wellbeing it implies.)](p. 348). This is an extraordinary vision in the brothel, where sex and love bear no connection; indeed, it is an extraordinary image in Radrigán's work where love dies with poverty and deprivation, where Rafael fears that Sabina's rancor may be motivated by his sexual impotence, where Pedro and Sara cannot make love because of the presence of El invitado.

The divide between the religious and political message is fluid, and it is not until the last scene that the seeming confusion of political and religious allegory turns into a parable for redemption. For the dramatic community El Milagrero plays Christ to El Hombrón's God the Father. El Milagrero tells how he had begged El Hombrón to free him: "Usté es Dios, no me puee condenar, suélteme, suélteme" (p. 352); and at the moment of his death he cries: "Usté es el rey de los reyes, no puee echar su fuerza contra mí, yo soy un pobre gallo" (pp. 362–63). Radrigán further casts El Milagrero as Salvador Allende to El Hombrón's Pinochet. El Hombrón, politically, is the authoritarian leader who employs El Milagrero to curb the desire for political change by providing realistically unattainable promises. Yet, from the beginning, El Milagrero is a potentially explosive creation. If the rule of El Hombrón is to be ensured by the repression of the masses' political expression, El Milagrero can only be effective while he is void of autonomous thought. As long as the power of "El" is not challenged, the existence and the livelihood of El Milagrero is safe, but as soon as the dividing line between the pseudo-religious and the political is crossed, El Hombrón brings all his power to bear. El Milagrero is political, then, in two ways: firstly as the creation of El Hombrón, and secondly when he begins to preach his own message of rebellion. If there were any doubt as to the symbolic value of El Milagrero, then it is dispelled in his dying moments when Radrigán has him echo Allende's vision of democracy: "¡Salgan, salgan! Llevan la vía por las calles, como lleva el padre al hijo, váyanse por las tremendas, las anchas alamedas!" (p. 362).

Radrigán has pointed to the importance of distinguishing between the perceptions from within the dramatic community and those of the reader or spectator looking on from outside. El Milagrero, in the context of the play, is a failure with nothing to offer and whose greatest disservice to the people in the brothel is to arrive, for he would have saved them from final disillusion if they had been allowed to hold on to their false hope. Yet this character,

who merely seems to serve the purpose of paying another instal-
ment on the characters' death, is the symbol of the author's belief in
humanity: "La esperanza, o sea el afuerino, no sabe por qué tiene
que morir ni se sabe por qué lo tienen que matar. Está muy cansado
ya de todo esto. Cree que no sirve para nada ya. Eso piensa él, pero
mirando la obra desde fuera, uno se da cuenta que pareciera que
sirve" [Hope, or rather the outsider, does not know why he has to
die nor does he know why he has to be killed. He's really tired with
all this now. He thinks he is worth nothing. That's what he thinks,
but looking at the play from the outside, you realize that it looks as
if he is worth something].[12]

The Ubiquitous "El"

Throughout his work Radrigán deals with the theme of marginality as it has never been dealt with before in Chilean theater.
This world is set apart on all accounts from the mainstream of
society; the characters have a constant awareness of their exclusion
from society, an exclusion that finds dramatic expression in the
physical setting of the plays. Radrigán explores this world as it
relates to a perpetual spiral of deprivation and worsening social
conditions, and in terms of the nature of human relationships in
such poverty. Characters find themselves more and more bewildered by life, for they feel that they, for their part, have continued
living in the same fashion as before, and yet still things get worse.
Why does this happen? Who is to blame? Can they blame anyone
apart from an impersonal being they can only refer to as "El" and
who, in his most extreme expression, may be God? Characters in
search of a conflict through which to resolve their situation can find
an antagonist nowhere.

In *Hechos consumados* [When all is said and done] (1981) the
major symbols come together. The play takes place on the outskirts
of town where a tramp, Emilio, has saved a woman, Marta, from a
canal where he presumes she tried to drown herself. In the distance
they can see a continual procession of people who walk endlessly
by, and they are visited on two occasions by a mysterious man, who
is perhaps mad and is dressed in rags with tins jangling from his
body. He has the unreal air of an apparition and speaks in tones that
they find hard to follow but that suggest doom and destruction in an
unjust world, and he predicts Emilio's closeness to death. Far more
real and threatening is the presence of Miguel, the watchman for the
boss of a nearby textile factory on whose land they are seated. The

boss, whom Miguel never sees, but who he knows must exist since he is in his pay, demands that Emilio and Marta quit his land by moving a few feet. Emilio refuses to do so, having decided that he must at last make a stand against his perpetual banishment from society, that moving two steps along signifies moving another two steps toward nothingness. Miguel, terrified at the prospect of the anger of his boss and of losing his job, beats Emilio to death.

Like all Radrigán's dramas, *Hechos consumados* works on levels of reality as defined by the characters' perceptions of life and death. Emilio and Marta are reminiscent of the prostitutes of *El toro por las astas,* for they believe themselves to be only partially alive. They seem to have little past other than vague memories of former partners and of children who have died "de muerte entera," that is, who have totally disappeared from their lives. Emilio describes people as "hechos consumados": ". . . no tuvimos arte ni parte en nosotros mismos; los hicieron y los dijeron: aquí están, vayan p'allá, pero no los dijeron por qué los habían hecho ni a qué teníamos que ir a ese lao que no conocíamos. . . . A ese lao aonde lo único seguro que había era que teníamos que morir . . ." [. . . we weren't given any say in ourselves; they made us and told us: here you are, get on with it. But they didn't tell us why we had been made or where we were supposed to go in this place we didn't know . . . In this place where the only sure thing was that we had to die] (p. 310). People are left invariably to their own sadly inadequate devices in the place called life, and those such as Emilio and Marta will never find the way into the center of life; they are destined to be "en la vía. Pero no al medio, al lao" [In life, but not in the middle, at the side] (p. 279). Marginalization is not only economic, it is emotional, physical, human. It is tangible, and these characters carry deep inside them the consciousness of marginalization. Emilio sees his life as being a search for the moment when he will be born truly to live, when he will enter life at its center, when he will have peace, but he is constantly moved on, constantly deprived of the opportunity to live as a human being. Marta recognizes in his eyes the soul of a person dehumanized by society, the soul of a stray animal, "O sea dos veces desgraciao po animal y botao" (p. 279).

Marta, by contrast, says she likes life, but life treats her badly, plays endless cruel jokes on her, repays her love with detestation and spite. Life is a lover that, like all lovers in Radrigán's plays, cannot be relied on, and it is external circumstances that dictate the strength and lasting power of love. Marta has more memory of a past, she has a greater notion of what has been forbidden her in her life, and like Sabina, she has a profound nostalgia for the illusion of a future home and family, which is translated, in her case, into the attempt to make the space by the river that she temporarily shares with Emilio into a semblance of a living space.

Hechos consumados develops around a vicious circle of death. Emilio fishes Marta from the water where he thought she had tried to commit suicide, but in fact she had been thrown there after having witnessed the dumping of a dead body. And when she finally recovers consciousness Emilio is not interested in her past, even in why she was in the river, but in what visions had passed before her eyes so close to death, so close to the other side. Then, as Miguel finally beats Emilio to death, he subjects him to the full force of the power that had thrown Marta into the river, but that now is the power of "El," of the boss. What cruelly absurd world is it that the characters live in when a man may be brutally murdered for refusing to move two steps along, and when the murderer is such for fear of losing his job?

As in *Testimonio de las muertes de Sabina,* the characters are acutely aware of a greater power that dictates their every move, they feel that they are being watched, but they do not know by whom until the arrival of Miguel, the caretaker of the site. With Emilio, Miguel shares a background of working in the textile industry, but while Emilio is now unemployed, Miguel continues to work in a textile factory, accepting lower wages and twice the amount of work he used to do. He is the boss's pawn, in his complete control and in perpetual fear of putting a foot wrong, for, like the protagonist of *Informe para indiferentes* [Report for the indifferent] (1983), an old man who spends his days guarding the empty garage of his boss, he knows that his every move is monitored night and day. The greatest difference between Miguel and Emilio is that the latter, regardless of how destitute he may be, has managed to keep a hold on the principles upon which he builds his dignity, whereas Miguel accepts everything the boss throws at him as long as he keeps his job. Miguel has assimilated "El's" philosophy of power, his prejudice against anything that suggests subversion of the established order; and he carries a long stick, the material prop of the power he wields in the employ of "El" and with which he will kill Emilio. Yet, neither does Miguel understand the power of "El": he does not know where he lives, nor can he fathom how the boss can be aware of his movements. He merely knows the limits of his own jurisdiction as "El" 's caretaker. It is through Miguel that Emilio and Marta are introduced to the existence of the boss, but he is a figure with whom they are all too familiar, the person who never appears, always represented by his employees. The person who commands their banishment from society.

In the distance there is a constant procession of people walking by. They are walking away from the city, which smells of rotting, but they look too calm to be fleeing. Emilio says that close up they look tired. They are seemingly unaffected by the police sirens that terrify Emilio and Marta and that are a constant reminder of distant persecution, nor do they respond to Miguel's interrogations, despite the stick. These people are threatening in their anonymity, they do not speak, they do not ask for anything, they merely walk. "El" does not like their presence, which is threatening, impinges on his tranquility and ignores the strict social order he has established. Miguel has been ordered to get rid of them.

The most important point is that they are walking away from the city, from society, where, according to the mad man, there exists only "la muerte y la nada." In this sense the procession is of people who have opted out of a rotten society and have set out on the road to achieving an as yet undefined goal. They are survivors in the desolate city, the uprooted inhabitants of a society so decayed and putrid they can no longer exist in it. Or have been banished by it. They, too, are finally on the margins, they do not belong to the new society that is being created and from which many must be cast out to make a "better world" (p. 285). Emilio feels somehow accused, guilty, unable to understand anything, yet he feels empathy with the wanderers; he likes their refusal to bow to repression; he feels there may be place there for him: "¿Qué cree que son? ¿Muertos? ¿Cesantes? ¿Sin casa? ¿Gente que tiene miedo que le pasa algo? En una d'esas poímos ser nosotros también . . ." [What do you think they are? Dead? Unemployed? Homeless? People who are afraid that something might happen to them? We could be there alongside them, you know . . .] (p. 312). And he sees the people as the archetypal exiles, the Jews, who, despite centuries of wandering in the wilderness, survive: "Me gustan los judíos, tienen el secreto de la unión en la sangre. ¿Sabe cuál puede ser ese secreto?" [I like Jews, they've got the secret of union in their blood. What do you think their secret could be?] (p. 308). Yet Marta's and Emilio's lack of access to the secret further heightens their sensation of total isolation.

In the course of the play, Emilio and Marta, camped on his land, are at the mercy of "El." It is clear that in all the plays studied here, "El" is the personification of a remote power, ultimately the symbol of the ruthless nature of the regime in its mission to create a "better world," a cleaner society. In *Testimonio de las muertes de Sabina* this remote power is the law, threatening and unjust; *El invitado* deals with a closed situation in which "El," the mysterious guest, is a symbol of total and unrelenting control, and in which there is little hope for future release. *El toro por las astas* is set in another closed situation, a brothel within whose confines "El" represents a hope of redemption and a deposit for the characters' already existing but almost forgotten superstitious religious belief, but this is a cruel deceit, for the real "El" lurks in the background, omnipotent, invisible, and feeding their hopeless illusions. And in both *Hechos consumados* and *Informe para indiferentes,* "El" is the boss, the archetypal representative of the ruling classes in the class struggle. All of these variations find echoes in other Chilean drama.

In the sixties there were many examples of the boss as antagonist. In plays such as *Los papeleros* by Isidora Aguirre, "El" is the owner of the rubbish dump where the protagonists live and work. He is the boss in the developing world who leaves his employees behind in their underdeveloped state, whose disregard for their welfare is total; his only ambition being for his own economic rise. As he fulfills his ambition, he becomes more mechanical and cold; he becomes alien as his powers, aided by technology, far outreach those of his employees. There can never be any dialogue since the worlds they inhabit and the language they speak grow farther and farther apart, and communication, based on demands for improvement, never welcomed by "El" in the first place, is made no more than a "noise of words." This is the "El" that Radrigán reproduces in *Hechos consumados* and *Informe para indiferentes,* a boss whose power has grown so much that he is more and more alien, and has in his hands the means of making and breaking people at will. He is paternalistic, allowing the meek to survive. demanding total loyalty and submission. Usually the majority of the dramatic community can learn to survive, and some even welcome his brand of paternalism, but some, like the protagonist, are doomed to failure as his power grows.

In *El toro por las astas,* Radrigán produces an "El" who is regarded as the salvation of the dramatic community. In Marco Antonio de la Parra's *Lo crudo, lo cocido y lo podrido,* there is also a character in whom the waiters believe as their redeemer and for whom they wait, endlessly preparing themselves for the moment he will come, reopen the restaurant, and declare the reestablishment of the old order to which they belonged and whose leaders they had served. Ossa Moya represents the oligarchy, a class in irreversible decline, and when he arrives he totally destroys any hope in the return of the old order. But, unlike the prostitutes, the waiters are able to exit through the door that had been opened for them.

The other category of "El" is in *El invitado,* and is the figure who relates most blatantly to the authoritarian regime of this period. The play is essentially a treatise on the dire consequences of military rule on the social class to which the protagonists belong, the greatest victims of the "economic miracle." If, in the sixties much of the drama was laced with the fear of the revolt of the dispossessed, those metaphorically "on the other side of the river," in the world of the seventies, there is no fear of such a threat, for after the appearance of "El," the uninvited guest, these sectors have been so totally repressed that they have no strength to revolt. Emilio in *Hechos consumados,* uses the central metaphor of *El invitado,* that somewhere a door was opened to let in such misery and suffering, and although the connection with the present period is not made in such an explicit fashion as in *El invitado,* the implication is clear: ". . . en alguna parte se abrió una puerta y entró de golpe too lo malo que hay. Del hambre, de la soledad y de las patás, ya no te salva ni Cristo" [. . . a door opened somewhere and evil came pouring in. Not even Jesus Christ can save you now from hunger, loneliness and beatings] (pp. 289–90).

That the existence of "El" governs all else is undisputable. The characters always behave with a mind to the future reaction of the seemingly omnipotent figure in the background, generally invisible and unknown to the dramatic community. Their progressive loss of dignity echoes the development of the characters in the plays dealing with work, reinforcing the argument that it is marginalization from the mainstream of the community and from forming a useful part of society that is the main cause of their demoralization at the hands of authority. But Radrigán does not stop at journalistic commentary, for his is also a theater of denunciation, accusation. *El invitado* is not a dialogue; it is a confrontation, emerging from what he calls the silence of injustice. Momentarily in the theater there is a coexistence of two parallel worlds that can never meet, where the challenge is the challenge of the voiceless. For the world of the audience in the independent theaters of Santiago is "el pueblo de los bien alimentados, bien instruidos y bien descansados"; it is a world of those who are paternisticaly allowed a small, restricted voice, and where the possibility of a solution may exist. It is the world of those who are at or near the center of life.

Radrigán's is a world that is, in itself, absurd. There is no coherence to the lives of the protagonists; the plays read as mosaics of fragmented conversations, characters speak to each other in fits and bursts, content to leave questions unanswered, following parallel, never connecting lines of thought, each one interpreting the other's words as these fit in to their respective perceptions of life. In this way idle chatter, taken at its most literal level, adds to the impression of the absurd, since simple questions hide a multitude of insinuations, and incessantly evoke the same images of alienation, injustice, and death. At the center of the symbolic world of Radrigán sits the imagery of death: coffins, holes, candles, blood, and forgetting. For his characters fight to forget and look to others to kindle life in them again. Yet, for Radrigán, forgetting is death itself, it is the digging of a grave, it is the true absurdity and cruelty of life, for it denies the process of history and change, the consciousness of existence, no matter how painful that can be. He says of his work, of words, "[Las] recojo y junto, no para usurpar el oficio a los historiadores, sino porque un pueblo que olvida lo que le hicieron, es un pueblo que no merece ni el cadáver de la libertad" [I pick them up and gather them together, not to usurp the job of the historian, but because a people that has forgotten what has been done to it is a people that is not worthy of even the cadaver of freedom].[13]

Radrigán's is among the most powerful theater of the Pinochet years. For his work is born of the acute awareness of defeat, not merely political defeat, but a grinding moral and human defeat that denies life itself to so many people. And it is made all the more unbearable because even the most profound belief in the possibility of life is not enough to revive it. Life is absurd because it *is* meaningless. His characters are "beside" life; there is little or no sense of the passage of time, for they are suspended in the limbo of a perpetual present. While their lives have no physical boundaries to define them—no home, no walls, no refuge—theirs is a symbolic world of closed doors, enclosed spaces, on the verge of the final hole. It is a world hit by a "crisis," a "war," which the protagonists are never sure has ended. In reality, for them it can never end, for they are the eternal losers in the struggle with "El" and the power he represents. Such is the nature of the absurd and grotesque limbo they inhabit. As outcasts and losers.

5

Exile and Return

The 1970s and Exile: Cultural and Political

The perception of defeat—the role, both imposed and assumed, of the defeated—is a constant of the drama of the mid seventies. This can be no truer than in the plays dealing with exile. Exile, in its most common contemporary Chilean expression, is a form of political repression involving banishment of a citizen from the native land. "Relegación," the banishment of a citizen to remote parts of the country, stripped of all civil rights, has also been a major silencer of dissidence under the Pinochet regime.

Figures for those in exile differ dramatically. It will shed some light on the perceptions of exile that we will find in the plays studied in this chapter if we have an idea of the disparity to be found: "The number of exiles is estimated at anything from 10.000 to 10m. *La Segunda* recently gave the figure, from police sources, of 200.000 people who are expressly banned from entering the country. The problem affects perhaps one family in five, particularly among the upper and middle classes."[1] Reports such as these reveal, on one hand, the difficulty of collecting specific information about the numbers of exiles and, on the other, the awareness of the scale of the problem.

In October 1982 General Pinochet announced that the situation of political exiles would be revised as a "measure for national unity" and that lists of those who could return would be drawn up.[2] The following month, however, the expectations raised by the announcement were dashed when it was made clear that, in the interests of national security, the cases of those exiles considered "políticamente inconvenientes o calificados como activistas o terroristas" would not be considered by the commission that had been set up to deal with the matter.[3] "Normalization," as the process was called, was not to be seen as a sign of weakness on the part of the regime; and the political cleansing campaign that had resulted in the exile of so many Chileans had not been abandoned for the sake of national unity.

While the publication of the lists (three in all) did little to solve the problem and was seen by many as a "cruel propaganda game,"[4] it did open up the question of exile to a public debate, which was reflected in the theater. Before 1984 exile had been referred to in passing in short sketches that were witness to the awareness of exile as a grave contemporary problem, but whose impressionistic nature showed the level of ignorance as to the experiences of those abroad.

A la Mary se le vio el Poppins [We saw Mary Poppins' bottom] by Teatro La Feria (1981), a collage of the events of the decade 1970–80, is a flight of memory that takes in, superficially, the exodus of part of the bourgeoisie fleeing from the Popular Unity government and the exile of the left after the coup. In one sketch, dedicated to a tale of political exile in France, a couple use their pitiful French to order breakfast in a café, a task made all the more difficult by the waiter's contempt for them. Around this simple sketch is painted the picture of some of the most typical problems of exile: isolation from the receiving community, complete lack of contact with the new culture, the growing distance from children who now speak a different language and reject all things Chilean, and the exile's inability to adapt, partly a result of the belief in a quick return to democracy in Chile. The sketch is a caricature of the contemporary Chilean political exile, and in its humorous portrayal of this couple, it reinforces the stereotype built around impressions of the most salient problems of exile.

The same theme is treated to much better effect in *La increíble y triste historia del General Peñaloza y el exiliado Mateluna* [The incredible and sad story of General Peñaloza and the exile Mateluna] (1976), with which Aleph had its first production in France. Like the rest of its work, this is a collective creation relying on its members' personal experiences of exile. Although I do not intend to deal here with groups working in exile, I want to look briefly at this play as an example of the perceptions of the state of exile that are absent from the above sketch written and performed in Chile.

Oscar Castro describes the evolution of the play:

La pièce durait environ deux heures trente et racontait deux histoires qui se melaient: celle d'un dictateur et celle d'un exilé latino-americain à Paris. A la fin, le dictateur tombait, abattu sous la poids de sa con-science, ce qui correspondait davantage a notre espoir qu'à la réalité. Nous sentions que le thème du dictateur manquait d'originalité mais que celui de l'exilé était plus riche, plus nouveau. . . . Dans sa version définitive la pièce dure une heure et le Général n'est qu'un personnage dans une pièce jouée par une troupe de comediens éxilés—le théatre dans le théatre. Par contre nous avons développé dans divers registres les mésaventures de Mateluna et son histoire."[5]

[The play lasted about two hours and thirty minutes and told two interweaving stories: the story of a dictator and the story of a Latin American exile in Paris. In the end the dictator fell, crushed under the weight of his guilt, which had more to do with our hope than with reality. We felt that the theme of the dictator was lacking in originality but that the story of the exile was richer, newer. . . . In its final version the work lasts one hour and the general is only a character in a play performed by a group of exiled artists—a play within a play. On the other hand we developed the story and the misadventures of Mateluna on several different levels.]

So, the general's intended fate is revealed as an invention of the exiles' self deception, of the exile's illusion of returning home once the general has fallen, betrayed by the strength of the guilt on his conscience. But the authors distanced themselves from the myth-making tendencies that had initially tempted them, and from these roots the play grows in another direction. The exile, Mateluna, who, like many and as an act of political faith, refuses to open his suitcase as a demonstration of his belief that the return will come soon and as a symbol of his resistance to integration into the new country, finally, in the last scene, opens his case. Once he has recognized the durability of the regime, the character is in a position to start a new life in the receiving country. And Mateluna finally belies the image of the perpetually disoriented exile who refuses to accept his present situation.

In no other area is the feeling of severance from a past and a culture so great. In the Chilean case, this rupture in artistic circles meant the break from a politically committed art and the destruction of the possibility of creating a "new culture." Yet the whole experience of exile has, as we have seen, been shrouded both in vagueness about the reality of the experiences and awareness of the problem, reflected in what has been called "las dos mitades del silencio."[6] This is the lack of communication between those who stayed in the country and those who left, which is translated into impressionistic and often misleading interpretations of how "the other half" lives. In this scheme of things, while those in exile thrive on what the poet Enrique Lihn called "una leyenda más o menos dorada" of the country they had left behind,[7] relating specifically to the Popular Unity years, and even talk of the "collaboration" with the regime of those who stayed in the country, the latter face official silence about the question of exile. And the myths that are created as a way of explaining a grave social injustice are left to grow unabated.

Enrique Lihn, in the letter quoted, points to an important aspect of the impact of exile on art when he accuses exiles of believing that culture was not split in two, "escindida," but "exiliada," to be brought back with the exiled artists. Bitterly, he revealed the tensions that exist around the question of political exile and the debate about who has lost the possibility for real freedom of expression. The possibility that Chilean culture will only be revived at some vague moment in the future when the country has been reunited, brings us to the problematic question of return, and to "desexilio." "Desexilio" is one of a number of expressions coined to describe different experiences within the state of exile. It has been used by Mario Benedetti as a way of describing the new exile encountered on return to the native country: "Y menos seguro estoy de poder habituarme, si algún día regreso a ese país distinto que ahora se está gestando en la trastienda de lo prohibido. Sí, es probable que el desexilio sea tan duro que el exilio" [And I am less sure that I will be able to adapt, if one day I return to that different country that is being created behind the scenes of the prohibited. Yes, it is possible that disexile will be as difficult as exile].[8] The state of "desexilio" is that of an extension of external exile; it fills the future with disillusion and further feelings of marginality. It is the ultimate tragedy of the exile, exiled on return, from the past, the present, and looking vaguely to an uncertain future of renewed adaptation.

Here, through the plays, *José* (1980) by Egon Wolff; *¿Cuántos años tiene un día?* [How many years are in one day?] (1978) by Ictus; *Primavera con una esquina rota* (1984) also by Ictus, based on the novel by Mario Benedetti; *Regreso sin causa* (1984) by Jaime Miranda; *Cinema-Utoppia* (1985) by Ramón Griffero, I want to examine the perceptions of exile as abandonment, defeat, survival, and adaptation. Through the study of these plays, it will become clear that exile applies to a variety of states imposed by political, social, and economic circumstances, and that in theater there is an awareness of the whole spectrum of the experience of expulsion, be it voluntary or enforced.

José: A Drama of Return and Intrusion

José[9] is a drama of return from abroad. The central character, after living in the United States for seven years, returns to Chile

where his mother, Isabel, and his two sisters, Estela and Trini, live
dependent upon Estela's husband Raúl, a successful businessman.
The arrival of José is awaited with high expectations by the family,
for whom the United States is synonymous with progress and
wealth. But he is a great disappointment to them all, for he is the
antithesis of all that North America means to them. He has fore-
gone all worldly possessions and is concerned only with rekindling
the values of love and caring that, in his loneliness in the United
States, he had seen to be undermined, and that he hopes to find
again in the modest family he had left behind. The initial disappointment is mutual, for José finds himself with a family that is no
longer satisfied with a modest, simple life and has embarked on a
socially upward mobile course. Part of this is the relegation of the
grandfather—of whom they are now apparently ashamed as part of
a rejected past—to an old folks' home, and the forthcoming marriage of Trini to a promising young social climber, with whom she
will emigrate to Sweden. When he finds out that his grandfather is
only out of the home for one day to greet him, José resolves to bring
him back to live in the house against the wishes of the family,
guided in their decisions by Raúl. As José attempts to reestablish
the family he once knew, he only causes problems, and his efforts
to make them face up to the lies they are living cause serious
conflicts and finally rupture, when he is asked to leave. The grandfather also leaves now that he is no longer welcome in the house,
and Isabel thinks it best to join him, but repents after Estela pleads
hysterically for her to stay. And Trini, who momentarily rebels
against her destiny with Cristián, is advised by José to turn back to
him and to love him. Finally, with the grandfather and José gone,
the dramatic community returns to the initial order.

In its dramatic format and development, *José* is the drama of the
intruder who upsets the dramatic status quo, who awakens deep
fears and inhibitions in the dramatic community, and who becomes
the personification of a threat they are all aware of but which they
have pushed to the back of their minds. In this case, the threat is of
renewed poverty and a return to a life they have all left behind and
now reject. The role of the central character is to expose the codes
according to which the family now live. Finally, the key question in
José is one posed in all these plays about exile: who, or what, has
changed, and how?

In the United States, José has undergone a change, a change so
marked that he conforms neither to the image his family has re-
tained of him nor to the fiction they had built around his life abroad.
All three women remark on the change in him in the same terms.

Trini remembers a brother she had idolized: "Recuerdo al hermano que fui a dejar al aeropuerto. Partiste tan confiado, tan feliz. Abrazaste a todo el mundo. Me tomaste la cara y me diste un beso, que me quemó durante días. Estaba tan orgullosa; hablé tanto de tí a mis compañeras de curso que dijeron que parecía enamorada de tí . . ." [I remember the brother I went to say goodbye to at the airport. You left so confident, so happy. You hugged everyone. You took my face in your hands and gave me a kiss that burned me for days. I was so proud; I talked about you so much to my school friends that they said I must be in love with you . . .] (p. 14). Not even the ritual games that they remember from her childhood and that they repeat as a way of recuperating the past can reinvent the José she remembers. Estela has the same impression: "Cuando partió a los Estados Unidos, no parecía tener problemas. Se fue feliz y tranquilo, lleno de posibilidades. ¡Ahora parece un patán!" [When he left for the United States, he didn't seem to have problems. He left happy and calm, full of possibilities. Now he looks like a layabout!] (p. 20). But it is Isabel who sees José's transformation as a sign of suffering: "Sin embargo, tienes una tristeza en los ojos. ¿Por qué es eso? Pareces un Lázaro" [Yet, there is a sadness in your eyes. Why is that? You look like as if you've risen from the dead] (p. 10).

The family had imagined José progressing materially as a result of the possibilities open to him once incorporated into the American dream. But, having lived in the United States, José has rejected all that the "dream" is supposed to represent; for him it signifies, above all, loneliness, and the loss of basic humanitarian values. In his own interpretation, he is a type of Lazarus, he sees his present state as a resurrection after the experiences and deceptions he had lived through in Chicago, a city he calls "un cementerio de cemento," a city of the living dead (p. 25). His very name is the token of his "death" in such a society: " 'Joe' es nada, ¿me entiendes? ¡'Joe' no existe! ¡'Joe' es cosa!" (p. 24). Joe is anyone who has not succeeded according to the rules of the capitalist game, who is left on the margins of society and is despised by even the most humble of those who are in the process of surviving.

The female characters share the destiny of a "Joe," of a nobody. They conform for fear of being banished and abandoned; they act in as insignificant a way as possible, hoping that their behavior will contribute to the success of Raúl's regime and save them from becoming impoverished nobodies. Estela is in the worst position. Hers is a world bound by the need to follow a certain set of rules: she "belongs" to Raúl. The primary emotion she feels for him is fear, a fear she can persuade herself does not exist if she submits meekly to his domination and constant humiliation of her. She can only recuperate the illusion of normality with the departure of her brother, for he does not allow her to hide her fear, he robs her of any illusion of tranquility, and adds guilt to her destructive emotions. More importantly, however, even though she is on the side of her husband, in his eyes she is contaminated by association with José and by the shame of belonging to the same stock. She has already proved herself to be a failure to Raúl through her inability to have children. If she proves herself, through contact with José, to be, over and above that, a misfit and a loser, she will suffer the fate of the loser: expulsion.

Trini, who has been brought up in this atmosphere, conforms most closely to what is expected of her in the world of Raúl, and genuinely aspires to the kind of life Cristián can provide. She is most shocked by José's alternative code of values to which she had never before been exposed. When she asks, "¿Por qué hace un tiempo siento como que no estoy viviendo mi vida?" (p. 41), she realizes that she has never been asked to voice her own opinions, that her thoughts are never taken into account. Like the other female characters, Trini will be protected from the realities of the world outside her family; she will never have to make decisions, will never be seriously asked her opinion, and her only role will be as a suitable and supportive wife for the correct husband. A rejection of all this would mean a certain "exile" for her, as the negation of the type of woman she is training to be, one who is wholly dependent, always protected from facing reality or making decisions.

The Chileans who now run the family are shown to have accepted unreservedly the materialistic values that accompany their advance into the modern capitalist world. José, at first, sees it as his duty to open Trini's eyes to the trap that she is falling into by marrying Cristián, the epitome of the new Chilean, on his way north and thereby up in the world, complying with the well-established rules, never doubting anything he is taught, never questioning his legitimate right to all his privileges, the perfect package, only awaiting the correct wife in order to compete in the world. José tries to make Trini aware of the pitfalls in her fiancé's "plan for the future":

Cristián tiene un solo problema: ¡Que nació en Chile! ¡Que aquí, fastidiosamente, aún se le da cierta importancia a las cosas inútiles; como querer a un amigo, por ejemplo, y eso le hace parecer duro, a veces, e inhumano, y teme que se le note! ¡Pero, para suerte de él, las cosas van cambiando! ¡El chileno de hoy se está volviendo práctico también, y realista! ¡Abrió una ventana a los Estados Unidos, y está recibiendo de allá todas sus fetideces, y le están oliendo a perfume! ¡Hoy el chileno está aprendiendo a parecerse al Americano, y eso le alegra el corazón! (pp. 34–35)

[Cristián has only one problem: he was born in Chile! It's annoying, but here people still give a certain importance to useless things; like loving a friend, for example, and that makes him seem hard, sometimes, and inhuman, and he's afraid that people notice that! But, luckily for him, things are changing! Today's Chilean is becoming practical too, and realistic. He opened a window to the United States, and is receiving all its filth, and it smells like perfume. Today the Chilean is learning to be like the North American, and that makes him very happy!]

This declaration highlights what is generally perceived to be an acute social problem in rapidly modernizing Chile, that is the loss of the values of caring and community to a dog-eat-dog environment, based in admiration for North American principles. José does not conform, refusing to accept a society based on competition and individual betterment, and preferring expulsion from the regime within the house to living in the family as the undeclared enemy whose lifestyle is held in contempt. This destines him to become a Chilean Joe.

Raúl, like Cristián, is among the winners and holds sacred the principles of ruthless economic gain. When challenged by José to defend his role, he justifies it by referring to his right to personal gain in a hard business world. José's reply highlights the reversal in expected roles that has taken place: "Yo ya había oído discursos parecidos, pero en inglés" (p. 42). This is one of a set of melodramatic oppositions, if the most dubious: the setting up of English as the language of the inhumane and Spanish as that of the humane values lies well within a recognizable Manichaeistic code of interpretation of the capitalist world.

By bringing his grandfather home, José is trying to destroy the model that has been imposed, that the grandfather had attempted to follow, and that had been his moral and economic ruin. But in fact he is submitting him to the ownership of Raúl, an ownership that José hopes to stop. The grandfather is a fellow in exile to José, and his reintegration into the family unit is equally impossible. With José he forms one side of the melodramatic oppositions that compose the drama. Before his grandson's arrival, he tells the rest of the family that there have been too many changes, that they have gone "muy jai," that they have divided the family into rich and poor, the presentable and the misfits. The grandfather's statement, "Ese niño se va a helar de frío en esta casa" [this boy is going to die of cold in this house] (p. 4), completes the melodramatic oppositions, the warmth of the past having been lost to the cold prosperity of the present.

If José, as exile returned, is the traditional intruder, he is also set up as a symbol of purity. In the words of Pedro Bravo Elizondo, *José* deals with "una lucha contra la enajenación del hombre, contra su embrutecimiento."[10] Seeing his next of kin alienated from their former values and having found peace with himself in Christianity and a world of socially marginalized people, José seeks to put his family in touch once more with the loving and caring attitudes he believes had once been theirs. But they have slipped into what for José is a form of barbarism, that of the individual fight to acquire more and more economic security and material wealth. The dichotomy of "civilización y barbarie" still exists, but which is which? The answer is ever more difficult. Does civilization mean modernization? Does it emerge in the grandfather's state after he has sold his land? If Egon Wolff presents José as a latter day apostle, preaching a forgotten creed, and points to the fact that the apostles gave up home, family, and belongings for a belief, then equally there are those who will see him as Raúl does, "un hippie de mierda," incapable of assuming real social responsibilities and only capable of pontificating from the sidelines about matters he does not understand.

Putting this into the context of modern Chile, Wolff's *José* does not deviate from the thesis often put forward in contemporary theater about the degradation of man in economic circumstances that promote a constant brutal fight for survival in which the weakest always lose. It is worth pointing out in passing that José's exile began in 1973 and that one of his places of exile was Chicago, the home of the theory of monetarism, the model on which Chile's economic "miracle" was built. In these terms, Chicago is the ultimate symbol of theory at the expense of humane values, and it is significant that José found his belief in God in this city. Taking these parallels even further, Raúl's language is reminiscent of that which we have seen in other plays. When he describes José, it is as a disturbance, a public nuisance who avoids responsibility in life and who does not allow others to live or work "tranquilos." He sees his brother-in-law in terms of a communist threat, giving away the goods and property of others, and as a contaminating influence: ". . . yo quiero una casa limpia. Nada de chascones amargados . . ." (p. 31). In the final scene, Raúl warns the remaining women of the consequences of adopting similar attitudes: "Cuando vuelva al almuerzo, quiero ver mi casa . . . despejada . . . y a todo el mundo, sonriendo" (p. 42). He forfeits everything to the all important illusion of cleanliness, tranquility, and harmony. The ethos of expulsion is clear.

Ultimately, *José* is a drama of intrusion and incohesion. If the respective worlds inhabited by the returned exile and by those he had left behind do not blend, then it is because the latter have been integrated into the new system while the former has lived with an image of a past before drastic economic upheaval. Note that it is to his grandfather, to a sector of a generation brought up on the values of old, that he turns, to a generation that has not been fully incorporated into the new society and that has the strength to retain an individual identity. Meanwhile, the weakest characters, the women, remain in a domain where they will be safe and not be subjected to the fight for survival outside the home, where they would surely lose as the weakest do. This is the role of José: as intruder to reveal the fears and insecurities of the rest of the dramatic community; and as exile in his own country to expose the "desencuentro" of two worlds. It is this double image of "desencuentro" and inner exile that we will find in *¿Cuántos años tiene un día?*

¿Cuántos años tiene un día: Cultural Inner Exile

¿Cuántos años tiene un día?[11] is set in two acts in a television studio. In the first act, the immediate aim of the protagonists, a team of journalists, is to record an anniversary broadcast of the current affairs program on which they work. For this occasion they are joined by a guest journalist who has worked in Europe for twenty years. The recording is disturbed by the absence of one of the group and by constant interruptions from the management. Despite the feeble insistence of the leader of the team, Ignacio, that this type of harassment does not normally happen, it soon becomes clear that it is, in fact, a daily occurrence. As a response to intimidation by the management and to the uncertain fate of the absent journalist, an extremely insulting and potentially explosive letter of protest is drafted. The first act closes with the recital of Pablo Neruda's "Oda al aire," as Ignacio takes charge of the letter and a fragile reconciliation between the journalists—divided as regards the response to intimidation—is contrived.

The second act follows the same pattern. The team sets about recording the program, but conflict continues. It is revealed that

Ignacio had not presented the letter to the management who, he knows, would use it as the excuse to sack the whole team and rid the channel of intrusive, potentially subversive forces. When the conflict reaches a climax, Ignacio decides to resign, but the arrival of the absent journalist and Cecilia's reading of a letter in which Ignacio declares his dedication to fighting to provide an intellectual and cultural alternative in modern Chile revitalizes the strength of the team.

The main prop of the play is the friendship between Ignacio and Cecilia, which goes back as far as the late fifties. This introduces the perpetual cultural problems faced in a country such as Chile, it suggests how these have developed over the intervening twenty years, and it reveals the archetypal dilemma: whether to stay in the country or to go abroad, normally to Europe. Even at a time when the cultural outlook for Chile had seemed positive, as represented in the flashback to 1961 and the First Congress of Latin American Writers, Cecilia had felt stifled by the cultural atmosphere, by the never-accomplished projects and by the lack of contact with other cultures. Her response had been that of many others, to leave in search of fulfillment abroad, in Europe, where she saw a promise of greater achievement and better possibilities for her own development. Then Ignacio had tempted her with visions of what Chile would be in ten years time, had tried to make her believe that her place was in her own country. But now the environment is radically different, the time of cultural expansion is over, and television has become a thinly disguised medium for government propaganda, where the journalists are merely struggling to survive, with little hope of professional satisfaction.

Ignacio, who best expresses the belief in the cultural strength of television, is also the best expression of how the medium has evolved. He is a man with a deep involvement in one of the most significant social and cultural innovations in Chile in the second half of the twentieth century, the introduction of television, which had taken place at a time of cultural expansion, of optimism in the possibilities of the newly introduced medium, which, in university hands, was to mean "a guarantee for culture" (p. 184). In the new circumstances he seeks to hold on to this concept of television. While the more radical members of his team will accuse him of the treasonous act of "adapting" to the new repressive circumstances, Ignacio believes that it is more profitable for the cultural health of his country to provide some means of reflection and expression than to opt out completely. He describes the task he now has as that of filling a basic gap, and not, as he had done before, as a complement to other media of expression and information: "Hoy sólo puedes intentar usar tus facultades para expresar lo que los otros no pueden expresar, para incitar el pensamiento; cuando unos pretenden eliminarlo no es una tarea fácil . . ." (p. 192).

The pressures on the journalists to respond to the new role of television are huge and are represented here by a group of vigilantes called "El Comité de Saneamiento Interno," whose purpose should be no mystery by now: they provoke and denounce, accusing their victims, for example, of bad personal hygiene, of any behaviour that deviates from their rigid norms, that is politically "unhygienic," and that they believe to belong to "tiempos afortunadamente sobrepasados para siempre" (p. 157). By this stage, these need no further clarification.

Cecila is amused but bewildered by the ridiculous nature of the tactics, which are no longer amusing to the members of the team. This is a fundamental point of the play. Cecilia's first "exile" had been voluntary, an intellectual option to develop her talents in a more promising environment. To a large extent she will not have considered herself an exile, for her movement to and from the country was not restricted, since her exile was not politically enforced. Yet, on return to authoritarian Chile, she begins to feel the sentiments of the real exile. She finds it difficult to break the codes that govern the working lives of the journalists; she finds ridiculous the self-nominated "Comité de Saneamiento Interno"; she does not fully appreciate the level of harassment experienced by the team; and their demoralization is alien to her. She will stay in Chile for four days; she will understand little and see little other than superficial changes, results of the modernization of the city, the outward facade of progress. Hers will be the outsider's view of her own country, her experience that of "desexilio," exile encountered on return.

The use of the space on stage is vital for the development of the argument. The higher level is the domain of the management, where the director of the channel governs its daily business and guards the interests of politically correct reporting, of decency and morality. The conflict that motivates the action is directed toward this area, where the journalists are called to be reprimanded. This is the level that represents the reality of the country, rigid, repressive, impersonal, governed by uninspired projects for the nation's future. The lower level, the television studio, is where the fight against the silencing of dissident cultural expression takes place. Here the spectator is provided with a view of the reality of the difficulties faced reporting everyday events. Each time the journalists try to resume recording, an interruption by the management or by the impassioned outburst of a journalist adds to the impression that the initial stages are part of a frustrating ritual of beginnings with no apparent possibility for continuation.

In the working space, too, flashbacks underline the contrasts between past and present. In the first act, a flashback to the late fifties—when Ignacio and Cecilia covered the end of dictatorship in Argentina and debated the possibilities of the Chilean people understanding the nature of a country dominated by authoritarian regimes—provides a stark contrast to the present atmosphere. If we compare Martín, the youngest member of the team, to the younger Ignacio and Cecilia; we will see that the present environment is not conducive to grand projects and hope in the future. Whereas Ignacio at twenty-five was full of optimism, Martín, at the same age, is bitter and disillusioned, obsessed with the idea of leaving Chile, of going to Europe where cultural roots are more "solid," making everything possible. He echoes Cecilia's need to go abroad, but his is not born of a strong conviction in the richer possibility of self-development, but of despair and constant intimidation in the only working environment he has known. Like the other members of the team, he works in the constant awareness that all his actions are watched, with the perpetual intuition that he is doing something wrong. Martín finds the world he lives in small and mean. The other journalists are remnants of a past time. They had good careers in the late sixties and early seventies, had subsequently been blacklisted, lost their jobs, and one—demoralized by the battering his career had taken and by the attacks on his self-esteem after a number of years of unemployment—is an alcoholic. They personify the diminishing relevance of their intellectual experience; their careers are pared to nothing and their professional lives dominated by the day-to-day pettiness of the channel.

During the recording Ignacio repeats Cecilia's words of twenty years before, "Estoy cansado. . . . Cansado hasta la locura," but the dilemma has moved from the purely personal sphere to a political one, for the decision to stay in the country is now a decision to fight against a dominant ideology which is repressive of freedom of expression and which encourages art as a good for consumption and not for reflection, as a means of creating absolute uniformity of opinion. Ignacio tells Cecilia, ". . . estoy aterrado frente a la posibilidad de que conviertan a todos en esa tropa de mediocres que han perdido hasta la facultad de soñar" [I'm terrified of the possibility of them making us so mediocre that we lose even the faculty of dreaming] (p. 188). Martín echoes this, fearful of imperceptibly becoming one of the mediocre people.

The working space is also the space where a vision of another Chile, of an alternative reality is created. This is represented on one level through the flashbacks that show the existence of the intellectual potential within the country. On another level it is created through the demonstration of the intrinsic strength of the team and their deep commitment to taking advantage of the drastically reduced space for comment. The central question is still whether to go or to stay, to fight armed with the ideological baggage of previous years or to adapt, synonymous for some with a betrayal of ideals, but which, finally, means working within a strict ideological code while defying that very code.

It is Ignacio who, in a letter to Cecilia, declares that, having weighed all the pros and cons, he still thinks that staying in the country is the correct decision, even if that means inner exile:

> Sé donde estoy. . . . Sé lo que me falta. . . . Sé lo que tengo. . . . Sé lo que me han quitado. . . . Sé lo que tengo. También sé que puedo parecerte un iluso, o peor, un agachador de moño. . . . Más de alguno ya me lo ha dicho. Pero una cosa es agachar el moño y otra, muy distinta, rendirse. Y yo no quiero rendirme ante lo que siento como un gran desafío: contribuir a que mi gente mantenga viva la facultad de pensar . . . que nadie piense por nosotros. Es la forma que yo entiendo mi contribución a defender la cultura, que no es otra cosa que la facultad que tiene un pueblo para reflexionar críticamente en torno a su propia realidad. Por muy poco que se pueda hacer, hay que hacerlo y nadie lo puede hacer por tí. (p. 192)

> [I know where I am. . . . I know what I need. . . . I know what I have. . . . I know what they've taken away from me. I know what I have. I also know that I may well look like a dreamer to you, or worse, a conformer. . . . More than one person has said that to me. But it is one thing to bow your head and conform and another completely to give up. I do not want to give up in the face of what I feel to be a great challenge: helping my people to keep the faculty of thought . . . so that nobody thinks for us. That's how I understand my contribution to the defence of culture, which is nothing other than the faculty of a people to reflect critically on their own reality. No matter how little you can actually do, you have to do it, and nobody can do it for you.]

This becomes a direct communication with the real theater audience. This speech enters into the public debate about how best to describe and reveal the national reality and also enters into the

ongoing debate of the cultural possibilities of those who stay and
work in the country. With *Primavera con una esquina rota* (1984),
Ictus turned to the theme of political exile, dealt with in terms of an
overall experience of living in dictatorship.

Primavera con una esquina rota: The Arms of Dictatorship

Primavera con una esquina rota [12] refers to Uruguay, which also
suffered a military coup in 1973, followed by similar patterns of
political repression and exile. This is the story of one family, a
family from a middle-class, left-wing intellectual background. Santiago, who was involved in an underground terrorist movement, was
arrested and imprisoned after the coup, as was his friend, Rolando,
who was later released. The rest of Santiago's family—his wife
Graciela and their daughter Beatriz—are in exile with his father,
Don Rafael, in Mexico, where Rolando also goes upon his release.
At the beginning of the play, after four years, five months, and
fourteen days, painfully counted by Santiago, the situation has not
changed except for a glimmer of hope for Santiago's release.

The first act deals with the coup and the positions of the characters in exile, and it reveals Graciela's growing despair and guilt as
she admits that time and the length of separation have distanced her
from her husband who, on the other hand, shows in his letters how
much he longs to be with her and Beatriz again. The second act
concentrates on Graciela's dilemma, her love for Rolando and the
news of Santiago's imminent release. It is with the complex emotions of guilt and betrayal, of continuing feelings of loyalty to the
past and of the awareness of insecurity in the future that the play
finishes, in the airport on Santiago's return.

Santiago's is the most problematic role to translate to the stage,
for in Benedetti's novel, he speaks through letters to Graciela and
his father. This problem was solved by taking him out of his cell in
dramatizations of his letters in which he remembers the time before
the coup and relives past experiences in the time "antes de que el
futuro se pusiera decididamente malsano" (p. 37). As a dramatic
device this heightens the awareness of enclosure when he returns to
his cell. Furthermore, it is a dramatization of the prison censorship
by which his permission to write and receive letters may be taken
away at any time.

The question at the heart of *Primavera con una esquina rota* is
normality, and in these circumstances, especially, "normality" cannot be easily defined. Santiago has to fight to remain sane or normal

despite the disintegration of his world, and he has fought against mental collapse primarily by looking to the future. He knows that the normal course of his life has been interrupted, but hopes that, in exile, a normal life together may be renewed. While his life revolves around this one hope, those outside begin to aspire to other possibilities from the future, at the same time trying to make sense out of the experience of exile. Exile becomes a chaos that plagues each life.

Dictatorship with "sus dos brazos más expresivos, la Cárcel y el Exilio" [Its two most expressive arms, prison and exile][13] plays havoc with people's lives and undermines the values they had accepted before. Part of Graciela's problem is guilt at the fact that she feels she bears exile too easily, that her life is good and that she has a good future, if only she were let loose from the confines of her past. With her new relationship, she enters into what is called "un ping-pong de la conciencia," the constant conflict between loyalty and abandonment, normality and its counterparts. The ideas of exile and imprisonment become increasingly contradictory, for, if Santiago is imprisoned in an inner exile, then Graciela, for her part, feels that she is denied absolute freedom: "Y eso hace que me sienta como cercada. El está preso allá, pero yo también estoy aprisionada en una situación" (p. 130). Freedom, exile, and imprisonment are key words in this play, yet they are words whose meaning can never be taken for granted, as Don Rafael explains: ". . . también hubo lindas palabras que ellos torturaron o ajusticiaron o incluyeron en las nóminas de desaparecidos" [. . . there were also pretty words that they tortured and sentenced to death or that they included in the lists of the disappeared] (p. 104).

As in much literature that deals with themes of dictatorship, language is a theme in itself and, in *Primavera con una esquina rota,* the exploration of the meaning of these key words is a vital way of coming to terms with the circumstances. In this respect, the pivot of the work is the daughter, Beatriz. Through her child's drawings and essays on life, her family, her status in her new country, and her deliberations on the immensity of words and ideas, the audience is given a very special image of the meaning of exile. Beatriz is a well-developed character and a clever device. As a device she is a way of expressing opinions about the state of exile with humor and, albeit well-orchestrated, innocence. As a child she need bear no responsibility for her thoughts which, in turn, are a projection of adult bewilderment in the face of changing circumstances.[14]

It is Beatriz who opens our eyes to many of the sad ironies of the fate of the adults in her life. "Libertad es una palabra enorme," she tells her school class of dolls. In her experience it is related to the time she spends out of school, it is an image of countries where people can do as they please, but where they must justify any misdemeanors. But it is more than that: "Libertad quiere decir muchas cosas. Por ejemplo, si una no está presa, se dice que está en libertad. Pero mi papá está preso y sin embargo está en Libertad, porque así se llama la cárcel donde está hace ya muchos años. A eso el tío Rolando lo llama qué sarcasmo" [Freedom means lots of things. For example, if a person is not a prisoner, you say that that person is in freedom. But my father is a prisoner and he's still in Freedom, because that's the name of the prison where he's been kept for a long time now. My uncle Roland calls that really sarcastic] (p. 119). Her understanding of the reasons for her father's imprisonment are confused and reflect the explanations given by the adults, who tell her that he is in prison for his ideas. She is proud of this and proud of her own ideas, but has learned the lesson that it is better to keep them to herself if she is to remain in liberty. Her mother is a personification of the immensity Beatriz reveals in words, free but still trapped.

The play shows Beatriz's first encounters with certain words, when her understanding of them is purer, more innocent, and in some ways more concrete because her world of words is built around visual images, images that she expresses in her drawings. "Amnistía es una palabra difícil," she informs her class: "Amnistía es cuando le perdonan a una la penitencia" (p. 191). In order to understand this, she relates it to her world, to the punishments and forgiveness of her mother, to quarrels with her friends and to a bullfight she sees on television. When she tries to relate it to her father's possibilities of freedom, she finds in the dictionary that amnesty is the pardon of political prisoners, more importantly, "el olvido de los delitos políticos," a definition that she finds ominous, for perhaps the general in charge has a good memory and remembers everything. Yet, her interpretation of these words, which she feels to be huge, are no more than an opening to the true and cruel range of meaning they hold.

The representation of the plebiscite in November 1980, in which the Uruguayan people voted against the regime, becomes in the play in Chile an extremely important scene, given that in the same year the Chileans voted in favor of the regime's new constitution.[15] Here again the value of one word is demonstrated, this time by Don Rafael: ". . . la dictadura decidió abrir no una puerta sino una rendija, y una rendija tan pequeña que sólo pudiera entrar en ella una sola sílaba, y entonces la gente vio aquella hendedura y,sin pensarlo dos veces, colocó allí la sílaba NO" [. . . the dictatorship decided to open a door, but just a little, and so little that only one syllable could enter, and the people saw the crack and, without a second thought, placed there the syllable NO] (p. 190). Like Beatriz's pictorial versions of words, this one syllable becomes something concrete. Words are enormous and the shades of meaning, which can be easily perverted, are not to be found in the conviction behind a seemingly insignificant syllable.

The incident is doubly important since, in the play, the news of the No vote is received in prison. The prisoners bang their plates and shout the slogan of the opposition, "y va a caer." Like Don Rafael, they feel that a door has been left ajar, but that it may be opened completely is still a mad illusion. The very word door is almost an obsession with the prisoners, for it evokes the possibilities of enclosure and freedom, it evokes the attempts to destroy their spirit, which they defy with letters, fantasies, and projects for when it will finally open, when they will finally begin to recuperate real life.

The generation gap between grandfather and granddaughter is bridged by their special relation with words. One of these is the word *country* itself, which holds within it implications about the right to live freely in the native country and the difficulties of adapting to the host country. The incorporation into the new country means, for Don Rafael, making his exile his own by defying the defeat that the regime wished to impose on him; it means taking over the streets, first and foremost by giving up the walking stick he began to use when he arrived; it means appreciating local ways of speech. Is he a stranger in the country? Not even he can answer that. His most vital way of reaching the people of the host country is through a woman called Lydia, and through her, with "un país llamado Lydia," the country having become his only when he felt part of something created there, and not merely an onlooker in an alien state, created and governed by people with whom he has had no previous contact.

For Beatriz, the notion of country poses obvious problems and confusion. As a child she represents the generation that will grow up in exile and that will have only tenuous links with and notions of her parents' home. When she talks of "este país," it is of a country that she inhabits but that is not hers: "Este país no es el mío pero me gusta bastante. No sé si me gusta más o menos que mi país. Vine muy chiquita y no me acuerdo de como era" [This is not my country, but I like it quite a lot. I don't know if I like it more or less than my own country. I came here when I was very little and I don't remember what it was like there] (p. 21). She asks adults to clarify the problem for her but they can only confuse the matter, for there is no real answer and if there is one, then Beatriz has already guessed it: she has two countries, one that she knows little of, her mother country, and one that she knows very well but of which she is not a natural citizen. Her knowledge of her mother country is mixed in her mind with her father, with dreams of going to the zoo with him and seeing the animals behind bars, and her father telling her, "así también viví yo" (p. 92). Her country is synonymous with imprisonment.

Beatriz's greatest contribution to the science of language is her discovery of the word "elotoño." Like many of the words she explores, it is a mystery to her. Yet, while other words can be explained, at least partly, through her own life experience and reading the meaning in dictionaries, not so "elotoño." It is a season, she knows, but she cannot relate to the word as a season, for she has never experienced it in the same way as she has spring, summer, and winter; therefore, she cannot create a visual picture of it: "Graciela, es decir mi mami, porfía y porfía que hay una cuarta estación llamada elotōno. Yo le digo que puede ser pero nunca la he visto. . . . Elotoño es la más misteriosa de las estaciones porque no hace ni frío ni calor y entonces uno no sabe qué ropa ponerse. Debe ser por eso que yo nunca sé cuando estoy en otoño" [Graciela, that is my mummy insists and insists that there is a fourth season called theautumn. I tell her that that may be so but that I've never seen it. . . . Theautumn is the most mysterious of the seasons because it isn't hot or cold and so nobody knows what to wear. That must be why I never know when it's theautumn] (p. 30).

Autumn is, for Beatriz, a time that does not exist, that is far beyond the reach of her experience and even of her imagination. This is where the real meaning of autumn is to be found, for she goes on to tell us: "Donde está mi papá llegó justo ahora elotoño y él me escribió que está muy contento porque las hojas secas pasan entre los barrotes y él se imagina que son cartitas mías" [Where my father is now theautumn has just arrived and he wrote to me to say that he's very happy because the dry leaves fall through the bars in his window and he imagines that they are little letters from me] (pp. 30–31). Autumn, then, is a season that she does not recognize, it is a season characterized by its lack of identifying factors, by its nothingness.

The seasons are symbols of specific states. Spring, for Graciela, according to Beatriz, is the time of year she hates because it was then that Santiago was taken prisoner. But spring for Santiago, in the words of Don Rafael, is the time when he finds "su termómetro, su patrón, su norma." Despite the changing seasons perceived from behind bars, he will only regain this measure of spring in his life when he is free: "Aunque no lo mencione sino rarísimas veces, sé que para él los aconteceres del mundo en general y de su mundo en particular se dividen en primaverales, poco primaverales y nada primaverales" [Although he may not mention it very often, I know that for him the events of the world in general and of his world in particular are divided into spring-like, quite spring-like and un-spring-like] (p. 209). Autumn, then, is a state that Beatriz's father recognizes from behind his bars, one that he is living, and that for him is totally abnormal. Upon his release, Santiago thinks of his return to normality as the coming of spring after five years of winter. He imagines that "la primavera es como un espejo," a mirror of his life, but just as the normal course of his life has been broken, so has the mirror: ". . . todo recomenzará normalmente naturalmente aunque el espejo tenga una esquina rota eso sí la tendrá seguro la tendrá" [. . . everything will begin again normally naturally even if the mirror has a broken corner for sure it will have a broken corner] (p. 217). Spring was the mirror of his life, it is now a shattered mirror, a shattered spring, a shattered life. Broken by the two arms of dictatorship, exile, and imprisonment.

Regreso sin causa: The Black, the White, and the Gray

Regreso sin causa by Jaime Miranda,[16] takes place in two parts, the first in Sweden, the second in Chile. In the first act the author unveils the life of a couple, Mario and Chela, who are in exile in Sweden with his bedridden father, Don Octavio, and their two children, Rody and Carla. With fastidious and often very funny attention to detail, this act shows a life in exile that revolves largely around political and solidarity activities. In the first scene the couple are preparing for a farewell dinner for an exile who has appeared on one of the regime's lists of those who can return. In the second Mario is on his way to a congress of exiles and Swedish human rights and government representatives that is meeting in protest of the Chilean regime's decision to suspend the lists and set up a commission in their place. This scene introduces his dilemma of conscience about whether to attend the congress, when he finds out that he has been given permission to return and realizes that attendance at the congress could jeopardize that. In the third scene, as they are packing, they find out that Don Octavio has been suspended from the list. The reason given is his participation in the congress, but since he had not been present, it is evident that a mistake had been made and that, in fact, it is Mario who should have been suspended. Mario and Chela then have to decide whether to return, leaving Don Octavio behind in a nursing home or in the care of Mario's brother. For Chela there is no choice, for now that the possibility exists, she must go back to Chile, and the final decision is insinuated when the act closes with a phone call from the brother.

Back in Santiago in the second act, the material quality of the couple's life has fallen drastically in comparison to the standard of living they had enjoyed in Sweden. They rent a flat, it is winter, there is no work, there are numerous blackouts, and the only communication they have with other people, it seems, is when they are warned of the times of the pot-banging protests. On the day that Don Octavio's permission to return is refused again, they hear of his death in Sweden. In the second scene, the emotional climax of the play, the couple are invited to talk of their experiences in exile at a "Velada por el Gran Reencuentro" when, instead of talking of the joy of being back in Chile compared to the agony of living outside, Mario talks of the disillusion of return to a country where they feel like strangers, and of the belated recognition of the worth of their host country in exile. He talks of the tragic irony of Don Octavio's fate, for he had received permission to return after his remains had been brought back to be buried. Yet, there is some hope, for their son has written to say he is coming to Chile, and Mario has found a job.

Even within the same family, exiled for the sake of one of its members, experiences of exile differ greatly. The difference between Mario's experience of exile and Chela's is that of the gulf between a traditional male and female experience of the immediate environment, whereby the male experience is primarily outside the home and that of the female confined to the home and family. Mario becomes increasingly loud and domineering; Chela quiet, silent, and submissive. She has few means to help her incorporation into a wider community, Mario has work, his bread-winning role and his political militancy. Through his political activities, Mario is able to prove himself, to show that he belongs to the exiled community and that he truly hopes for both the return of the exiles and the return to democracy. When the permission to return is given, Chela's first reaction is to dissuade Mario from attending the congress, recalling the circumstances of his brother, who lost his permission to return after having declared in public the right of all Chilean citizens to live freely in their country. Their conflict is defined, ultimately, in the play, in terms of the tension between a female concept of what is best for the family, that is return at any cost, and a male concept of personal self-respect, that is return in the right circumstances. Yet, the whole situation is wrought with conflict. In the last scene of the first act, when Don Octavio's permission is suspended, Mario concedes that his decision to attend the congress had been a serious mistake, but explains it in the following terms:

> MARIO: Reconozco, Chelita . . . soy un idiota. ¡Pero, por favor, entienda . . . [*le ruega*] . . . entiéndame! [*se siente en la cama*] . . . Hay cosas . . . hay momentos. . . . Un momento donde se define todo en una sola pregunta: ¡tengo las bolas bien puestas o no las tengo! . . . Y la pregunta se siente aquí, en la nuca . . . entra como una aguja y se va clavando . . . clavando . . . ¡Ese momento, Chelita, donde no se puede dar un paso atrás! Más todavía cuando es uno . . . uno, el que tiene la razón . . . el derecho! [*pausita*] ¿Es así o no es así? (p. 37)

> [MARIO: I know, Chelita . . . I'm an idiot. But, please, try to understand . . . [*Pleading*] . . . hear me out! [*Sitting down on the bed*]. . . . There are things . . . there are moments. . . . Times when there's only one question: have I got balls or not!. . . . And you feel the question here, in the back of your neck . . . it's like a needle digging right in. . . . That's the moment when you can't give in, Chelita! Especially when you're right, when you have the right to do it! [*Pause*] Can't you see that?]

Chela will never be able to comprehend or share his view of the dilemma.

Finally, Mario's actions must be understood in the context of his loss of identity, of his feeling of anonymity in a country where he does a menial job far below his intellectual capabilities, in which he misses the human contact he had formerly experienced. In Sweden he has become, he says, "vulgar y gritón." He strives to retain his sense of identity through links with the remnants of his past, which are also a hope for the future.

Chela's life in Sweden is built into the structure of the play. While we see Mario come and go, while he has contact with the community and has a place in the group of exiles, Chela never leaves the main set. She says she lives frozen, "numb," isolated from her friends and family, with no social support and no new social contacts that would provide warmth or affection in her life. Physically, her vision of the world is partial, through a window: her world is reduced to visions of things to which she has little or no access. Because her domain is the home, she has a greater awareness of the differences that separate their individual experiences of Sweden:

> CHELA: Nada me quita de la cabeza que para tí es distinto. ¡Tiene que ser distinto! [*pausita*] Mario, ven acá. Díme qué se puede ver a través de esta ventana. (*pausita*) ¡Blanco! ¡Todo blanco! ¿Y a lo lejos? . . . ¡Sombras! ¡Yo no quiero pasar mi vida en blanco! ¡Tampoco a oscuras como un ciego! ¡Ni me conformo en blanco y negro porque voy a terminar viendo un tablero de ajedrez! (p. 41)

> [CHELA: I can't get it out of my head that it's different for you. It has to be different! [*Pause*] Mario, come here. Tell me what you see through this window. [*Pause*] White! Everything is white! And in the distance? . . . Shadows! I don't want to spend my life in white! And I don't want to spend it in darkness as if I were blind! I'm not ready to live in black and white, if I do, all I'll see in the end is a chess board.]

The way Chela's role is defined reduces her possibilities of integration into the new society. Her ability to express herself is limited, not because of ignorance of Swedish, but because she has little opportunity to speak. More than once she says that she might as well cut off her tongue. When Mario is making translations of "testimonial voices" of exiled Chileans, he omits to ask Chela to record her experience, because these are "entrevistas serias" to which her meager contribution would add nothing. Her life, as far as Mario can see, is inactive and passive, and she is regarded as being "egoísta" when she actually voices her own opinions and desires. She conforms to the stereotype of the exiled "mujer-madre": ". . . resignada a ver crecer sus hijos en un mundo extraño y extranjero que ella no puede penetrar ni siquiera a nivel de la palabra. . . . Siempre al servicio de su familia. . . . Es decir, un ser pasivo, objeto de las acciones de los otros, incapaz de aprehender la realidad que la rodea, victima propiciatoria por excelencia" [. . . resigned to seeing her children brought up in a strange and foreign country that she cannot enter even verbally. . . . Always at the beck and call of her family. . . . That is to say, a passive being, an object of the actions of others, incapable of understanding the reality that surrounds her, the well-disposed victim *par excellence*].[17]

The family is developing in an environment that has nothing to do with that in Chile, and in Mario's eyes she has failed with *her* children, has failed to instil in them the proper values, to inspire them with love for their homeland and to keep the family united. It is she, however, who faces up to the fact that they have lost their children to a new way of life. Their son has become a dope-smoking dropout, fully preoccupied with evading reality. And their daughter has demonstrated her extreme distaste for the exiled community. The children are victims of the exile imposed on their parents, but they are also proof of the severance from the Chilean past, a past with which Mario had tried to inspire them. For, instead of describing reality, he had created an idealized image of the country, of "un país donde todo era bello, perfecto y bueno y en el cual la historia de Chile se reduce al período de la U.P., al vino tinto, a la cordillera y a las empanadas, repitiendo hoy en el exilio los clichés que antaño hacían reír" [a country where everything was beautiful, perfect, and good and in which the history of Chile is reduced to the history of Popular Unity, to red wine, the Andes mountains and *empanadas,* repeating now in exile the clichés that would have made them laugh before].[18] But demonstrations of a violently macho culture and false values of morality have alienated the daughter who, having been beaten by her father for sleeping with her boyfriend, denounced him to the police, as a result of which he spent six weeks in jail. She is now moving to study in Denmark. Mario avoids confrontation with his failure with the children, a failure born of his inability to develop a new set of social responses, for which he compensates by reinforcing traditional patterns of behavior that are unacceptable or, in the case of the beating, illegal in the receiving country.

The bedridden Don Octavio embodies the most extreme case of exclusion from the host society. While Mario and Chela find themselves in constant conflict between loyalty to links with the native country and the need to integrate somehow into the receiving community, Don Octavio has eliminated from his mind all that has to do with the time after leaving Chile. In his senility he imagines himself traveling in a train through Chile. When Mario tells his father that he is to be present at the congress where, in a symbolic gesture, a place will be kept empty for him, he wants his son to tell the driver to let him off the train in Talca (a town in central Chile). His voicelessness in Sweden is a token of the withdrawal of his right to express his now subversive opinions in his own language. His only means of expression in the play is a little bell, but this is the weapon of a sick, incontinent old man, with which he communicates his most basic needs. The bell ties Chela to him, and it becomes an instrument of alienation, not of communication. When she hides it, in a fit of rebellion against the constant "torture" of answering his every beck and call, she severs his links with everything outside his bedroom, completing the voicelessness imposed on him as a prolonged punishment for his political beliefs. His death in exile, after spending the last years of his life in isolation, is no more than the physical completion of his nothingness.

On their return, the black and white areas that had symbolized Mario and Chela's rejection of the host country and their adherence to the idealized past, now become shades of gray—like the Chilean winter, not white with snow but gray and bleak with rain. The same preoccupations, those of the children, the fate and the health of Don Octavio and the experience of exile, still fill their life. Chela is a housewife in a poorly furnished rented flat, but now her role is more in tune with the expectations of the society of which she is part. Although her isolation is still marked, she is near her family, she is recuperating her world and her identity. In Sweden she had seen her only possibility as that of "una vida inútil realmente" (p. 44). Now, in Santiago, it is Mario who uses these same words. For him, the humiliating, mechanical work he had done in exile now seems a vast improvement on the degradation of tramping the streets in search of work, and meeting only with constant refusals.

This last act is a testimony to "desexilio" in modern Chile, where Mario and Chela cannot fit in: "¡Este es otro país, mihijita! ¡Hasta cuándo nos seguimos mintiendo! ¡Nos cambiaron todo!" [This is another country, my dear! How long are we going to go on lying to ourselves! They've changed everything on us!] (p. 56). The "Velada del Gran Reencuentro" is a social evening in which returned exiles recount anecdotes about life abroad, giving the impression that life away from Chile is reduced to a succession of disconnected, unhappy, incidents. The testimonies are supposed to show "lo terrible que es vivir afuera" (p. 62), to demonstrate the suspension of life until the return. But Mario has realized that they had lived what has been called a "ghost reality," "a personal past which prevents them (exiles) from realizing and accepting the present dynamic Chilean reality as well as their actual present reality in their new society". [19] Now, after two weeks of "the madness of return," consisting of "empanadas y vino," followed by three months of loneliness and despair, of coming to terms with yet another new country, he can tell the audience, "Se produce al volver un nuevo exilio" (p. 63).

In the last scene, the tables are turned on the audience. They may have agreed with most of the sentiments expressed and may have been in sympathy with the characters, and many will have lived similar experiences, but the message of the play is that it is the audience as real people, outside the cosy bounds of the dramatic fiction, that create the atmosphere of "la locura del regreso." Mario tries to break the silence between the two parts of the broken country, to be the first in a "clamor of voices" that will provide the truth that so much silence had hidden and that had left a gap filled by myths of false paradises.

Mario and Chela, who had come to the "Velada del Gran Reencuentro" to provide the black and white story of exile and return, show the audience, both fictitious and real, the gray areas lived by those who return to a type of inner exile. It is the meeting of two mistaken visions, the paradise the exiles paint of home and the paradise those in the country paint of the "exilio dorado" (p. 63). In this sense the last scene does indeed call for, as Mario says, "un clamor de voces" to bear witness to the problem and to solve it. The play finally moves from theater to melodramatic reality. The last scene is, in effect, a political speech.

Two Silent Parts or a Mutual Deafness?

Cinema-Utoppia (1985) by Ramón Griffero is one of the most imaginative plays around the theme of exile. The absence of a manuscript makes it impossible to comment closely on the text, but in this section I want to look at the major points of the play and the way it relates to the other plays studied here.

Cinema-Utoppia is set in a cinema, El Valencia, in the age before television, when it was common to attend performances of a serialized soap opera every week. The regulars at this cinema—a Down's syndrome woman, a 'Señora,' an alcoholic, a lonely spinster, and a man who is always accompanied by his rabbit—are all solitary people looking for fantasy, escape, company. The other character, the usher, has lived there all his life and is totally absorbed in the world of the cinema, and his fantasy companions are the figures from the films, with whom he dances and converses.

The film the characters are watching is a serial about exile in Paris, the tragic existence of a lonely, isolated young man, Sebastián, an antihero with no future and only remembrance of a past love, which never loses its vividness, despite separation, loss, death. He lives in a squalid apartment for which he cannot pay and which he can keep as long as he indulges the landlord's sadomasochist fantasies. He is a drug addict, and a friend has become a drug dealer and a male prostitute as a means of economic survival. His best friend, Esteban, with whom he has a homosexual relationship, is repelled by most of the underlife he sees around him, and it is he who survives while Sebastián destroys himself.

The serial evolves around Sebastián's growing dependence on drugs and on his attempts to resist the alienation from his past, but these are futile, for the past, primarily in the shape of the dream image of his lover, lost in a distant and irretrievable time, returns to haunt him in an endless torment. In each episode his despair is deeper, his attachment to this life weaker, and finally the only solution is self-destruction.

At the moment Sebastián's suicide becomes inevitable, the fates of the two dramatic communities become intertwined. A sailor, who had entered the cinema hoping to watch pornography, leaves when he finds the serial does not provide the scenes he had been looking for; different aspects of the spectators' worlds begin to disintegrate: the rabbit dies, it becomes clear that a relationship between two of the characters was no more than a fling; the usher leaves his fantasy world briefly when he breaks down, wondering why it is always the good and the simple who suffer most. But, this time at least, he is saved from his insight by the appearance of a dancing couple from his fantasy world. In the final scene, it is only Mariana, the Down's syndrome woman, and the usher who are left in the innocence of the cinema watching the last episode of the extraordinary serial. Meanwhile, the other characters have become voyeurs at the death of Sebastián. The fiction of the serial is thus finally turned into nonfiction, and somehow the story had influenced the destruction of the world in the cinema stalls. But can the characters in the cinema audience distinguish between reality and irreality?

Cinema-Utoppia helps us to understand the dramatic treatment of exile by adding a new perspective to the main themes addressed in other plays. Firstly, there is the question of the existence of two distinct worlds, portrayed in some plays in terms of melodramatic oppositions that duplicate common real-life manichaeistic interpretations of the period since 1970. These interpretations are no more than a reversal of the regime's equivalent oppositions: thus, good is the past between 1970 and 1973, good is in Chile at that period, bad is anything after 1973, and bad is in Chile after 1973. Good is a future, often seen as a return to the past. In each one of the plays we find a nostalgia for this past, the severance from which has had great psychological repercussions. At the most common level, integration into the receiving society of exile brings with it feelings of guilt and the fear of losing all contact with the past.

But if we look at different visions of the past it soon becomes clear that they have long been subjected to a process of myth-making. Mario in *Regreso sin causa* accuses Chela of having failed with the children by not building a positive identification with their country and cultural heritage, while she accuses him of alienating them with tales of the paradise left behind. The adults, nevertheless, share a common view of the country, if not a common interpretation of how to transmit it to their children. This common view of Chile is shaped by the image of a country totally destroyed by the new regime, it is molded over the years by the exiles' political activity, which provides a sense of purpose and community in relation to the society they left behind. As they pack, Chela hides casettes of Chilean protest song among the underwear in case it should be discovered and confiscated, but the audience will find this a laughably naive precaution since, by this stage, 1984–85, the music was widely available, even if the artists were not allowed to perform in the country. The protagonists' frozen image of Chile is further demonstrated through the huge talking doll they take as a present for Chela's niece in the understanding that such a toy will be a novelty. Again the irony will be all too evident for the audience after the huge boom of imported consumer goods, and it is heightened by the fact that the doll is later sold in order to buy the girl her school uniform. In the exterior, images of the country had rested on vague notions of underdevelopment, but had not been transformed into concrete ideas of poverty. On another level, however, the episode of the doll is a comment on the impoverishment of some middle sectors in the course of the regime, for it is to be supposed that Chela's family had not previously suffered such economic hardship as to have been forced to sell a toy to provide basic necessities.

For the exiles portrayed in these plays, the past becomes summed up in certain symbols and images, smells, tastes, and sounds. For Graciela in *Primavera con una esquina rota,* the past is her relationship with Santiago. Her sense of betrayal as she adapts to the present and begins a new relationship is mixed with her inevitable distancing from another time and another country. This is somehow transferred to Beatriz, the child, the person with little first-hand knowledge of the country left behind. Autumn for the adults around her means Uruguay; it evokes smells, colors of a season that does not exist in their present home. Beatriz, with no experience of autumn, cannot imagine it through her senses, but she evokes it in pictorial images of leaves falling through the bars of her father's cell, the bars that she, in turn, relates to a zoo in Montevideo. Hers is an image of the home country that is in some instances visually vivid, born of symbols of imprisonment and confinement, but essentially vague since she has no conscious recollection of experiencing her country. As her mother rediscovers her sensuality, Beatriz clings more to the past, perceiving the imminent destruction of the suspended world she inhabits as they await her father's release from jail. While Graciela's sense of self is returning, Beatriz is threatened with the loss of a sense of identity.

At times these symbols of home are apparently superficial. When the characters in these plays talk, for example, of the dreamed-of great madness of weeks of "empanadas y vino," they evoke, in effect, a sensual memory through which they seek to find a link with their own history. Chela looks forward to satisfying her husband's stomach with Chilean delicacies, yet on their return these lose the strength they held as memories, for the wine and *empanadas* do not compensate for the disillusion experienced as the mythical image of the country is exploded. The protagonist in *José*, on return, is tempted by the new delicate fare the family now eats as befitting their higher position in society, but he had fed his image of the family on the earthiness now to be found only in the grandfather. And in *Regreso sin causa,* the old father, Don Octavio, excluded for so many years from living a worthwhile life, begins to sense things again when he is in possession of the air tickets, regaining the experiences of the senses with the illusion of return.

The revelation on return of the emptiness of these symbols is shown to be one of the principle symptoms of "desexilio." As the characters rediscover that the country cannot solely be defined in terms of clichés, this becomes the final proof that history and the essence of the country had not been moved abroad to be brought back with the end of exile. Both parts of the country have evolved, the future cannot be built on the foundations of a regression to the mythical version of the democratic past.

Cinema-Utoppia introduces to better effect than any of the other plays the reality of two silent halves, and the question of the impact of exile on the younger generation. The protagonists of the serial are young people, probably in their mid to late twenties, who went into exile in their teens. They are alienated from the experience that brought them to Europe, distanced from the ideological principles of the period and, thus, from the country painted by the older generation. This is a problem of generations, of the inability of the younger generation to assimilate completely their situation and identity as exiles. Like the older generation, they feel betrayed. But these exiles have been betrayed by their own, by those who adhere to the belief in an absurdly obscure and, for them, irrelevant past, identified by what José Donoso has described as the "cifras de un código emocionalmente inerte para ellos."[20] Their assimilation into

the new country is shown to be into a subculture: marginal, sometimes criminal, and ultimately destructive. Unlike the son in *Regreso sin causa,* supported by his family in a country (Sweden) that
is renowned for its advanced welfare state and its welcome of Latin
American exiles, they do not have any family structure to fall back
on and feel rejected by the receiving culture (France). The son is
tempted back to Chile with his family, but the characters of the
serial in *Cinema Utoppia* have no such option, no such pretext.
Their access to the receiving culture has been into a subworld; they
can aspire to no more, nor can they realistically aspire to renewed
access to their expelling country. Notably, they have very little
contact with the political groups of exile and view their activities
with more than a touch of cynicism.

Finally, *Cinema-Utoppia* offers the greatest metaphor for the
"desencuentro" of the two parts of the country. The audience goes
to the cinema to escape and fantasize, to be transported to another
exciting, romantic, and satisfying life. Instead they are transported
to a harsh futuristic reality. The clash of past and present, of reality
and fantasy is doubly important, for it is the juxtaposition of a past
age of innocence—the audience belongs to a bygone age—with a
contemporary age of cruelty and destruction. The function of
cinema-going is reversed, for the utopian image, albeit tainted, is to
be found in the stalls and, ultimately, in its purest expression, in the
ghosts that populate the usher's fantasy world.

Cinema-Utoppia provides a vision of two parts of a world that
are so alienated that there is virtually no possibility of welding them
together. Even when the audience become voyeurs the characters
are looking through a window, and thus the illusion of cinema still
exists. Above all, the protagonists of the serial and the cinema
audience belong to two different ages, two periods in which the
respective protagonists have different experiences and different
fantasies to fill their lives. Sebastián at the beginning of the serial
was for the cinema audience a fantasy. As the hero of the serial he
should have had a bright future, with problems along the way but
with the inevitability of long life, success, love. But they are distanced from him as the hero when his imperfections, the effects of
exile and the disintegration of his world become clear. The final
scene may be one of the nearness of the encounter of the two
worlds, but it is one also of the impossibility of this encounter and
one of destruction as Sebastián's death is witnessed as yet another
spectacle that hardly affects their lives. *Cinema-Utoppia* can be
interpreted as a metaphor for the inability to grasp the realities of
exile imposed as a consequence of dictatorship. The story of the

protagonists in Paris is told, but not understood; it is related as another, slightly disturbing aspect of life and is not internalized by the spectators who, after all, have no means of understanding the problem, just as the experience of exile cannot be fully understood by those who have not left the country.

Cinema-Utoppia is unlike the other plays that deal with exile. These are testimonies; they deal with the survivors in a political confrontation, and they hope to fulfill the purpose of replacing with images of the real experience the misconceptions about exile caused by the suppression of the truth. In one way or another, the plays dealing with political exile—*Primavera con una esquina rota, Regreso sin causa, ¿Cuántos años tiene un día?*—search for ways of exploring experiences of exile and breaking down the myths created in the vacuum of information. They seek to provide testimony untainted by political interest and peppered with the inevitable accusations of betrayal, collaboration, adaptation. The theater of exile is a theater of the expression of the defeated, of those who have suffered prolonged ostracism. The authors ultimately hope to recuperate the strength and vitality of expression they feel existed before, and finally they hope to end the silence between the two parts of the country.

6
Rupture and Continuity, Memory and Forgetting

The Space for Theater

It is perhaps paradoxical that theater, with its long commitment to portraying Chilean reality, has been allowed such freedom of expression and has used this space since 1973 in such a way as to express overt dissent. The relative freedom from repression of the theater has been explained in terms of the perception of its impact on society, which is deemed to be minimal. Theater, it is recognized, can be dangerous and can have a strong impact, especially when outside events somehow enter the theater world; but there are effective mechanisms to deal with the few cases when this happens. And it must be recognized that the military regime was aware of the political importance of the middle sectors that make up the audience, among whose demands on the state is a certain degree of freedom of expression.

These reasons and those discussed in chapter 1, such as theater being used as a democratic showpiece and as an escape valve, may go some way to explaining the actual freedom of expression that existed in the years 1973–89, but it does not explain why theater has been so dynamic. The answer lies in the nature of the impact of the reduction of the space for community activity and the perceived retreat of individuals from a public space into isolated shells. While political gatherings were not allowed, unless subject to strict rules and monitoring, it was in the nature of the Pinochet regime that sectors not posing any serious immediate threat be left alone. This is vitally important, for it means that while the collective political sphere distintegrates, the individual may be left in peace, and the inner self of thoughts, ideas, creation, remains private.

The special importance of theater lies in the union of the expression of the private thought with the freedom to express this to a relatively small audience. This is why theater has been so vital in the last years. I do not mean this as an apology for the Pinochet regime but as another way of explaining how the dramatist has used the space of inner life that is his or her creative space to its best advantage in an otherwise severely restrictive atmosphere. This is all the more important because the value of this inner life has in itself been expressed as a constant subtheme throughout the period, in the game-playing, the dreaming, and the fantasizing; in, for example, Efraín's almost heroic gesture as he leaves the restaurant. It is an expression of the power of the individual within the collective, and that it is not translated to the collective is a measure of the wider social impasse. This inner self is often best expressed in the realms of memory and forgetting, where the past is recalled as a better age and as an alternative for the present and the future. It is this I want to concentrate on in this final chapter, firstly through Marco Antonio de la Parra's *Toda una vida* [An entire life] (1979).

Memory and Forgetting

Sí, si sé, . . . pero igual son leseras . . . si el doctor me dijo . . . yo le pregunté ¿oiga qué tiene don Eustaquio? y me dijo . . . así . . . clarito "tiene la memoria destrozada por una atrofia de la corteza cerebral y vive clavado, anclado en sus mejores recuerdos, como encerrado para siempre en un álbum de fotografías que el viento hubiera deshojado de un sólo manotazo . . ." ¡qué lindo que habla! . . . ¡qué amor sus ojitos de cielo!¹

[Yes, yes, I know that, . . . but all the same it's nonsense . . . the doctor told me so . . . I asked him, look, what's wrong with don Eustaquio? . . . and he said . . . just like this . . . as clear as day "his memory has been destroyed by an atrophy of the cerebral cortex and he lives stuck, anchored in his best memories, as if he were shut for ever in an album that the wind had blown open, and all the sheets had flown away in one gust. . . ." He talks so nicely! . . . and he's got the most gorgeous blue eyes!]

This quotation holds the essence of the picture of contemporary Chile painted in Marco Antonio de la Parra's *Toda una vida* (1979). The speaker (Marilin) is a nurse in a sanitarium where the subject of her concern, an old man named Don Eustaquio, is an inmate who is lost in a world of perpetual remembering. In this speech we encounter the essential frivolity of the nurse and her clear word-for-word recollection of the description of Don Eustaquio's state, prompted nevertheless by the attractiveness of the doctor. In the juxtaposition and play between the nurse's frivolity and the repeated memories of Don Eustaquio, we find the parallel juxtaposition and play between characteristics of two starkly contrasting periods of Chilean history, the democratic years of the thirties and the election of the Popular Front government of Pedro Aguirre Cerda and the authoritarian years of the seventies.

Toda una vida takes place in a sanitarium at the change of shift between Marilin and another nurse, Leontina. The inmates are primarily geriatrics whom it is easy to control with drugs and tranquilizers. Not so Don Eustaquio, for he lives continually reenacting his favorite memories, which refer to the fall of the dictator General Carlos Ibánez in 1931, the short-lived Socialist Republic of 1932 led by Marmaduque Grove, and the election in 1938 of the Popular Front government of Pedro Aguirre Cerda. Don Eustaquio, we are informed, is perfectly healthy apart from the tricks his memory plays on him. He is an affectionate old man, left in the asylum by his family because he represents a danger: "Se asustan . . . no ve que se les arranca y después se larga a hablar esto del presidente y lo toman por qué sé yo" (p. 24). His favorite position is on top of a ladder where he is discovered at the beginning of the play shouting, "¡Cayó, cayó! . . . ¡cayó el general Ibáñez! ¡abajo el general!" (p. 1). But inevitably, at a certain point in his memory he becomes stuck, "clavado, mirando al vacío," as in a trance, only to begin again with the same story later.

The two nurses are in constant conflict. Leontina finds Marilin an enigma, immersed as she is in the Chile of the late seventies; in love with consumer goods, with Americanized fast food, and with imported soap operas. She calls herself "joven de alma y cuerpo," is coquettish, determined to remain attractive, and detests the testimony the patients provide of the ugliness of growing old. This is a world to which the apparently older Leontina has no access, which is alien to her, and even the language Marilin uses, contaminated with Americanisms, is incomprehensible; but above all this world is synonymous with falling standards, for Marilin shares it with men who are not her husband (the husband, Nelson, travels a lot) and she seems obsessed by material acquisition and with sex. She torments Leontina with visions of how the clinic is to be modernized, how the old, time-served but unattractive nurses are to be replaced by young attractive women, Dallas-clones. But this cruelty is countered and surpassed by Leontina, for she accuses Marilin of sharing Don Eustaquio's problem, of being "pegada en la edad." In reality Marilin is forty, not twenty-eight as she had claimed; Nelson has abandoned her; and in the new order of things she will suffer the same fate as Leontina. As the facade crumbles, Don Eustaquio begins to represent an alternative companion for Marilin, his world a new fantasy for her to take refuge in. Finally she enters his world, painting the clinic with Don Eustaquio's beloved sea gulls that remind him of Valparaíso. And it is he who must be convinced that the sea gulls are real, that Marilin has not gone mad. It is only when he hears along with her the sound of singing that he joins her at the top of the ladder.

Toda una vida develops around the absorption of Marilin into Don Eustaquio's world of perpetual remembering. For her it is the replacement of one fantasy world—that of her youth, her continuing sexual attractiveness, her place in the new society—for another that implies an escape from the trap of her former environment into one of joy, tenderness, and belief in the promise of democracy. It is important that for Marilin this is a fantasy, while for Don Eustaquio it is a memory, a dream and an evocation of a possible alternative. Locked in this one prolonged memory, Don Eustaquio is awaiting its return in reality, and when Marilin enters his world, *Toda una vida* begins to suggest the possibility of its realization. But how does his "dangerous" memory work?

The essential point is that it is akin to a dream that can be reenacted until a certain point and then is lost and cannot be remembered, no matter how much of an effort the dreamer makes to continue, even to invent a continuation. His is an exclusive memory that spans the decade of the thirties, at times recalling the fall of Ibáñez, at other times the Socialist Republic, then the great earthquake of Chillán in 1939, the presidency and death of Pedro Aguirre Cerda. What these memories have in common is an intrinsic sense of optimism in the promise of socialist government as represented in the political developments of the thirties. Each time he becomes stuck, it is a token of how his dream became stuck, suffering the same atrophy as his memory and relegated to the photograph album that "el viento hubiera deshojado de un solo manotazo" (p. 11).

"Oiga mi reina," he asks Marilin, "¿por qué será que yo siempre sueño el mismo sueño?" (Listen, my dear, why do you think I always dream the same dream?, p. 23). But Marilin knows nothing of Pedro Aguirre Cerda, of Marmaduque Grove, of Ibáñez. When Don Eustaquio shouts that the general has fallen, she warns that his big mouth could land him in prison, yet, she feels attracted by his descriptions of people rejoicing, of the processions, of the daring with which he participated in opposition to unpopular measures. When she enters his game as a way of indulging him, he accuses her of being mad—how can she suggest that a bed is a "lancha" (the small boats that are used in the port of Valparaíso)? She tries to follow his line of thought by recalling the political slogans that have become part of the linguistic heritage of her country, but when she answers his question, "¿No sabe quién mandó el buque?" with "Don Marmaduque," he tells her, "¡No me haga enredos con la historia mi reina, por favor!" (pp. 20–21). At this level, by trying to intervene with the popular refrain, she fails because she has not assumed the internal logic of the memory, ordered as it is around real happenings of which she knows nothing. But she is on the verge of sharing Don Eustaquio's vision of the world. No longer does she want him to share the pleasures the seventies can provide; now she wants to learn about the old, dead things that had depressed her previously. The ship was not Don Marmaduque's, as the old man explains, but was one sent by the Mexicans to celebrate democratic victory; it brought gifts, acrobats, Mexican singers and, above all, angels:

EUSTAQUIO: ¡Sí, pero, sobre todo traía ángeles!

MARILIN: ¡No esté leseando! (Muy impactada).

EUSTAQUIO: Y bajaban por los cerros de Valparaíso, por los funiculares . . . por las escaleras . . . todos tomados de la mano y cantando . . . y yo estaba en medio de todo. . . . Y los ángeles gritaban. . . . ¡Viva don Pedro, abajo el demonio! Y pintaban las murallas. ¡Gobernar es educar; Pan, Techo y Abrigo! Y después organizaban un desfile por las calles de Santiago. ¡Por Carrascal, por Mapocho, por Quinta Normal, por Dieciocho!

MARILIN: ¿Y también por aquí, frente al hospital?

EUSTAQUIO: Sí. ¡Por todas partes! Y la gente que los seguía, cientos de miles de personas, les gritaban: "Angel, amigo, el pueblo está contigo". Y los ángeles les contestaban: "El que no salta es el demonio". Y de repente aparecía en el balcón don Pedro. Y yo como un loco me sacaba el jockey y gritaba: "Viva don Pedro, abajo el demonio pelado." Y de repente me quedaba solo.

MARILIN: ¿O sea, que la gallá se iba?

EUSTAQUIO: La multitud desaparecía. Y quedaba sólo un auto grande y coludo con un demonio gordo y calvo que lo manejaba y se me venía, se me venía . . .

MARILYN: ¿A atropellarlo a usted . . . ?

EUSTAQUIO: Sí . . . yo estaba como trancado en la tierra y transpiraba y transpiraba. . . . Y de repente se me aparece un angelito vestido de obrero y me dice: "No se asuste compadre; que el miedo es la escopeta del demonio. Mientras usted no se asuste, estaremos siempre juntos. Nosotros bajaremos de la historia, cada vez que sea necesario. . . . Bajaremos como un sueño de su memoria . . .

MARILIN: ¿De la memoria suya? (pp. 21–22)

[EUSTAQUIO: Yes, but the important thing is that they brought angels.

MARILIN: Don't be daft! [*Very moved*]

EUSTAQUIO: And they came down the hills in Valparaíso, in the funicular railways . . . down the stairs . . . all holding hands and singing . . . and I was in the middle of it all. . . . And the angels were shouting. . . . Long live don Pedro, down with the demon! And they painted the walls. Government is education! Food, Shelter and Clothing! And then they organized a parade through the streets of Santiago. Carrascal, Mapocho, Quinta Normal, Dieciocho!

MARILIN: And did they come by here, in front of the hospital?

EUSTAQUIO: Yes. They went everywhere! And the people followed them, hundreds of thousands of people, shouting out: "Angel, our friend, the people are with you." And the Angels shouted back: "Anyone who doesn't jump is a demon." And all of a sudden don Pedro appeared on the balcony. And I threw my hat in the air and shouted like mad: "Long live don Pedro, down with the bald demon!" And then all of a sudden I was alone.

MARILIN: You mean the folk left you?

EUSTAQUIO: The crowd dispersed. And all that was left was a big long car with a bald fat demon driving it and he was driving toward me . . . closer and closer . . .

MARILIN: He was trying to run you down?

EUSTAQUIO: Yes . . . I felt as if I was stuck to the ground and I was sweating and sweating . . . And all of a sudden an angel dressed as a worker appeared and said to be: "Don't be afraid, my friend; fear is the weapon of the demon. As long as you are not afraid we will always be together. We will come down from history, each time it is necessary. . . . We will come down like a dream from your memory . . .

MARILIN: From your memory, don Eustaquio?]

If we examine the dream more closely, it becomes clear that it is Don Eustaquio himself who muddles history. The boat referred to was sent for the victory of Popular Unity in 1970, not for that of the Popular Front; the slogans evoke those of the Popular Unity period, "demonio" suggesting "momio," the name given to right-wingers; and the angels are both the angels of salvation, evoking the name of Salvador Allende, and symbols of popular rule. The imagery of Allende's evocation of the return of democracy, of the "grandes Alamedas" (hence the switch from Valparaíso to the great avenues of Santiago), is once again to the fore and the violent end to the processions, with the appearance of the "demonio," unequivocally sets the date for the violent end to Don Eustaquio's distant dream of democracy. By superimposing the imagery of Popular Unity upon the memory of the Popular Front, De la Parra creates an impression of former progress and continuity in history, which adds greater emphasis to the impression of later rupture and stagnation that is created through the dream "stuck" in the old man's memory.

Don Eustaquio is locked in a cyclical memory that will eternally be renewed and frozen. Not so Marilin. For her the dream becomes a beautiful fantasy of another world, a free, hopeful world where people like herself will not be kicked aside as too old or too ugly. She enters Don Eustaquio's world as a rejection of the cold, restrictive, hopeless environment to which she belongs. For her, then, the image is not cyclical; it is a progression toward the freedom she paints in the last scene when she covers the walls with sea gulls and when she begins to see the angels. Yet Don Eustaquio knows the angels cannot have arrived, he worries about Marilin's sudden madness and does not recognize his dream in Marilin's words, for coming from someone else they represent only a sad reminder of failed democracy. He knows that the angels can thrive only in an atmosphere of freedom: "para que bajen los ángeles, la gente tiene que cantar"; but Marilin's new hope allows him to hear the song of joy being sung. "¡Están cantando . . . entonces es cierto . . . bajaron de la historia . . . después de tanto . . . tanto tiempo esperándoles. . . . Y ahí están todos . . . Marmaduque . . . Don Pedro . . . y tanto resucitado glorioso! ¡Qué lindo día de septiembre, mi reina! ¡Como para inventarlo de nuevo! ¡Como para inventarlo de nuevo!" [They're singing . . . so it's true . . . they've come down from history . . . after so long . . . I've been waiting for so long. . . . And here they all are . . . Marmaduque . . . Don Pedro . . . and so many wonderful people revived from the dead! What a beautiful September day, my dear! Someone should invent it again!] (p. 33).

Once he is back on his steps Don Eustaquio enters his memory again. Perhaps he reenters the memory's essential circular quality. Perhaps Marilin has assumed his memory and will also remain "clavada" in the moment before the coming of fear. And perhaps she has gone mad as the only way of escaping the reality of her Chile with its false values and its perverted codes of behavior. But the message of the play is clear: the singing is the end of fear; the voice of the angels will ward off the demons. Only the loss of fear will open the way for a return to democracy.

The strength of *Toda una vida* lies in the play off between fantasy and memory. To all intents and purposes Marilin, before her "conversion," lives in a fantasy world, for she longs to belong completely to the new world, she lives locked in a distorted mirror image of herself, which reflects the film-star appearance and sexual attraction her name suggests should be hers (her mother named her Marilin for this very reason, as if as a means of cheating fate). Her boldness hides her deep insecurity; it camouflages the torment of the awareness that her future is basically the same as that of Leontina's; it hides the absolute emptiness of her life. Don Eustaquio, on the other hand, is not part of the new order; he holds no affection for material wealth; his is a world of sensitivity and concern for the state of democracy, it is a world that was halted when history stopped and his interest for what was happening—for example in the Congress, suspended—became irrelevant.

Despite his age, his weakness, his being locked in the past, it is Don Eustaquio's personality and his sensitivity to the state of his country that begin to invade the stage and take over, so much so that Marilin's music, the music of "the average Chilean" (p. 12), seems intrusive, extraneous, crass. Marilin escapes from a world that, by the end of the play, is revealed as ugly and vacuous, into a beautiful fantasy, but this fantasy is really a vision of an alternative reality, one that did exist but that somehow became "clavada en la historia". It is a vision of a day that should be invented again, the fourth of September, election day.

Rupture, Continuity, Change

Memory and forgetting, rupture, continuity, and change—all of these are at the heart of the preoccupations of Chilean theater since 1973. In these final pages I want to highlight broad ways in which they have affected theater, all too aware that I can only look at perceivable trends.

Nineteen forty-one is a key year; it is regarded as the beginning of modern theatre in Chile and as the year when a definite break with the past took place. In some senses this is true since there was a concentrated effort to shake off old negative aspects of theater. The theater empresario was scorned as forsaking art for financial gain, shoddily improvized drama was abhorred as an insult to the art, the social elite was revealed as the sole consumers of theater. Yet, despite the aim of popularizing it, still theater remained an art for an elite, now drawn from the middle sectors, and only sporadic efforts succeeded in effectively broadening the social extraction of its audience. However, perhaps for the first time in the forties and certainly in the fifties, theater was being regarded as a genuine art and literary form, as a worthy part of the intellectual life of the country, and the creators of the university theaters consciously mapped out a future for their theater, a future that was to include new dramatists, new plays, a cultivated audience, wider appeal.

In the fifties the dramatists of the university generation came into their own, and their work was born largely of the social preoccupations of the middle sectors, from where these dramatists came. Plays were set within a bourgeois social framework, often relying on a fundamental melodramatic situation, set within the boundaries of the family in society. Conflict arose from the intrinsic fears and inhibitions of these classes, and this drama indulged constant themes of doubts about their position in society, their moral codes, about their human values. Theirs was a social sector portrayed as at once secure and fearful. Dramatic communities were attacked and intruded upon by a changing society, by the erosion of moral codes, by social pressures from above, and finally by the threat of intrusion by the lower classes.

By the sixties the role of theater in society was being challenged again, plays were often seen to be an integral expression of bourgeois models, and the major impulse was again one of rupture with this past, of the creation of a "new" theater, one that spoke of the people and was written by the people. The bourgeois dramatist was often regarded as linked to the forces of imperialism, the middle-class audience likewise, and the latter was seen anew as a narrow elite. Collective creation became the mode of democratic expression, and new audiences were actively sought from among the lower and working classes. Dramatic conflict became clearly set within the context of the fight against economic and cultural dependency, against imperialism and capitalism. By the time of Popular Unity, revolution was a key issue in the arts as well as in politics, and in the theater there was a creeping sense of an imposed revolutionary form, especially in the organization of amateur theater.

The "crisis" in theater, to use a much abused word, had not been overcome and the problems remained the same—not enough dramatists of contemporary national reality, too few theater venues, a small and narrow theater-going public, and lack of funding for new initiatives. A pattern emerges of repeated cycles of perceived breaks with the past, of the "old" being replaced by the "new." This is reflected in the themes of the plays, in the changing procession of protagonists on the stage, in the mode of creation best favored at any given time. A sense of the disappointing superficiality of these breaks was expressed in the disillusion of the students in

Vodanović's *Nos tomamos la universidad,* in which their final "Vendrá el día" ["The day will come"] is a call of despair at the pervasive power of old institutionalized forms.

The military coup of 1973 was a major point of rupture. The essential difference being, obviously, that this break with the past was imposed by political circumstances, not by a natural artistic process of questioning methods of production, of creation, or of the role of theater in society. One impact of this in terms of the theme and the preferred methods of creation has been to sharpen the sense of rupture with the past, while at the same time strengthening the need to look for some sort of artistic continuity. So, whereas the perception of a break is more acute since it was imposed by political upheaval, there is little effort to break culturally with the past as in the forties and the sixties, rather there is a strong tendency to create symbolic, artistic, and formal links with a past that can be identified in general terms as democratic and, in more specific terms, as the Popular Unity years. This in itself puts the playwrights and groups who have been studied in this book on the side of the losers, for the victors of 1973 have concentrated on defiling the image of the Popular Unity years that may persist in the collective memory.

The "new" is imposed; it is the invention of an authoritarian regime; and it is the new, not the old, that is generally rejected in artistic creation. The building of links with the past, the forging of a perception of continuity has become a central principle of what is deemed to be a counterculture, that is, anything that does not conform to the cultural expression promoted by the regime through subsidized art, the media, and television. In the following pages I want to suggest the "inquietudes colectivas"[2] that have continued to preoccupy dramatists and groups, those that have disappeared or been transformed and those new collective preoccupations whose appearance suggests that they reflect deep changes in society.

"Inquietudes colectivas"

Marginality has been a constant theme since the early sixties. On one level it takes the form of social realism, set within the context of the possibility of social reform through political consciousness raising and organization. It delivered both a political message and a warning aimed at directing the collected audience toward an ideology of left wing change, ultimately toward a "new" future. The characters from plays such as Isidora Aguirre's *Los que van que-*

dando en el camino and *Los papeleros,* María Asunción Requena's
Pan caliente, and Jorge Díaz's *Topografía de un desnudo* were the
people literally and metaphorically on the other side of the river,
the fear of whose organization and subsequent power haunted the
protagonists of Wolff's *Los invasores* and destroyed the female
protagonist in *Flores de papel.* Given the sociopolitical reality of
the sixties, this threat seemed to be well on the way to being
realized and by 1970, with the election of the Popular Unity government, some of the middle and upper sectors were genuinely afraid
that the consolidation in power of the Marxists would be carried
out with the malevolence of such as Wolff's character El Merluza,
The Pike, in *Flores de Papel.*

The growing place of popular amateur theater after 1968 was
linked to the strength of the left; the expansion of popular culture
became an aim of those artists committed to the Popular Unity
program; it was the fortieth point of the Popular Unity manifesto.
But more and more in the years 1970–73, workers, peasants, students, and youth groups were asked to limit expression to the
"new" ideology, and, although the strength of the popular theater
organization, ANTACH, cannot be denied, the majority of the
plays produced were along the lines of agitprop and rigorously
politically monitored. It was this as a form of popular expression
that was savagely repressed after the coup as a part of the eradica-
tion of all organizations linked to Popular Unity.

When new plays began to be performed after the coup, the
marginal sectors came to the fore. In plays such as *Pedro, Juan y
Diego, Los payasos de la esperanza,* and *Tres Marías y una Rosa,*
this was an expression of real social problems, but also an expression of intellectual unease at the way society was developing. It
was a way of revealing the poverty and deprivation that lay beneath
the decontaminated upper crust of society. It was an expression
also of the constant awareness that all is not what it seems; the
portrayal of the marginal sectors was a portrayal of the ugly under-
side of a society that has been transformed into a palatable parcel,
handed back to the country for its consumption. And the people in
receipt of such a parcel are also the public in the theater. The
predominance of popular characters on stage, furthermore, speaks
of the traumatic impact of the economic recession of the mid-
seventies, and it highlighted major changes in the structure of the
lower classes as a result of massive unemployment. If, before, there
were plays that concerned the unemployed, they did not deal with
the impact of the loss of employment on family life, cultural expression, the sense of identity of the working classes. These were

new themes to deal with new, important social problems. The characters were people relegated to a position of extreme marginality, who had no access to the "new" society being built by the regime, epitomized for them by the *caracoles* and the consumer boom, the economic miracle. These plays spoke of disintegration, the break-up of the family, the adherence to small and demeaning plans for everyday survival. These new marginal sectors were the first theatrical expression of the prolonged period of impasse: no longer was political organization a credible solution, and the characters were left to struggle against a powerful but invisible antagonist. But neither do they pose a serious threat, for no longer are they symbols of rebellion, but of defeat.

In the dramas of the fifties and sixties—in Wolff, Cuadra, Debesa, Vodanović—the family was the most important single unit in society, essentially closed, defensive, and hostile to outside influence. The household was a place into which the outside inevitably intruded in the form of untested values, questioning attitudes, rejection of the old for the new, and this was the source of a common dramatic conflict. The strength in this world came from the mother, who, constantly aware of the precarious position of the family, usually middle- or lower-middle-class, and always fearful of losing the family's relative security and comfort, would urge her children on in an upward social struggle.

Fernando Cuadra's *La familia de Marta Mardones* (1976) saw the continuation of this type of portrayal of the family unit, guarded by the overpowering, ultimately stifling mother from whom the characters, in variously drastic moves, escape, while she fights to save the solidity of the home for the time when they will, inevitably it is implied, return to the nest. There is no other play in this period that presents such a strong family unit, which, although it breaks up, does so for reasons extraneous to the immediate sociopolitical environment. By contrast, Egon Wolff's *José*, set within a family that is seemingly strong and well-established in the contemporary framework, gradually reveals it to be wrought with problems, doubts, tensions, and nostalgia for simpler days, and in this context the women are, more than ever, trapped in the prison of their dependent condition. When José leaves, the family ostensibly returns to the same "tranquility" as at the beginning, but nothing will ever be the same, for the unity of the family has disintegrated, although the cracks are hidden behind the perfect facade of the men's making.

In *El último tren*, the family unit has broken down completely in the context of the new society in which the adults cannot cope, and the daughter has to save the family from total destitution. It is a cruel irony that Ismael, as he retreats into madness, looks to Violeta's childhood for hope, in the belief that children adapt more quickly to new circumstances. In fact her young, dependent role has been robbed from her, and she does adapt, but in a much more brutal way than Ismael can imagine or accept. Violeta finds a temporary release from her present role in the evocation of the idyllic childhood she had known, but this is a calculated, at times cynical, act. She takes refuge in this past identity in order to please her father and her aunt, and she enters into its spirit as an escape from the true circumstances of her life. These rituals from her childhood act as a contrast to the terrible failure of the family to protect her and guarantee a better future. Mercedes, her aunt, had taken refuge in this idyllic past as an evasion of the failure of her own life, she had sought refuge in the past she knew before the all-important point of rupture, but in the end, she had only looked to a world that existed in her imagination. The family unit must be reconstructed in fantasy to exist at all.

In *Tres Marías y una Rosa,* the *arpilleristas* have moved out of the home. But this, in itself, is a result of the deep changes in their immediate community, for their partners must be unemployed for them to join the tapestry workshop: the male world must be in a process of decay before the female world assumes importance. *Tres Marías y una Rosa* is in this way a testimony to profound and perhaps irreversible changes in society. Work now defines the women's lives; it is the means by which they attempt to retain the last remnants of the family together. Yet, they have found a new strength in work and a community of women that had not existed before, they have found an alternative and a future.

The theater of Juan Radrigán encompasses all of these themes. The family has totally disintegrated, characters wander the streets, or live alone in squalor in rooms and shacks, they remember lost partners, they have been forgotten by children, or they choose not to have children because the circumstances are too difficult. Work is a thing of the past; nobody works, and when they do it is in grotesquely ridiculous circumstances. One play, *Cuestión de ubicación* (1980), gives a graphic example of this disintegration of the family. In it a girl dies of malnutrition while the rest of the family debate where they should put their new color television. Although this play oversimplifies references to consumerism, it does provoke reflection on the use of consumer goods to deny marginalization. For the family it is more important to conceal their poverty from the old meat-eating lady next door who, they believe, only eats to torment them (reduced to a diet of tea and bread), than it is to do something about bettering their standard of living. It is a symptom of the nature of consumer society that the only access the protagonists have to the community is through material goods, the most prominent expression of the new. And it is indicative of the perverse nature of modern society that the shiny symbols of belonging exist in such close proximity to squalor and unnecessary death.

It is a characteristic of the period that old people have also been prominent as protagonists—Ismael, Andrés, Don Octavio, Don Eustaquio, the aging and ageless waiters, Radrigán's characters. Don Eustaquio is a personification of the perceived wasting away of Chilean society, of its stunted development. This idea is also embodied in characters such as Don Octavio in *Regreso sin causa* and Ismael in *El último tren,* both of whom belong to a democratic past and who have been silenced and ostracized. And the symbolic similarities go further than this creation of a stereotype of democracy, for the symbol of the train is present in all three of the plays. This is coherent on one level as a metaphor for the march of history, and on another it is a reminder of a strong tradition of political organization, one that, through the railway, is explicitly linked with the central valley and the south of the country.

In *Toda una vida* the train is used in joking fashion as part of the imaginary journey of Don Eustaquio when Marilin, trying to enter his fantasy, tells the old man that he will travel on the ultramodern "tren japonés," but he reacts violently to his foreign intrusion into the respected world of the Chilean railway and demands to travel on a "tren democrático." Likewise, Don Octavio in *Regreso sin causa* in his senility in Sweden travels Chile "en un tren imaginario." In these two instances the train is a peripheral symbol, part of the old men's memories of past Chile; it speaks of their present immobility, as a result of which the only movement they can make is through their imagination. To this extent the ladder and the bed in *Toda una vida* are indications of Don Eustaquio's limited scope for physical movement in contrast to the journeys he embarks on in his imagination at all hours of the day.

In *El último tren* the train is the central symbol of rupture, of change, marginality, and submission to a new and cruel reality. Ismael's whole life has revolved around the culture attached to railway society. As long as Ismael can carry on in the way established by his forefathers, he remains the embodiment of family tradition. But from the beginning of the dramatic action, small incidents show that the atmosphere has changed and that the cosy structure of before has disappeared. The most significant of these is that Ismael is bitten by a dog for the first time in his life. It is an incident that he brushes aside at the time, but that he will remember when he finally takes the last train from reality: "¿Sabes por qué muerden los perros, Rafael? . . . ¡Por el miedo! Los perros huelen el miedo y por eso muerden. . . . Así es que no hay que tener miedo, porque ahí es cuando los perros muerden" [Do you know why dogs bite, Rafael? . . . Fear. Dogs smell fear and that's why they bite. . . . So you shouldn't be afraid, because that's the only time that dogs bite] (p. 138). Yet, in his "madness" he refers to the time when his daughter Violeta was bitten, not himself, for he has taken refuge in a lost past where his role and that of the railway were secure. And he has subconsciously sought a flicker of hope in the awareness that children forget and adapt with greater facility than adults. For Ismael the future has been well and truly killed and he opts for a frozen past into which is built a false illusion of continuity.

The fate that affects these old people is translated as a steady progression into ritual existence, obsessive remembering, madness. They are isolated from society as a deliberate means of diminishing the possibility of their contaminating other minds with subversive ideas. This is an echo of the reasoning by which, in *Baño a baño*, "preso" becomes synonymous with "loco," because both types of social misfit "Perjudican la tranquildad pública." What is missing from these old characters' lives is the element of choice; there is no acceptable alternative to the state they are in; choices and movement are limited. The acts of Ismael signify the acceptance of defeat, and Don Rafael in *Primavera con una esquina rota* temporarily accepts defeat in exile when he starts to use a walking stick. In *Toda una vida*, meanwhile, Don Eustaquio shows a certain lucidity about the fact that his memory is only a dream, that it cannot become reality until fear has gone from society. The old men portrayed in these plays are ostracized by the dominant ideology as part of a sickness in society, but the evidence provided otherwise reveals that it is society that is in fact sick.

Old people are the protagonists of Egon Wolff's *Alamos en la azotea* [Poplars in the attic] (1981) and *Kindergarten* (1977). *Kindergarten* revolves around the rivalry between two aging brothers of an old family "de estirpe de la sociedad santiaguina" who now live from the takings of an umbrella shop. Theirs is a life of constant mutual torment, of game-playing and ritual. Into this world enters their long-lost sister, returned home after many years, in search of the family, her youth, and the daughter that she had either aban-

doned or had had taken from her. She threatens to upset the fragile
balance of the ritual abuse between the two brothers, but, in effect,
her arrival really means the closing of the family circle, decaying
and isolated from the world.

This decaying family has been seen as an allegory for the demise
of the old aristocracy and for a social stagnation that afflicts the
country. Undoubtedly, there is something of this in the play, but, as
Frank Dauster says of *Kindergarten:* "Toño, Mico and Meche, por
podridos que se les vea, rebosan voluntad de sobrevivir. Por eso, y a
pesar de la chatura y la ordinariez de su vida, tienen una fuerte nota
de humanidad, y se alzan más arriba de cualquier significado al-
egórico. Serán muy poca cosa, pero son seres humanos, como
todos nosotros, y tienen que importarnos." [Toño, Mico and
Meche, no matter how rotten they may seem inside, overflow with
the desire to survive. That's why, despite the smallness and or-
dinariness of their lives, there is a strong note of humanity, and the
characters rise above any allegorical meaning. They may not be
very much, but they are human beings, like all of us, and they must
mean something to us].[3] This was written in response to Juan
Andrés Piña's affirmation in the introduction to the printed edition
of the play that, "Ya no hay aquí tránsito ni evolución, lucha de
distintas posiciones vitales, sino mostración dramática de sólo una
de ellas: la antiquilosada, decrépita, falta de vitalidad, condenada
ya irremisiblemente" [There is no longer change or evolution, a
fight between different life positions, but a dramatic demonstration
of only one of them: the decayed, decrepit lack of vitality, a vitality
now irredeemably condemned].[4] The characters may be trapped to
all appearances, in a sordid ritual rooted in the decay of the society
to which their family belonged, but they are surviving, they have
seen through the ritual nature of their life and turned it to their
benefit, for they play the games in full knowledge of all the rules.
They need the games, they need each other, and game-playing is the
space for invention and renewal: the assuming of the ludic quality of
life is their saving grace. As in the case of all these old characters,
redundancy in life is counteracted by a strong inner life that simul-
taneously provides optimism and anguish.

One of the outstanding impressions in these plays is of massive
marginalization. There is no work; therefore the male role is undermined, young people are silent, old people who belong to a subversive past are ostracized and silenced, many are exiled, the family
disintegrates. The stage is populated by the losers in a society in
which the dominant social preoccupation of the winners is to keep

the losers in their place. And nothing seems to happen. The conflict seems to have gone from the stage, and in this prolonged suspension it is the inner life of the protagonists that is most important, the space in which they remember, plan, fantasize, create alternatives.

In the plays about power and, to a lesser extent, throughout the rest of the drama, we have seen that language is infinitely malleable, and as such is a weak weapon of dissent when used by itself. If the regime talks of the old and the new, the opposition talks of the new and the old, if the regime talks of war and peace, of freedom and enslavement, so does the opposition. Isolated words can be manipulated, violated, and so the power of theater lies in its use of visual and contextual imagery as well as words.

The lower sectors on stage play an important role in this context. The use of Chilean slang is one of the best expressions of dissent through language; it is a language of its own, inventive, ever-changing, beyond the comprehension of many people. It is the antithesis of the clinical language of political propaganda with its clear-cut images and adherence to worn out key words—freedom,peace, prosperity, modernization. The Chilean slang on stage in the seventies and eighties is far richer and far more representative of colloquial speech than any slang of the sixties; it is full of almost impenetrable images, of cruel humor, it is a language expressive of a different approach to and experience of life, both of which transcend the barrier of 1973. This is best expressed in Radrigán's work, where the dialogues act as transcriptions of the language of the people he best knows. But in the plays about work, for example, the election of working-class people, of shanty town dwellers, and of the lumpen and their language is a conscoius attempt to subvert the dominant social order through visual and linguistic means.

One of the other overwhelming characteristics of Chilean theater in this period is the impression of stagnation. Characters feel they can do little to change their immediate circumstances, and in some cases they may do nothing at all. The present and the future are no longer a simple continuation of the past: the present is empty and the future looms as a worthless repetition of the present. This suspension of time is filled with "palabrería," with story-telling, games, remembering. The memories form a touchstone for a sense of identity, they contrast with the image of a period of depression and disintegration, and they invariably act as a sign of an alternative to the contemporary state of society. If the reasons for the characters' immobility, their lack of purpose, and the senselessness of their existence are not explained, it is because, generally, that is not necessary, for the other codes and references to contemporary circumstances inevitably place the drama in the present period and indicate the cause of the protagonists' state.

This lack of conflict can be interpreted, in the initial period, as a safeguard against censorship, since it would have been impossible on stage to give the oppressive antagonist his true identity. On one level this would seem to be an idle preoccupation, for in the context of the recent history of the country and, more specifically, with a knowledge of the history and therefore the broad political allegiances of groups with a longer history (Ictus, Imagen, La Feria), the identity of the off-stage antagonist is blatantly obvious. Furthermore, naming the protagonist would add an artistically unwelcome political note to plays that, while being testimony, did aim at a greater understanding of the deeper preoccupations of the protagonists, at examining and creating visions and perceptions of the effects of authoritarianism. Even when censorship became more selective, the off-stage antagonist was still "anonymous."

While the antagonist is absent from the stage, his presence is constantly evoked in terms of the codes, of the sirens, sounds of helicopters, of bombs, that shatter the protagonists' peace and intrude into the make-believe world of the theater. The lack of conflict on stage is countered in this way by references to the real, suspended, conflict in society, the conflict of the winners against the losers. The sirens, bombs, and intrusions are the voice of the unnamed antagonist whose society is essentially unjust, violent, and, in its continued stagnation, increasingly cruelly absurd.

When *Todo una vida* begins, Don Eustaquio's words are heard in the dark, divorced from the environment in which he lives and from his identity as a deranged old man. They are received as a part of the audience's general experience of real life: when they hear, "cayó el general," taboo words expressive of a real hope, the audience will feel uneasy, Don Eustaquio will be perceived as an intruder into the facade of conformity. An atmosphere of tension is created, temporarily the illusion of theater is broken down, but this is relieved as the lights come up on the stage and the "madness" is revealed. This is repeated throughout. Don Eustaquio is gifted with seemingly unbounded energy: he may seem to be asleep, or "clavado," but he awakes shouting, and the respite and lapse into present-day normality is shortlived. These lapses are interspersed with what are the most common images of contemporary Chile, the images of rampant consumerism, the loss of human values of community, the importance of appearances. These are the codes that create a complicity between audience and actors against those that have created a society for which both parties in the theater feel extreme distaste.

Yet, while this may provide an illusion of opposition, of the lost community of political thought, is it not rendered less meaningful by the knowledge that the actor on stage, playing the role of a demented old man, may be allowed to shout "cayó el general" so that the regime may point to the group and ask, "So there is no freedom of expression in Chile?" Without another level of meaning, the performance would be a futile exercise; it would be a way of conforming to the regime's image of the clean and free paradise it has created. It would become part of the facade so many plays have sought to uncover. So, the allusions to the consumer society that are present in almost all the plays studied, the noises of war that can be heard beyond the confines of the enclosed and isolated spaces where the characters live out their "insignificant" existences, become part of a system of codes that, in a perverted way, conform to and bolster the false image of the construction of a free and democratic society. But this is not the case. For, while this may weaken the strength of overtly political phrases as opposition pure and simple, the fact remains that these are part of a script that still stands as an expression of the wish of both actors and audience that, for example, the general will fall. Like language, whose words are finally the only words available, the signs, symbols, and codes are employed as an integral part of subjective portrayals of society, and they are part and parcel of the complicity between group and audience.

The capacity of theater to adapt and its resilience as an art of immediate communication with a public hungry for a means, even only symbolic, of expressing some form of dissent, has been great throughout this whole period. If the fact that the role of the theater in Chile has been socially defined for a long period meant that it was subject to the dictates of the social and political environment, this has not seriously restricted the range of expression experienced, for Chilean theater since the forties, with its ups and downs and many crises, has been a diverse and revealing reflection of society. It is its constant applicability to the age and the timeliness of some of its best plays that have made it an important form of artistic and cultural expression. Over the whole period studied, the major preoccupation has been to reflect on society, it has encompassed the quest for "chilenidad." And in recent years there has been a pervasive sense of suspension of action, of marginality and of stagnation in the face of a conflict against an "invisible" antagonist. Yet, transcending this there has been a constant study of the inner self of the individual, where hope and renewal may lie, where the regime cannot penetrate, and through whose expression and externalization theater finds its strength as an art form.

Notes

Introduction

1. Juan Andrés Piña, *Seminario: situación y alternativas del teatro nacional en la década del '80* (Santiago: CENECA, 1983), p. 40.

Chapter 1

1. Exhaustive accounts of the birth of the university theaters can be found in Julio Durán Cerda, "El teatro chileno de nuestro días," in *Teatro chileno contemporáneo: Selección y prólogo de Julio Durán Cerda* (México City: Editorial Aguilar, 1970), pp. 9–57; Elena Castedo Ellerman, *El teatro chileno de mediados del siglo XX* (Santiago: Editorial Andrés Bello, 1982); Teodosio Fernández, *El teatro chileno contemporáneo* (Madrid: Editorial Playor, 1982); Carlos Ochsenius, *Teatros universitarios: 1940–1973* (Santiago: CENECA, 1982); Jorge Sánchez V., "A cuarenta y un años del teatro experimental", *Atenea* 446 (1982), p. 151; Rebeca Torres Rivera, "El teatro chileno desde 1941 hasta 1981" (Ph.D. thesis, University of California, Riverside, 1983).
2. Carlos Miguel Suárez Radillo, "El teatro chileno actual y la influencia de las universidades como sus fuerzas propulsoras," *Revista Interamericana de Bibliografía* 22, no. 1 (1972), p. 18–29.
3. Ricardo A. Latcham, "Psicología del caballero chileno," in *El carácter chileno*, Hernán Godoy ed. (Santiago: Editorial Universitaria, 1976), p. 372. The article was originally published in the *Revista Indice* 1, no. 4 (1930).
4. Hernán Godoy, *La cultura chilena: Ensayo de síntesis y de sociología* (Santiago: Editorial Universitaria, 1984). See Chapter 10, "La hegemonía mesocrática y las corrientes modernas 1903–1950," pp. 491–532.
5. See Mariana Aylwin et. al., *Chile en el siglo XX* (Santiago: Ediciones Emisión, 1985), p. 213.
6. Hugo Montes and Julio Orlandi, *Historia y antología de la literatura chilena* (Santiago: Editorial del Pacífico, 1965), p. 287.
7. In the first decades of the century, there had been a large amount of drama, often written by people who were journalists, poets, novelists. A few names stand out from the period, however, namely, Eduardo Barrios (1884–1936), Antonio Acevedo Hernández (1886–1962), Armando Moock (1894–1942) and German Luco Cruchaga (1894–1936). Luco Cruchaga was a costumbrist dramatist who, in plays like *La viuda de Apablaza*, provided deeper psychological studies of rural life than the ordinary costumbrist. The other three are best described by Durán Cerda: "Eduardo Barrios nos descubrió la burguesía santiaguina, Acevedo Hernández hace lo propio con los sectores más desposeídos; Armando Moock, con su agilidad de virtuoso de la escena, nos muestra la aldea chilena y luego ambientes más refinados." See Julio Durán Cerda, *Panorama del teatro chileno 1841–1959*

(Estudio crítico y antología) (Santiago: Editorial del Pacífico, 1959), p. 62. For a comprehensive review of theater in Chile since independence, see Raúl Silva Castro, *Panorama literario de Chile* (Santiago: Editorial Universitaria, 1961), pp. 394–432.

8. Julio Durán Cerda, "Actuales tendencias del teatro chileno," *Revista interamericana de bibliografía* 13, no. 2, (1963), p. 166.

9. Julio Durán Cerda, "El teatro chileno de nuestros días," p. 14.

10. See Mario Cánepa Guzmán, *Historia del teatro chileno* (Santiago: Editorial Universidad Técnica del Estado, 1974), p. 179.

11. The wars in Europe brought other benefits to the Chilean arts. In 1940 the company Ballet de Kurt Joss visited the country, and by 1946 the Cuerpo de Ballet de la Universidad de Chile had been created with the involvement of some of the members of Ballets Joss. Also in 1940, in the "época brillante" in the universities, the Orquesta Sinfónica de Chile was founded (1941). See Hernán Godoy, *La cultura chilena,* pp. 508–14.

12. See Carlos Miguel Suárez Radillo, "El teatro chileno," p. 19.

13. For descriptions of these aims see Julio Durán Cerda, "El teatro chileno de nuestros días," pp. 17–23, and Jorge Sánchez V., "A cuarenta y un años del teatro experimental", p. 153.

14. Julio Durán Cerda, "El teatro chileno de nuestros días," p. 24.

15. Raúl Silva Castro, *Panorama literario de Chile,* p. 429. Other Chilean works to be mounted were, *Como en Santiago* (1875) by Daniel Barros Grez, *El tribunal de honor* (1877) by Daniel Caldera, *El jefe de la familia* (1858) by Alberto Blest Gana.

16. For further information on the generation of university dramatists, see María de la Luz Hurtado, "Teatro y sociedad chilena: La dramaturgia de la renovación universitaria entre 1950 y 1970," *Apuntes* 94 (1986).

17. See Teresa Cajiao Salas, *Temas y símbolos en la obra de Luis Alberto Heiremans* (Santiago: Editorial Universitaria, 1970), p. 173.

18. For information about Lucho Córdoba, see María de la Luz Hurtado, "Teatro y sociedad en la mitad del siglo XX: El Sainete," *Apuntes* 92 (1984), 39–47. Lucho Córdoba was well regarded as a director. In 1980, at the age of 78, he was asked to direct the vaudeville *Hotel Paradiso,* by Georges Feydeau, for the Teatro Nacional Chileno (ex-DETUCH). A year later he was called again, this time to direct the classical work *Lisistrata,* but he died soon after its debut. See Rebeca Torres Ribera, "El teatro chileno," pp. 183–84.

19. William Knapp Jones, "Chile's Drama Renaissance," *Hispania* 44 (1961), p. 94.

20. In 1961 of twenty-six plays produced twelve were of national origin, while in 1969 of the twenty-four produced this was the case of only six. While some plays attract audiences of more than sixty thousand, the average is much less than this, about ten thousand.

21. Orlando Rodríguez B., "Realidad y perspectivas del teatro chileno," *CEREN,* Centro de Estudios de la Realidad Nacional 2 (1970), p. 61.

22. Carlos Ochsenius, *Teatros universitarios: 1941–1973* (Santiago: CENECA, 1982), p. 138.

23. *Huaso* is the name given to the rural people of the central valley of Chile and is the adjective used to describe the form of Chilean they speak and all that pertains to them.

24. Hans Ehrmann, "Theatre in Chile: A Middle Class Conundrum," *The Drama Review* 14, no. 2 (1970), p. 83. He reports outrage from the Opus Dei,

attack on provincial tours, tear gas and stink bombs in Santiago on the opening night, demonstrations, masses to ask divine forgiveness (pp. 82–83). The play was a great success, with an audience of around 41,500. As the Pinochet regime learned, repression in the theater is often counterproductive. See also Louis P. Falino, "Theater Notes from Chile," *Latin American Theatre Review* 3, no. 2 (1970) 67–70.

25. The Christian Democratic government of Eduardo Frei undertook a land reform program, based on the *asentimiento*, "the transitory cooperative ownership of an expropriated estate until further transfer of the land to its workers." See Markos J. Mamalakis, *The Growth and Structure of the Chilean Economy: From Independence to Allende* (New Haven and London: Yale University Press, 1976), pp. 139–40. For the extreme left wing this was too slow, hence the comparison with 1934. See Mamalakis, *Growth and Structure*, pp. 236–37.

26. The title and the political moral taken from Ernesto "Ché" Guevara's *Pasajes de la guerra revolucionaria.* This play was intended as the university theater's contribution to the Popular Unity campaign. See Teodosio Fernández, *El teatro chileno*, pp. 115–16.

27. Raquel Cordero in interview with Edmundo Villarroel, "Expediente de jubilación para teatros universitarios," *El Mercurio*, 13 Nov. 1971.

28. "Un jardín no tan ideal," *Ahora*, 20 July 1971.

29. "Primer estreno DETUCH: El jardín de los cerezos," *Telecran* 23 (July 1971).

30. Domingo Piga T., "El teatro popular: Consideraciones históricas e ideológicas," in *Popular Theater for Social Change in Latin America*, Gerardo Luzuriaga ed. (Los Angeles: UCLA Latin American Publications, 1978), p. 9.

31. Sergio Vodanović, "Nos tomamos la universiad," in *Teatro* (Santiago: Editorial Universitaria, 1972), p. 74.

32. *Tomas* are illegal takeovers of land or factories. These escalated in the Allende years, taking on a dynamic that was beyond the control of the government. Experiences such as that of the Teatro Nuevo Popular were important indications of the way *tomas* had become autonomous from government control, for Teatro Nuevo Popular belonged to the more moderate Communist party and *tomas* were often organized by the Movimiento de Izquierda Revolucionario (MIR). Agitprop such as this fell on deaf ears.

33. Virginia Vidal, "Interesante experiencia: El Teatro Nuevo Popular," *El Siglo*, 18 May 1972.

34. In the Teatro de la Universidad de Concepción, a five-point program was organized: touring the region with new works, and reaching new audiences; introducing unknown Latin American drama; interdisciplinary research; a Taller Experimental to study new ways of representing the reality of workers of the south; and a program of monitors associated with the already established program of the Central Unica de Trabajadores (CUT).

35. "Acontecer penquista," *Ahora*, 13 Oct. 1971.

36. Orlando Rodríguez B., "Caminos nuevos en el Cuarto Festival Nacional del Teatro Aficionado e Independiente," *Apuntes* 14 (1961), pp. 1–5.

37. "Festival de Teatro Universitario-Obrero de la Universidad Católica" (Santiago: ANTACH Document, 1968).

38. 1968: Festival Universitario Obrero. 1969: Primera Convención Nacional de Teatro Aficionado. 1970: Primer Festival Regional de Teatro Popular in Greater Santiago; Primer Festival Nacional de Teatro Aficionado, Temuco; Segundo Festival Nacional de Trabajadores y Universitarios. 1971: Segundo Festival Nacional,

1972: Tercera Jornada Nacional de Teatro Nacional, Coquimbo. May 1973: Asamblea General de Coordinadores; Primer Festival de Sketches.

39. "Informe Evaluativo y Apreciativo: Jornada Nacional de Teatro de Trabajadores y Estudiantes, Provincia de Coquimbo" (Santiago: ANTACH Document, 1972).

40. Orlando, Rodríguez B., "Notas sobre el teatro actual y el teatro popular," Primera Convención de Teatro Aficionado (ANTACH, 1969).

41. See Domingo Piga T., "El teatro popular," p. 9.

42. Sergio Vodanović, "El teatro que hace falta," *Ahora*, 10 Aug. 1971.

43. Sergio Vodanović in "10 críticos," *Primer Acto* 161 (1973), p. 42.

44. See the discussion of the relationship between Jorge Díaz and Ictus in *Maneras de hacer y pensar el teatro en el Chile actual: Teatro Ictus*, María de la Luz Hurtado and Carlos Ochsenius (Santiago: CENECA, 1984), pp. 14–21. Also, José Monleón, "Diálogo con Jorge Díaz," *Primer Acto* 69 (1965), 32–37.

45. "La Manivela" was important in the development of Ictus since the rigorous television schedule contributed to the perfection of its method of collective creation and gave it access to a mass audience, calculated at 1.5 million.

46. See *Teatro Ictus*, p. 36.

47. Juan Andrés Piña, "El tema del trabajo humano en siete obras chilenas durante el autoritarismo" (Working paper, CENECA), p. 9.

48. See *"Las Criadas,"* by Cyrano, *Ultima Hora*, 12 May 1972, and *"Las sirvientas* escandalizan a Santiago," *Puro Chile*, 7 May 1972.

49. Alejandro Sieveking, "Teatro chileno antifascista," in *Primer coloquio sobre la literatura chilena (de la resistencia y el exilio)*, Poli Délano ed. (México: Editorial Universitaria Autónoma, 1980), p. 103.

50. María de la Luz Hurtado, *La dramaturgia chilena: 1960–1970* (Santiago: CENECA, 1983), p. 99.

51. "Aleph: Para atacar la injusticia y la frustración; para promover la lucha y la esperanza," in *El teatro Céspedes* ed. (La Habana: Casa de la Américas, 1978), pp. 381–87.

52. "Antídoto contra la tensión política," *Ercilla*, 21 Feb. 1973.

53. *Paula*, 21 Sept. 1973.

54. A quick glance at the titles gives an indication of the objects of their humor. Lucho Córdoba poked fun at the plight of the right wing, known as *momios* (mummies), in *¿Qué haremos con los momios?* (What shall we do with the mummies?, 1969) and at government bureaucracy in *No me atropelle soy de la UNCTAD* (Don't run me over, I'm from the UNCTAD, 1972). The UNCTAD is an ugly building in the center of Santiago built in 1970 for a meeting of the United Nations Committee for Trade and Development. It then became the Gabriela Mistral house of culture, and after the coup and the bombing of the presidential palace, La Moneda, it became the Diego Portales, the new seat of government. Américo Vargas conjured up images of comments on state intervention with *Cabezas intervenidas* by Max Regnier and Andrés Gillois, but although there were puns based on the overuse of "intervenir" and "interventor," the play had nothing to do with the Chilean political situation. See *"Cabezas Intervenidas," Plan*, 31 May 1973.

55. " 'Full' de público en el teatro," *El Mercurio*, 15 April 1973.

56. Hans Ehrmann, "Chilean Theater 1971–73," *Latin American Theatre Review* 7, no. 2 (1974), p. 43.

57. Sergio Vodanović in "10 críticos," p. 42.

58. *La Revolución Chilena y los Problemas de la Cultura*, p. 6. Political document. No author. No date.

59. "Otra vez con Jorge Díaz," *Primer Acto* 153 (1973), p. 60.

60. Alejandro Foxley, *Latin American Experiments in Neo-Conservative Economics* (Berkeley, Los Angeles, and London: University of California Press, 1983), p. 1.

61. Ibid., p. 15.

62. Jorge Edwards, "Books in Chile," *Index on Censorship,* no. 2 (1984), pp. 20–23. One of the favorite examples of the absurd nature of book burning is the banning of a book on Cubism for fear that it had to do with the Cuban Revolution.

63. "¿Un teatro sin autores?" *Las Ultimas Noticias,* 27 Dec. 1973. According to figures provided by the actors' trade union, SIDARTE, about 25 percent of actors went into exile and around 90 percent were unemployed immediately after the coup.

64. Juan Andrés Piña, "La vuelta a los clásicos," *Mensaje* 239 (1975), p. 264.

65. Juan Andrés Piña, "El boom de los clásicos," *Mensaje* 153 (1976), pp. 256–58.

66. Juan Andrés Piña, "La vuelta a los clásicos," p. 263.

67. "Orfeo y el desodorante o el último viaje a los infiernos," in *No son farsas: Cinco anuncios dramáticos* (Santiago: Editorial Universitaria, 1974), p. 66.

68. The best examples have been *The Fiddler on the Roof,* presented by the Casino las Vegas, and *Cabaret Bijou* by Tomas Vidella, both of which had over 120,000 spectators.

69. María de la Luz Hurtado and Carlos Ochsenius, "Transformaciones del teatro chileno en la década del setenta," in *Teatro chileno de la crisis institucional 1973–1980 (Antología crítica)* eds. María de la luz Hurtado, Carlos Ochsenius and Hernán Vidal. Santiago: CENECA and University of Minnesota Latin American Series, 1982, p. 31.

70. "Teatro chileno antifascista," p. 109.

71. See Ariel Dorfman, "El teatro en los campos de concentración: Entrevista a Oscar Castro," *Araucaria de Chile* 6 (1979), pp. 115–46.

72. José Rodríguez Elizondo, "¿Dónde está la 'cuestión social'?" *La Quinta Rueda,* December 1972, pp. 12–13.

73. The members of Ictus voiced this opinion in a program for the BBC. See Edward Goldwyn, "Chile's Forbidden Dreams: 'Dictatorship Is Not a Political Problem but a Human Problem,'" *The Listener,* 7 June 1984, p. 9.

74. "The Theatre in Chile: Before the Coup and After," *Theatre Quarterly* 5, no. 20 (1976), pp. 103–7. See also Sergio Céspedes, "Theater in the Concentration Camps of Chile," *Theatre Quarterly* 6, no. 24 (1976–77), pp. 13–21.

75. ACU was formed in the University of Chile in 1977, originally with the name, Agrupación Folklórica Universitaria. It aimed to group workshops of different creative arts and survived until about 1982 when, with the graduation of its founding members, it began to disintegrate. See Beatriz Duque Videla and María Verónica García Huidobro Valdés, "El teatro aficionado universitario chileno (1968–1983): Un teatro alternativo," Tesis de Título, Escuela de Teatro, Pontíficia Universidad Católica de Chile, 1983, pp. 37–40.

76. See "ACU: El teatro universitario de hoy," in *Seminario del teatro Chileno de la década del 80,* María de la Luz Hurtado and Carlos Ochsenius eds. (Santiago: CENECA, 1980), pp. 176–78.

77. See "El teatro aficionado universitario chileno (1968–1983): Un teatro alternativo," p. 9.

78. "Los estragos del IVA," *Hoy,* 14 Jan. 1981.

79. "Suspensión de obra teatral provoca polémica en la Universidad Católica," *La Segunda,* 28 June 1978.

80. "Cerrada ovación recibió estreno de *Lo crudo, lo cocido y lo podrido,*" *Tercera de la Hora,* 30 Oct. 1978.

81. The bilingual institutes played an important role in providing support for theater and cultural groups after the coup.

82. See *Maneras de hacer y pensar el teatro en el Chile actual: Teatro Imagen,* María de la Luz Hurtado and José Roman (Santiago: CENECA, 1980), p. 24. Chilean theater was ostracized from the international theater community until 1980, when it was reintegrated into the International Theater Institute after five years absence.

83. See *Maneras de hacer y pensar el teatro en el Chile actual: Teatro La Feria,* María de la Luz Hurtado and Carlos Ochsenius (Santiago: CENECA, 1979).

84. "*Hojas de Parra:* Despues del café-teatro el teatro circopoesía," *En Cronista,* 20 Feb. 1977.

85. "Temporal desata *Hojas de Parra,*" *Las Ultimas Noticias* 1 March 1977.

86. Padre Alberto Hurtado was well known for his left-wing ideas and for his support of the Popular Front Government of Pedro Aguirre Cerda. He had a great influence among the Catholic youth of the country and became the Asesor Nacional para los Jóvenes de la Acción Católica. In his book *¿Es Chile un país católico?* he exposed the suffering of the poorest sectors of the community and called for true Christian values among those who professed the Catholic faith. One of his most lasting achievements was the founding of the Hogar de Cristo, a charity that runs homes for the elderly.

87. "Los directores ponen nota," *El Mercurio,* 29 Dec. 1976.

Chapter 2

1. All references will be made to the following editions: *Pedro, Juan y Diego,* manuscript; *Los payasos de la esperanza, Apuntes* 84 (1978), 27–80; *Tres Marías y una Rosa,* in María de la Luz Hurtado, Carlos Ochsenius and Hernán Vidal, *Teatro chileno de la crisis institucional,* pp. 196–248. See glossary at the end of the book for unfamiliar terms or chileanisms in the quotations from the plays.

2. *Chile: Series estadísticas, 1981* (Santiago: Instituto Nacional de Estadísticas, INE) p. 49. The sectors worst hit were building and manufacturing.

3. See Patricio Frías, "Cesantía y estrategias de supervivencia," Documento de Trabajo, 1977, FLACSO, Santiago.

4. To be eligible for this scheme, a person has to be the head of a family or the principal breadwinner, resident in a local authority *(comuna),* and provide proof of unemployment. The wage is one-third of the national minimum. At the time in which *Pedro, Juan y Diego* is set, the number employed in the scheme in Greater Santiago had risen from 4,748 in April 1975 to 31,572 in April 1976; it had taken on a more permanent nature, was incorporating more highly qualified people, and the beneficiaries worked a full working week instead of the original fifteen hours. See *Series Estadísticas* and Patricio Frías, "Cesantía," p. 30.

5. The Church played an increasingly important role in the years following the coup. As early as October 1973 the Catholic, Protestant, and Jewish communities set up the "Comité para la Paz en Chile," whose aim it was to provide legal and economic support for political prisoners and their families. In 1975, however, Pinochet demanded its dissolution, and the work performed was taken over by the "Vicaría de la Solidaridad," a Church organization that provides "legal and health services, manage(s) between 40 and 50 farm cooperatives in rural areas and

support(s) soup kitchens for 113,000 adults and children in major urban areas."
See Hernán Rosencrantz, "The Church in Chilean Politics: The Confusing Years",
Chile After 1973: Elements for the Analysis of Military Rule, D. E. Hojman, ed., p.
79. Liverpool: Centre for Latin American Studies, 1985.

    6. See María de la Luz Hurtado and Carlos Ochsenius, *Taller de Investigación
Teatral,* (Santiago, CENECA, 1979) p. 14.

    7. *Teatro La Feria,* p. 38.

    8. *Teatro Ictus,* p. 117.

    9. In so-called middle-class drama of the sixties walls, high partitions, divisions abound as the protagonists try to protect themselves from the perceived imminence of popular revolution. See Wolff, Vodanović, Díaz.

    10. See Benjamín Subercaseaux, *Chile o una loca geografía,* 16th ed. (Chile: Editorial Universitaria, 1973). This is but one of the many interpretations of the meaning of the name *Chile.*

    11. Taller de Investigación Teatral, p. 13.

    12. Ibid, p. 15.

    13. I refer here specifically to the Centro de Madres, CEMA Chile, a government-funded scheme run by the Secretaría Nacional de la Mujer under the direction of the president's wife, Lucía de Pinochet. The shops where these interpretations of popular culture are sold have a strict hierarchy and all creations are regulated to comply with the official version of the progress the country is making now that it is out of the hands of Marxist rule. They demand scenes of social equality and picturesque costumbrism.

    14. The women work in workshops or *talleres,* each one part of a centrally organized network and each one developing different themes, defined as religious, "vivenciales" or traditional. After realizing that the workshops were becoming a permanent, rather than a temporary, feature of life in certain sectors, "controles de calidad" were created and the commercial market for the work, especially abroad, was exploited more fully. See Cecilia Moreno Aliste, *La Artesanía Urbana Marginal* (Santiago: CENECA, 1984).

    15. Dagmar Raczynsci and Claudia Serrano, "La cesantía: Impacto Sobre la Mujer y Familia Popular," *CIEPLAN* 14 (1984), pp. 94–95.

    16. Ibid., p. 71.

    17. Marjorie Agosín, "Agujas que hablan: Las arpilleristas Chilenas," *Revista Iberoamericana* 132–33 (1985), p. 251.

    18. A *caracol* (literally snail) is a shopping arcade built in a spiral shape, the inner rim of which opens onto a central well while the outer is formed by rings of shops and boutiques.

    19. "Fondas bien endieciochás" refers to the fairs set up all over the country by local communities to celebrate the national independence day, 18 Sept.

    20. *El último tren* by Gustavo Meza and Imagen in *Teatro chileno de la crisis institucional,* pp. 102–38.

    21. The name Marcial Contreras is deliberately reminiscent of the name of the former head of the secret police, DINA (Dirección Nacional de Inteligencia). Manuel Contreras. Despite the fact that the Christian name is changed, his role as personification of the economy is underlined by a name that leaves no doubt as to his military connections.

    22. *Taller de Investigación Teatral,* p. 19.

Chapter 3

1. All references to plays will be to the following editions: *Una pena y un cariño*, in *Teatro Chileno de la Crisis Institucional: 1973–1980 (Antología Crítica)*, pp. 308–39; *Baño a baño*, id., pp. 287–305; *Lo crudo, lo cocido y lo podrido*, id., pp. 250–86.

2. See *Teatro La Feria*, pp. 17–18.

3. "En Orden y Paz Chile Avanza," is one of the most common and most visible of the regime's propaganda posters all over Chile.

4. See Joan E. Garcés, *Allende y la experiencia chilena: Las armas de una política* (Barcelona-Caracas-México: Editorial Ariel, 1976), pp. 391–92. The specific statement to which these images refer is: "Sigan ustedes sabiendo que, mucho más temprano que tarde, se abrirán las grandes alamedas por donde pase el hombre libre para construir una sociedad mejor."

5. Graham Greene has described Pinochet as "the greatest character actor of them all." He describes Pinochet's presence at the signing of the Panama Canal Treaty in 1977: "Like Boris Karloff, he really had attained the status of instant recognition: he was the one who could look down with amused contempt at the highly paid frivolous Hollywood types below him. His chin was so deeply sunk in his collar that he seemed to have no neck at all; he had clever, humorous, falsely good-fellow eyes which seemed to be telling us not to take too seriously all those stories of murder and torture emanating from South America. . . . Like Karloff he didn't have a speaking part—he didn't even have to grunt." See *Getting to Know the General: The Story of an Involvement* (London: Bodley Head, 1984), pp. 121–22.

6. All this echoes feelings of frustration and impotence in real life, when new outrages perpetrated by the security forces are denied in full knowledge that the denials of blame are transparently false. This kind of dismay and disbelief was witnessed after the murder of three Communist party leaders in March 1985, and the subsequent investigations that implicated high ranking members of the carabineros, the military police. In what is a graphic illustration of the distribution of power and the laying of blame, the head of the *carabineros* General Mendoza, resigned as a result of this incident.

7. El Restorán de los Inmortales is modeled on a famous old traditional restaurant in Santiago called El Torres, from where even the stage props for the play were borrowed. The walls of the restaurant El Torres, which was founded in 1879, bear inscriptions such as that quoted here.

8. Gerald Mars and Michael Nicod, *The World of Waiters* (London: George Allen & Unwin, 1984), p. x, 2.

9. Frederick B. Pike, "Aspects of Class Relations in Chile," *Hispanic American Historical Review* 43 (1963), p. 22. The most recent example of this use of serving classes is to be found in José Donoso's allegorical and, unusually for him, overtly political novel, *Casa de campo* (Barcelona: Seix Barral, 1978). Set in a country mansion belonging to a large aristocratic family, it is an allegory for the Popular Unity period and the breakdown of democracy. An excellent description of the plot and study of the novel's allegorical potential can be found in Pamela Bacarisse, "Donoso and Social Commitment: *Casa de campo*," *Bulletin of Hispanic Studies*, 60, no. 4 (1983), 319–32. It is interesting to quote from her description of the role of the servants, which can also be applied to the waiters: "The great discipline of their lives leads to a loss of individual identity on their part: they seem to be interchangeable. . . . They do not constitute an undivided group and

. . . they are afraid of those above them and impressed by their own clandestine power. They are ultimately proved to be inflexibly conservative and strongly attached to the social hierarchy which exploits them, as well as showing themselves to be dedicated to puritan values. . . . Individuals are forgotten—in fact the *mayordomos* have no individual personality—but the uniform is eternal" (p. 322).

10. See Paul Ilie, "Dictatorship and Literature: The Model of Francoist Spain," *Ideologies and Literature* 4, no. 17 (1983), p. 253.

11. Ibid.

12. It has not gone unnoticed that the character of Eliana is reminiscent of that of La Japonesita in José Donoso's short novel *El lugar sin límites* (Barcelona: Editorial Euros, 1975). Hernán Vidal has pointed to the fact that they are both the "accidents of homosexual fathers." See Hernán Vidal, "Teatro chileno profesional reciente," in *Teatro chileno de la crisis institucional*. But more significant is the climate in which each one is brought up. La Japonesita was born as a result of a bet by which her mother, La Japonesa Grande, would win the ownership of her brothel from the local landlord if she could make love with a transvestite dancer. At the time of the novel, La Japonesita, born and bred among prostitutes, is the virgin madam of her mother's brothel. The old order associated with the landowning classes who frequented the brothel in former days is dying out, the town is backward, chronically underdeveloped, business is almost nonexistent. La Japonesita shares a sterile legacy with Eliana, for the latter, born and bred among waiters, cannot belong to *la garzonería secreta;* she has no useful role to play. Furthermore, they both introduce a strain of ambiguity into the environment to which they belong, both as a result of their origin, and their dubious role. Both are the sad remnants of a past age.

13. Agustín Letelier, *"Lo crudo, lo cocido y lo podrido,"* *El Mercurio,* 28 July 1985.

14. Translated into Spanish as *El pupilo quiere ser tutor* in *Primer Acto* 131. References here will be to *No +*, *Apuntes, Revista de Teatro* 93 (1985), 171–204.

15. See in *Krítica* 17 (1985), "Graffiti" by P. Brodsky, pp. 37–39, and "Por qué soy un rayado," pp. 21–23. Note that "rayar" is the word used to refer to the painting of graffiti. "Rayado" is, furthermore, slang for mad.

16. See introduction to *No +*, "Obra *No +*," Apuntes 93 (1985), p. 168.

17. References will be to the manuscript of the work. *La mar estaba serena* was written by Ictus in collaboration with Sergio Vodanović and Carlos Genovese.

18. See "La obra que nació de una consulta psiquiátrica al revés," *El Mercurio,* 27 Oct. 1978.

19. Jacqueline Eyring Bixter, "Games and Reality on the Latin American Stage," *Latin American Literary Review* 12 (1984), p. 26.

Chapter 4

1. As a result of the popularity of Radrigán's work, an edition of his eleven plays to 1984 was published. All references will be to *Teatro de Juan Radrigán: 11 obras* (Santiago: Editorial Universitaria, 1984). In 1984 he presented *Las voces de la ira,* in 1985. *Made in Chile,* in 1986, *Los borrachos de luna* and *Pueblo de mal amor,* and in 1988, *La contienda humana.*

2. See Pedro Bravo Elizondo, "El dramaturgo de *Los olvidados:* Entrevista con Juan Radrigán," *Latin American Theatre Review* 17, no. 1 (1983), p. 61.

3. Agustín Letelier, *"Los borrachos de luna* de Juan Radrigán," *El Mercurio,* 17 Aug. 1986.

4. Juan Radrigán in interview. See Rosario Guzmán B., "Juan Radrigán, el mejor dramaturgo de 1982," *El Mercurio Internacional*, 20–26, Jan. 1983, p. 7.

5. *"Testimonio de las muertes de Sabina," El Mercurio*, 2 Apr. 1979.

6. "Juan Radrigán, el mejor dramaturgo de 1982."

7. Ibid.

8. Agustín Letelier, *"Los borrachos de luna* de Juan Radrigán."

9. *Redoble fúnebre para lobos y corderos* (1981) consists of *Isabel desterrada en Isabel, Sin motivo aparente,* and *El Invitado.*

10. See Patrick Brantlinger, *Bread and Circuses: Theories of Mass Culture as Social Decay* (Ithaca and London: Cornell University Press, 1983), p. 23.

11. AFP, Administradora de Fondos de Provisión. These are firms that administer privately the social security system.

12. "Borrachera de luna para quedar limpios," *El Mercurio*, 1 Aug. 1986. An interview with Juan Radrigán.

13. This is quoted from an unpublished article by the author, "Fragmentos contra el olvido" (Hamburg, 1988).

Chapter 5

1. "Pinochet opens doors for some exiles," *Latin American Regional Report*, 19 Nov. 1982, p. 4. *La Segunda* is a Santiago daily newspaper.

2. "Como medida de unidad: Gobierno revisará la situación de exiliados," *El Mercurio Internacional*, 21–27 Oct. 1982.

3. *El Mercurio Internacional*, 13–19 Jan. 1983.

4. See "El retorno de los exiliados: Un cruel juego propagandístico de Pinochet," *Chile-América* 84–85 (1983), pp. 84–85.

5. Jacqueline Baldran, "Entretien avec Oscar Castro (Grupo Aleph)," *Caravelle* 40 (1983), p. 171.

6. Carlos Cerda in interview, "Carlos Cerda, narrador: Chile y el exilio: dos mitades de silencio," *Apsi*, 3–9 April 1984, pp. 34–35.

7. Enrique Lihn, letter addressed to the Primer Encuentro de Poesía Chilena en Rotterdam 1983, in *LAR: Revista de literatura* 2–3 (1984), p. 6.

8. Mario Benedetti, *Primavera con una esquina rota* (México: Nueva Imagen, 1982), p. 104.

9. All references will be to the manuscript of *José*, 1980.

10. Pedro Bravo Elizondo, "Reflexiones de Egon Wolff en torno al estreno de *José*," *Latin American Theatre Review* 14, no. 2 (1981), p. 68.

11. *¿Cuántos años tiene un día?*, in *Teatro Chileno de la crisis institucional*, pp. 139–95.

12. References to *Primavera con una esquina rota* will be to the edition of the novel quoted above. The complete manuscript of the work was not available, but the study here refers to the play, since it deals only with those scenes from the novel that were adapted for the stage.

13. This is taken from the program of the production.

14. The effect of the double deceit of an adult actress playing a child—in whose mouth the evils of dictatorshp, imprisonment, and exile were expressed—was a major success of this production.

15. This is all the more significant, for, while there were fears of massive electoral fraud in both cases, the Uruguayans still had a No vote, and the Yes vote was seen in Chile as a major propaganda coup for Pinochet.

16. All references will be to the manuscript of the play, dated 1984. There has been, however, a publication of the text, *Regreso sin causa* (Santiago: Sinfronteras, 1986).

17. Myre Silva Labarca, "Mujeres chilenas exiliadas: Procesos de transformación ideológica y de comportamiento," *Chile-America*, 74–75 (1981), pp. 46–47.

18. "Mujeres chilenas exiliadas," p. 45.

19. Liliana Muñoz, "Exile as bereavement: Socio-psychological manifestations of Chilean exiles in Great Britain," *British Journal of Medical Psychology* 53 (1980), p. 231.

20. José Donoso, *El jardín de al lado* (Barcelona: Seix Barral, 1981), p. 52.

Chapter 6

1. See *Toda una vida* by Marco Antonio de la Parra, a sketch from the Ictus production *Lindo país esquina con vista al mar* (1979), p. 11. All references will be to the manuscript.

2. I have borrowed this idea from Teodosio Fernández, *El teatro chileno contemporáneo* (Madrid: Editorial Playor, 1982).

3. Frank Dauster, "Concierto para tres: *Kindergarten* y el teatro ritual," *Caravelle* 40 (1983), p. 14.

4. See Juan Andrés Piña, "Egon Wolff: El teatro de la destrucción y la esperanza," in *Egon Wolff: Teatro—Niñamadre, Flores de Papel, Kindergarten* (Santiago: Editorial Nascimento, 1978), p. 30.

Glossary

The aim of this glossary is to provide a comprehensive listing of those terms and colloquialisms encountered in the plays studied in this book that may be unfamiliar to readers. Invariably spelling imitates pronunciation, so the variety of versions of the same word is huge. I have tried to provide as many variations as is possible. In the case of general variations and distortions of vowels, consonants and verb endings, the most common fall into the following categories: consonant changes, such as f>j (fuerte > juerte), h>g (huaso > güaso), b>gü (buenas > güenas), n>l (nos > los); the loss of the final d, as in usté, the loss of the intervocalic consonant as in todos>toos, sabe>sae, para>pa; vowel changes such as e>i, (cabrear>cabriar), and commonly the distortion of the dipthong ue, which becomes u as in cuestión > custión. In some cases the *voseo* is used (often vos becomes voh), and the second person singular of the verb is distorted, for example, tienes > tenís, sabes > sabís.

Many of the "chileanisms," especially in the theater of Juan Radrigán and the plays about work, belong to a closed lumpen slang and can often only be understood with reference to the context in which the term or word is used. In these cases I have repeated the relevant quotation and, when there is more than one meaning, I have given examples of the different usages.

AGACHAR EL MOÑO: Literally, to bow one's head, to defer or yield to authority. "También sé que puedo parecerte un iluso, o peor, un agachador de moño. . . . Pero una cosa es agachar el moño y otra, muy distinta, rendirse." (*¿Cuántos años tiene un día?* p. 192).

AGARRAR PAPA: To fall for something hook, line, and sinker. "Y parece que la gallá agarró papa y le tuvo fe porque lo seguían como moscas a la miel" (*El toro por las astas*, p. 328).

ALLEGADO/A: A person who has come to live with relatives as a result of homelessness, economic problems, and destitution. It is most commonly used in shanty towns, where people are worst hit by sudden homelessness and is supposed to be a temporary arrangement. The expression used then is "vivir allegado". "De que la fábrica quedó en estado de crisis económica vivimos allegados donde mi cuñada." (*Tres Marías y una Rosa*, p. 202).

AL TIRO: At once, immediately.

BALSUDO: A distortion of *bolsudo*, meaning stupid. In *El invitado*, *balsúo* is substituted for *tonto* in the popular expression, "tonto con ropa y todo," meaning ridiculous through and through. "Claro, eso es cierto: si no existiera el Colo Colo los diarios tendrían que salir con la mitá de las páginas en blanco. ¡Y son balsúos con ropa y too!" (*El invitado*, p. 258).

BOCHE: A row, noise.

CABEZAS DE PESCADO, HABLAR CABEZAS DE PESCADO: Absolute nonsense. "SABINA: . . . Soñé que me venía a ver. RAFAEL: ¿Qué te venían a ver? Pucha tiene que ser otra cuestión rara. Voh too el tiempo andái soñando puras cabezas de pescao. Unas veces ti'andan siguiendo y no podís correr, otras veces que te caí a un hoyo y no llegái nunca abajo. ¿Por qué no soñái que te sacái la polla gol mejor?" (*Testimonio de las muertes de Sabina*, p. 78).

CABREARSE, ESTAR CABREADO: To get angry, to be angry. The *e* is often distorted to become *i*, cabriar, cabriado.

CACHAR: (1) To catch the meaning of something. "Me gustaría recitarles el poema del payaso . . . ¡entero! Pa que cacharan la movía de lo que cuesta ser toni." (*Los payasos de la esperanza*, p. 56). (2) To catch someone out. "Me sirve pa que no cache que la pega era fácil." (*Informe para indiferentes*, p. 370).

CACHETEAR: To hit, beat. "¿Y usted don Rafael ¿promete solemnemente ante este altar sagrado no cachetearla . . . ?" (*Tres Marías y una Rosa*, p. 233).

CAMPANILLERO: Doorman-cum-lookout in a brothel. Antonio in *El toro por las astas*.

CURADO, CURAO: Drunk, drunkard.

CURARSE: To get drunk.

CHAMULLO: Waffle. (As noun)

CHASCON: Long-haired, by extension left-wing. "¡Porque me cargan estos chascones intelectuales, que se creen tan inteligentes y tan buenos!" (*José*, p. 31).

DAR BOLA: To play along with somebody's game in order to humor them.

EMBARRAR: To mess something up. "¡Así que yo nomás tengo la culpa? Si veíai que yo l'estaba embarrando teníai que haberte metío, teníai que haber apechugao." (*El invitado*, p. 274).

EMPANADA: A type of cooked pastie, made with minced beef and onion (more and more in poor areas the onion is becoming more of an ingredient than the meat) or cheese. A typical Chilean snack, usually eaten with wine.

ENCACHADO/A: Dressed smartly and of general good appearance.

ENTRABADO/A: Deep, well set. "DON CARLOS: No se vaya a mandar guardabajo no más. PEDRO: Pa eso la construí entrabá." (*Pedro, Juan y Diego*, p. 37).

FALLOS AL CALDO: Skin and bone.

GALLADA: Crowd. "MARILIN: ¿O sea, que la gallá se iba? EUSTAQUIO: La multitud desaparecía." (*Toda una vida*, p. 22).

GORRO/PONERLE EL GORRO A ALGUIEN: To cuckold. "¿Y usted, Don Rafael . . . promete solemnemente ante este altar sagrado . . . no ponerle el gorro?" (*Tres Marías y una Rosa*, p. 233).

HALLULLA: A bread bun, in the shape of a halo.

HUASO, GÜASO: A rural person from the central valley of Chile and the form of Castilian they use. As an adjective it applies to all that belongs to them. It also has connotations of vulgar, stupid, a simpleton.

HUEVADA: Usually pronounced and written either güevá or huevá. A stupid statement; a piece of nonsense. It also means a bad time, as in, "Yo he pasao por cualquier cantidá de güevás malas, he estao pa la cagá, pior que ahora, queriendo morirme . . ." (*Los payasos de la esperanza,* p. 49).

HUEVAS, GÜEVAS, COMO LAS GÜEVAS: Like shit. "¿Cómo le voy a poner que estoy bien si estoy como las huevas?" (*Pedro, Juan y Diego,* p. 15).

HUEVEAR: Variously güevear, güeviar. To fool around; to act or talk stupid.

HUEVON: Variously güevón, güeón, ón, or just, ó. Can mean fool, idiot, bastard, sod. Also used in familiar terms of address as an expletive.

IÑOR/A: Señor/a.

JUERA / AJUERA: Fuera / afuera.

JUERTE: Fuerte.

LESERA: A piece of nonsense.

LESO, SER LESO: To be stupid; HACERSE EL LESO: To act as if unaware of what is going on around you.

LOS: Nos.

LOTE: A whole bunch of, as in "un lote de payasos." (*Los payasos de la esperanza*).

LUQUIADA, LUQUIA: A look. From the English. "¿Te cachái subir al cielo y pegarse una luquiá p'abajo." (*Los payasos de la esperanza,* p. 68). Also luqui and luquiar.

MAESTRO CHASQUILLA: A jack of all trades. The typical one is Polo in Radrigán's *Informe para indiferentes.*

MANDAR A ALGUIEN DE ESPALDA EL LORO, MANDAR CAER DE ESPALDA EL LORO: To make someone step back in amazement; to step back in amazement.

MANDAR GUARDABAJO: To fall to pieces. See entry for ENTRABA.

MARRAQUETA: The most common type of bread, a type of batch.

MEJORA: Literally improvement. A house in a shanty town that has gradually been enlarged over the years.

MOMIO: A name given to people of right-wing tendencies.

PAGAR EL PATO: To pay the consequences, usually for someone else's mistakes or bad humor, to take the stick. "Llegas maniático y soy yo la que tiene que pagar el pato. ¡Soy yo la que tiene que aguantar!" (*Regreso sin causa,* p. 17).

PEGA: A job, work.

PIRCA: A wall.

ROJELIO: A pejorative term for a communist, a commie.

ROTO: A person of lower-class origins.

TAITA / TATA: Father. God when capitalized. Affectionate way of addressing a more senior man, whether a relative or not.

TORRANTE, ATORRANTE: Down and out.

TORTA: Money, dough.

UPELIENTO: A pejorative way of referring to someone who supported the Popular Unity government. It comes from the initials, UP (Unidad Popular). "Estuve a punto de tomarlo por upeliento y echarlo cagando" (*El último tren,* p. 111).

Bibliography

Plays Consulted

Aguirre, Isidora. *La pérgola de las flores*. Manuscript, 1960.

———. *Lautaro, Epopeya del pueblo Mapuche*. Santiago: Editorial Nascimento, 1982.

———. *Los papeleros*. In *El teatro actual latinoamericano,* edited by Carlos Solórzano, pp. 245–90. Mexico: Edicones de Andrea, 1972.

———. *Los que van quedando en el camino*. Santiago: Ediciones Mueller, 1970.

Benavente, David, and Ictus. *Pedro, Juan y Diego*. Manuscript, 1976.

Benavente, David, and Taller de Investigación Teatral. *Tres Marías y una Rosa, Teatro chileno de la crisis institucional 1973–1980 (Antología crítica),* edited by María de la Luz Hurtado, Carlos Ochsenius and Hernán Vidal, pp. 196–248. Santiago: CENECA and University of Minnesota Latin American Series, 1982.

Castro, Oscar. *La increíble y triste historia del General Peñaloza y del exiliado Mateluna*. Manuscript, 1976.

Cuadra, Fernando. *La familia de Marta Mardones. Mapocho* 24 (1977): 103–66.

Debesa, Fernando, *Mama Rosa*. Santiago: Editorial Universitaria, 1983.

Díaz, Jorge. *El velero en la botella y El cepillo de dientes*. Santiago: Editorial Universitaria, 1967.

———. *Topografía de un desnudo (Esquema para una indagación inútil). Obra en dos actos de caridad)*. Santiago: Editora Santiago, 1967.

Griffero, Ramón. *Antes del fin o Recuerdos del hombre con su tortuga*. Manuscript, 1982.

Guzmán Améstica, Juan. *El wurlitzer. Mapocho* 19 (1969): 119–75.

Meza, Gustavo, and Imagen. *El último tren*. In *Teatro chileno de la crisis institucional 1973–1980 (Antología crítica),* edited by María de la Luz Hurtado, Carlos Ochsenius and Hernán Vidal, pp. 102–38. Santiago: CENECA and University of Minnesota Latin American Series, 1982.

Miranda, Jaime. *Regreso sin causa*. Manuscript, 1985. See also *Regreso sin causa*. Santiago. Sinfronteras, 1986.

Morales, José Ricardo. *Orfeo y el desodorante o el último viaje a los infiernos*. In *No son farsas: Cinco anuncios dramáticos,* pp. 13–78. Santiago: Editorial Universitaria, 1974.

Parra, Marco Antonio de la. *La secreta obscenidad de cada día*. Manuscript, 1984.

———. *Lo crudo, lo cocido y lo podrido*. In *Teatro chileno de la crisis institucional 1973–1980 (Antología crítica),* edited by María de la Luz Hurtado, Carlos Ochsenius and Hernán Vidal, pp. 308–39. Santiago: CENECA and Minnesota Latin American Series, 1982.

————. *Toda una vida.* Manuscript, 1979.

Pineda, José, and Alejandro Sieveking. *Peligro a 50 metros, Apuntes* 70 (1968): 4–60.

Radrigán, Juan. *El teatro de Juan Radrigán (11 obras).* Santiago: CENECA and University of Minnesota, 1984.

————. *Los borrachos de luna.* Manuscript, 1986. See also *Pueblo del mal amor: Los borrachos de luna.* Santiago: Editorial Nuke Mapu, 1987.

Requena, María Asunción. Pan caliente. Apuntes 71 (1968).

————. *Chiloé, cielos cubiertos.* In *María Asunción Requena: Teatro*—Ayayema, Fuerte Bulnes, Chiloé, cielos cubiertos, pp. 202–93. Santiago: Editorial Nascimento, 1979.

Rivano, Luis. *Te llamabas Rosicler.* Santiago: Ediciones de la Librería de Luis Rivano, 1976.

Sharim Paz, Nissim. *Cuestionemos la cuestión.* Mapocho 20 (1970): 131–80.

Sieveking, Alejandro. *Animas de día claro.* In *Teatro contemporáneo: Teatro chileno.* Selection and prologue by Julio Durán Cerda, pp. 357–423. México: Aguilar, 1970.

————. *La mantis religiosa.* In *Tres obras de teatro: La remolienda, Tres tristes tigres, La mantis religiosa.* Santiago: Editorial Universitaria, 1974.

Silva, Jaime. *El evangelio según San Jaime.* Manuscript, 1970.

Taller de Investigación Teatral. *Los payasos de la esperanza. Apuntes* 84 (1978): 27–80.

————. *No +. Apuntes* 93 (1985): 171–204.

Teatro Aleph. *Erase una vez un rey. Conjunto* 21 (1974): 68–83.

Teatro Ictus. *¿Cuántos años tiene un día?* In *Teatro chileno de la crisis institucional 1973–1980 (Antología crítica),* edited by María de la Luz Hurtado, Carlos Ochsenius, and Hernán Vidal, pp. 139–95. Santiago: CENECA and University of Minnesota Latin American Series, 1982.

————. *La mar estaba serena.* Manuscript, 1980.

————. *Lindo país esquina con vista al mar.* Manuscript, 1979.

Teatro La Feria. *Una pena y un cariño.* In *Teatro chileno de la crisis institucional 1973–1980 (Antología crítica),* edited by María de la Luz Hurtado, Carlos Ochsenius, and Hernán Vidal, pp. 308–39. Santiago: CENECA and University of Minnesota Latin American Series, 1982.

Todas las colorinas tienen pecas. Tres actos de teatro basados en *Obra Gruesa de Nicanor Parra. Revista EAC* 2 (1970): 80–106.

Torres, Victor. *Una casa en Lota alto.* La Havana: Casa de las Américas, 1973.

Vadell, Jaime, and José Manuel Salcedo, with texts by Nicanor Parra. *Hojas de Parra.* Manuscript, 1977.

Vadell, Jaime, José Manuel Salcedo, and David Benavente. *Bienaventurados los pobres.* Santiago: Ediciones Aconcagua, 1978.

Vadell, Jaime, and Teatro La Feria. *A la Mary se le vio el Poppins.* Manuscript, 1981.

Vega, Jorge, Jorge Pardo, and Guillermo de la Parra. *Baño a baño.* In *Teatro chileno de la crisis institucional 1973–1980 (Antología crítica),* edited by María de la Luz Hurtado, Carlos Ochsenius, and Hernán Vidal, pp. 287–305. Santiago: CENECA and University of Minnesota Latin American Series, 1982.

Vodanović, Sergio. *Nos tomamos la universidad.* In *Teatro: Deja que los perros ladren y Nos tomamos la universidad,* pp. 73–133. Santiago: Editorial Universitaria, 1972.

Wolff, Egon. *El signo de Caín.* Santiago: Editorial Universitaria, 1971.

———. *José.* Manuscript, 1980.

———. *Kindergarten.* In *Egon Wolff: Teatro—Niñamadre, Flores de papel, Kindergarten,* pp. 204–280. Santiago: Editorial Nascimento, 1978.

La balsa de la Medusa. Apuntes, Número Especial (1984): 81–215.

———. *Los invasores.* In *Teatro contemporáneo: Teatro chileno,* edited by Julio Durán Cerda, pp. 131–209. México: Editorial Aguilar, 1970.

Chilean Theater

"Acontecer penquista." *Ahora,* 13 Oct. 1971.

Alba de América. Special issue on Latin American Theater. Vols. 7, 12, and 13 (1989).

"Antídoto contra la tensión política." *Ercilla,* 21 Feb. 1973.

Baldran, Jacqueline. "Entretien avec Oscar Castro (Grupo Aleph)." *Caravelle* 40 (1983): 69–77.

Boyle, Catherine. "From Resistance to Revelation: The Contemporary Theatre in Chile." *New Theatre Quarterly* 4, no. 15 (1988): 209–21.

———. "Images of Women in Contemporary Chilean Theatre." *Bulletin of Latin American Studies* 5, no. 2 (1986): 81–96.

Bravo Elizondo, Pedro. "El dramaturgo de los olvidados: entrevista con Juan Radrigán". *Latin American Theatre Review* 17, no. 1 (1983): 61–63.

———. "El teatro en Chile en la década del 70." *Araucaria de Chile* 13 (1981): 127–35.

———. "El teatro obrero en Chile: Algunos antecedentes." *Araucaria de Chile* 17 (1982): 99–106.

———. "Entrevista a Alejandro Sieveking." *Latin American Theatre Review* 21, no. 2 (1979): 55–59.

———. "Reflexiones de Egon Wolff en torno al estreno de *José*". *Latin America Theatre Review* 14, no. 2 (1981): 65–71.

———. "*Regreso sin causa:* Jaime Miranda y sus razones." *Latin American Theatre Review* 19, no. 2 (1986): 79–84.

Cánepa Guzmán, Mario. *El teatro obrero y social en Chile.* Santiago: Editorial Universitaria, 1971.

———. *Historia del teatro chileno.* Santiago: Editorial Universidad Técnica del Estado, 1974.

Castedo Ellerman, Elena. *El teatro chileno de mediados del siglo XX.* Santiago: Editorial Andrés Bello, 1982.

"Cerrada ovación recibió estreno de *Lo crudo, lo cocido y lo podrido.*" *Tercera de la Hora,* 30 Oct. 1978.

Céspedes, Sergio. "Theatre in the Concentration Camps of Chile." *Theatre Quarterly* 6, no. 24 (1976–77): 13–21.

Cruz-Luis, Adolfo. "Para atacar la injusticia y la frustracíon, para promover la lucha y la esperanza." In *Teatro latinoamericano de colección colectiva,* edited by Francisco Garzón Céspedes, pp. 381–87. La Havana: Casa de las Américas, 1978.

Dauster, Frank. "Concierto para tres: *Kindergarten* y el teatro ritual." *Caravelle* 40 (1983): 9–15.

Díaz, Jorge. "Reflections on the Chilean Theatre." *The Drama Review* 14, no. 2 (1970): pp. 84–86.

Dorfman, Ariel. "El teatro en los campos de concentración: Entrevista a Oscar Castro". *Araucaria de Chile* 6 (1979): 115–46.

Durán Cerda. "Actuales tendencias del teatro chileno." *Revista Interamericana de Bibliografía* 13, no. 2 (1963): 152–75.

———. "El teatro chileno de nuestros días." In *Teatro contemporáneo: Teatro chileno,* pp. 9–58. Mexico City: Editorial Aguilar, 1970.

———. *Teatro contemporáneo: Teatro chileno.* Mexico City: Editorial Aguilar, 1970.

Durán Cerda, Julio, ed. *Panorama del teatro chileno 1841–1959 (Estudio crítico y antología).* Santiago: Editorial del Pacífico, 1959.

Duque Videla, Beatriz, María Verónica García Huidobro Valdés. *El teatro aficionado universitario chileno (1968–1983): Un teatro alternativo.* Tesis de título, Escuela de Teatro. Pontificia Universidad Católica de Chile, 1983.

Ehrmann, Hans. "Chilean Theater 1970." *Latin American Theatre Review* 4, no. 2 (1971): 65–68.

———. "Chilean Theater 1971–73." *Latin American Theatre Review* 7, no. 2 (1974): 39–43.

———. "Theater in Chile: A Middle Class Conundrum." *The Drama Review* 14, no. 2 (1970): 77–83.

"El teatro que surgió del silencio," interview with Juan Radrigán. *Pluma y Pincel* 12 (1984): 34–35.

Falino, Luis P. "Theater Notes from Chile." *Latin American Theatre Review* 3, no. 2 (1970): 67–70.

Fernández, Teodosio. *El teatro chileno contemporáneo.* Madrid: Editorial Playor, 1982.

"Festival de Teatro Universitario-Obrero de la Universidad Católica." Santiago: ANTACH Document, 1970.

" 'Full' de público en el teatro." *El Mercurio,* 15 Apr. 1973.

Goldwyn, Edward. "Chile's Forbidden Dreams." *The Listener,* 7 June 1984: 8–9.

"*Hojas de Parra:* Después del café-teatro el teatro circo-poesía." *El Cronista,* 20 Feb. 1977.

Hurtado, María de la Luz. *La dramaturgia chilena: 1960–1970.* Santiago: CENECA, 1983.

———. "Teatro y sociedad en la mitad del siglo XX: El sainete". *Apuntes* 92 (1984): 39–47.

———. "Teatro y sociedad chilena: La dramaturgia de la renovación universitaria entre 1950 y 1970." *Apuntes* 94 (1986).

Hurtado, María de la Luz, and Giselle Munizaga. *Testimonios del teatro. 35 años en la Universidad Católica*. Santiago: Ediciones Nueva Universidad, 1980.

Hurtado, María de la Luz, and Carlos Ochsenius. *Maneras de hacer y pensar el teatro en el Chile actual: Taller de Investigación Teatral*. Santiago: CENECA, 1979.

———. *Maneras de hacer y pensar el teatro en el Chile actual: Teatro Ictus*. Santiago: CENECA, 1980.

———. *Maneras de hacer y pensar el teatro en el Chile actual: Teatro La Feria*. Santiago: CENECA, 1979.

———. "Transformaciones del teatro chileno en la década del '70." In *Teatro chileno de la crisis institucional 1973–1980 (Antología crítica)*, edited by María de la Luz Hurtado, Carlos Ochsenius, and Hernán Vidal, pp. 1–53. Santiago: CENECA and University of Minnesota Latin American Series, 1982.

Hurtado, María de la Luz, Carlos Ochsenius, and Hernán Vidal, eds. *Teatro chileno de la crisis institucional 1973–1980 (Antología crítica)*. Santiago: CENECA and University of Minnesota Latin American Series, 1982.

Hurtado, María de la Luz, and Juan Andrés Piña. "Los niveles de marginalidad en Radrigán." In *Teatro de Juan Radrigán*, pp. 5–37. Santiago: CENECA and University of Minnesota, 1984.

Hurtado, María de la Luz, and José Román. *Maneras de hacer y pensar el teatro en el Chile actual: Teatro Imagen*. Santiago: CENECA, 1980.

Hurtado, María de la Luz, and Loreta Valenzuela. "Teatro y sociedad en la mitad del siglo XX: El melodrama." *Apuntes* 91 (1983): 11–77.

Jofre, Manuel. "Carlos Cerda narrador: Chile y el exilio: dos mitades de silencio." *Apsi*, 3–9 Apr. 1984: 34–35.

Jones, Willis Knapp. "Chile's Drama Renaissance." *Hispania* 44 (1961): 89–94.

Letelier, Agustín. *"Lo crudo, lo cocido y lo podrido"*. *El Mercurio*, 28 July 1985.

———. *"Los borrachos de luna de Juan Radrigán."* *El Mercurio*, 17 Aug. 1986.

"Los directores ponen nota." *El Mercurio*, 29 Dec. 1976.

"Los estragos de la IVA." *Hoy*, 14 Jan. 1981.

Maldonado, Carlos. "Cuando el teatro es algo vivo." *La Quinta Rueda*, no number (1973).

Martin, Alex. "Directing Chile, the Southern Cross at the Sherman Theatre." *Theatre Quarterly* 6, no. 24 (1976–77): 21–25.

Monleón José. "Diálogo con Jorge Díaz." *Primer Acto* 69 (1965): 32–37.

———. "Otra vez con Jorge Díaz," *Primer Acto* 153 (1973): 59–66

Noguera, Héctor. "En torno a *La balsa de la Medusa*." *Apuntes*, Número Especial (1985); 65.

———. "Visión de teatro aficionado." *Apuntes* 84 (1978): 14–23.

Ochsenius, Carlos. *Expresión teatral poblacional*. Santiago: CENECA, 1983.

———. *Teatros universitarios: 1940–1973*. Santiago: CENECA, 1982.

Peden, Margaret S. "Three Plays of Egon Wolff." *Latin American Theatre Review* 3, no. 1 (1969): 29–35.

Piña, Juan Andrés. "Egon Wolff: El teatro de la destrucción y la esperanza". Prologue to *Egon Wolff: Teatro—Niñamadre, Flores de papel, Kindergarten*, pp. 7–33. Santiago: Editorial Nascimento, 1978.

———. "El boom de los clásicos." *Mensaje* 253 (1976): 256–58.

———. "El tema del trabajo en siete obras chilenas durante el autoritarismo. Santiago: CENECA, 1982.

———. "Entrevista con Nissim Sharim de Ictus: Las razones de una primavera." *Apsi,* 17–30 July 1984: 34–35.

———. "La vuelta a los clásicos." *Mensaje* 238 (1975): 263–65.

———. "Teatro chileno de la década del ochenta: desarrollo de un movimiento innovador." Santiago: Instituto de Estudios Humanísticos, 1982.

"Principios del teatro aficionado chileno: Ante proyecto de estatutos para una Asociación Nacional de Teatro Aficionado." Santiago: ANTACH Document, 1969.

Rodríguez B., Orlando. "Caminos nuevos en el Cuarto Festival Nacional del Teatro Aficionado e Independiente." *Apuntes* 14 (1961): 1–5.

———. "Notas sobre el teatro actual y el teatro popular," Primera Convención de Teatro Aficionado. Santiago: ANTACH Document, 1969.

———. "Realidad y perspectivas del teatro chileno." *Centro de Estudios de la Realidad Nacional* (CEREN) 2 (1970): 60–69.

Rodríguez Elizondo, José. "¿Dónde está la 'cuestión social'?" *La Quinta Rueda,* no number (1972): 12–13.

Rojo, Grinor. *Muerte y resurrección del teatro chileno 1973–1983.* Madrid: Ediciones Michay, S.A., 1985.

———. "Muerte y resurrección del teatro chileno: Observaciones preliminares." *Caravelle* 40 (1983): 67–81.

Sánchez, Eduardo. "Primera convención de Teatro Aficionado (1969): Teatro Aficionado, creación colectiva." Santiago, ANTACH Document, 1969.

Sánchez V. Jorge. "A cuarenta y un años del teatro experimental." *Atenea* 446 (1982): 151–59.

Sieveking, Alejandro. "Teatro chileno antifascista." In *Primer coloquio sobre la literatura chilena (de la resistencia y el exilio),* edited by Poli Délano, pp. 97–113. Mexico City: Editorial Universitaria Autónoma, 1980.

Suárez Radillo, Carlos Miguel. "El teatro chileno actual y la influencia de las universidades como sus fuerzas propulsoras." *Revista Interamericana de Bibliografía* 22, no. 1 (1972): 18–29.

"Suspensión de obra teatral provoca polémica en la Universidad Católica." *La Segunda,* 28 June 1978.

"Temporal desata *Hojas de Parra.*" *Las Ultimas Noticias,* 1 March 1977.

"The Theatre in Chile: Before the Coup and After." *Theatre Quarterly* 5, no. 20 (1976): 103–7.

Thomas, Charles P. "Chilean Theater in Exile: The Teatro del Angel in Costa Rica, 1974–1984." *Latin American Theatre Review* 19, no. 2 (1986): pp. 97–101.

Torres Rivera, Rebeca. *"El teatro chileno desde 1941 hasta 1981."* Ph.D. diss., University of California, Riverside, 1983.

Valenzuela, Tito. "Shanty Town Theatre: Interview with Juan Radrigán." *Index on Censorship* 14, no. 1 (1985): 9–10.

Vidal, Hernán. "Cultura nacional y teatro chileno profesional reciente." In *Teatro chileno de la crisis institucional 1973–1980 (Antología crítica)* edited by María de la Luz Hurtado, Carlos Ochsenius, and Hernán Vidal, pp. 54–99. Santiago: CENECA and University of Minnesota Latin American Series.

————. "Juan Radrigán: Los límites de la imaginación dialógica," in *Teatro de Juan Radrigán (11 obras),* pp. 39–61. Santiago: CENECA and University of Minnesota, 1984.

Vidal, Virginia. "Interesante experiencia: El teatro nuevo popular." *El Siglo,* 18 May 1972.

Villegas, Juan. "Los marginados como personajes: Teatro chileno de la década de los sesenta." *Latin American Theatre Review* 19, no. 2 (1986): 85–95.

Vodanović, Sergio. "La experimentación teatral chilena: ayer, hoy, mañana." *Revista EAC* 1 (1972): 8–16.

Wolff, Egon. "Ideas dispersas sobre *La balsa de la Medusa.*" *Apuntes,* Número Especial (1985): 59–64.

————. "Sobre mi teatro." In *Teatro chileno actual,* edited by José Ricardo Morales, p. 164. Santiago: Empresa Editora Zig-Zag, 1966.

Latin American Literature and Theater

Albuquerque, Severino João. "Verbal Violence and the Pursuit of Power in *Aparaceu a Margarida.*" *Latin American Theatre Review* 189, no. 2 (1986): 23–29.

Bacarisse, Pamela. "Donoso and Social Commitment: *Casa de campo.*" *Bulletin of Hispanic Studies* 60, no. 4 (1983): 319–32.

Benedetti, Mario. *Primavera con una esquina rota.* Mexico City: Nueva Imagen, 1982.

Bixler, Jacqueline Eyring. "Games and Reality on the Latin American Stage." *Latin American Literary Review,* 12, no. 24 (1984): 22–35.

Dauster, Frank N. *Historia del teatro hispanoamericano: Siglos XIX y XX.* Mexico City: Ediciones Andrea, 1966.

Délano, Poli, ed. *Primer coloquio sobre la literatura chilena (de la resistencia y el exilio).* Mexico City: Editorial Universitaria Autónoma, 1980.

Donoso, José. *El jardín de al lado.* Barcelona: Editorial Seix Barral, 1981.

Edwards, Jorge. "Books in Chile." *Index on Censorship* 2 (1984): 20–23.

Jones, Willis Knapp. *Behind Spanish American Footlights.* Austin and London: University of Texas Press, 1966.

Lihn, Enrique. Letter addressed to the Primer Encuentro de Poesía Chilena en Rotterdam 1983. In *LAR: Revista de Literatura* 2–3 (1984): 6.

Montes, Hugo, and Julio Orlandi. *Historia y antología de la literatura chilena.* Santiago: Editorial del Pacífico, 1965.

Pérez Coterillo, Moisés. "10 críticos," *Primer Acto* 161 (1973): 31–44.

Piga T., Domingo. "El teatro popular: Consideraciones históricas e ideológicas." In *Popular Theater for Social Change in Latin America,* edited by Gerardo Luzuriaga, pp. 3–23. Los Angeles: UCLA Latin American Center Publications, 1978.

Silva Castro, Raúl. *Panorama Literario de Chile.* Santiago: Editorial Universitaria, 1961.

Suárez Radillo, Carlos Miguel. *Temas y estilos en el teatro hispanoamericano contemporáneo.* Zaragoza, Spain: Editorial Litho Arte, 1975.

Other Works

Agosín, Marjorie. "Agujas que hablan: las arpilleristas chilenas". *Revista Iberoamericana,* 132–33 (1985): 523–29.

Angell, Alan. "Why is the Transition to Democracy Proving so Difficult in Chile?" *Bulletin of Latin American Research* 5, no. 1 (1986): 25–40.

Attar, Samar. *The Intruder in Modern Drama.* Frankfurt am Main-Bern-Cirencester U.K.: Peter D. Laing, 1981.

Aylwin, Mariana, et. al. *Chile en el siglo XX.* Santiago: Ediciones Emisión, 1985.

Barraza, Fernando. " 'Canto nuevo': Vieja obsesión por decir verdades." *Mensaje* 317 (1983): 125–37.

Bianchi, Soledad. "El movimiento artístico chileno en el conflicto político actual." *Casa de las Américas* 130 (1982): 146–54.

Blakemore, Harold. "Back to the Barracks: The Chilean Case." *Third World Quarterly* 7, no. 1 (1985): 44–62.

Boyle, Catherine, M. "Chilean Song since 1973: An Overview." In *Chile after 1973: Elements for the Analysis of Military Rule,* edited by D. E. Hojman, pp. 43–64. Liverpool: Centre for Latin American Studies, 1985. Monograph Series No. 12.

Boyle, Catherine, and David E. Hojman. "Economic Strategies: Middle Sectors in Contemporary Chile." *Boletín de Estudios Latonamericanos y del Caribe* 38 (1985): 15–45.

Brantlinger, Patrick. *Bread and Circuses: Theories of Mass Culture as Social Decay.* Ithaca and London: Cornell University Press, 1983.

Brodsky, P. "Graffiti." *Krítica* 17 (1985): 37–39.

Brunner, José Joaquín. "Cultura e identidad nacional: Chile 1973–1983." Santiago: FLACSO, 1983. Documento de trabajo, 177.

———. "Vida cotidiana, cultura y política (1973–1982)." *Chile-América* 84–85 (1983): 63–78.

"Como medida de unidad: Gobierno revisará la situación de exiliados." *El Mercurio Internacional,* 21–27 Oct. 1982.

De Vylder, Stefan. *Allende's Chile: The Political Economy of the Rise and Fall of the Unidad Popular.* London: Cambridge University Press, 1976.

Faúndez, Julio. "The Defeat of Politics: Chile under Allende." *Boletín de Estudios Latinoamericanos y del Caribe* 28 (1980): 59–76.

Foxley, Alejandro. *Latin American Experiments in Neo-Conservative Economics.* Berkeley, Los Angeles, and London: University of California Press, 1983.

Frías, Patricio. "Cesantía y estrategias de supervivencia." Documento de Trabajo. Santiago: FLACSO, 1977.

Garcés, Joan. *Allende y la experiencia chilena: Las armas de una política.* Barcelona. Caracas and Mexico City: Editorial Ariel, 1976.

Gelderman, Carol. "Hyperrealism in Contemporary Drama: Retrogressive or Avant-Garde?" *Modern Drama* 26 (1983): 357–67.

Godoy, Hernán, ed. *El carácter chileno.* Santiago: Editorial Universitaria, 1976.

———. *La cultura chilena: Ensayo de síntesis y de interpretación sociológica.* Santiago: Editorial Universitaria, 1982.

Greene, Graham. *Getting to Know the General: The Story of an Involvement.* London: Bodley Head, 1984.

Ilie, Paul. "Dictatorship and Literature." *Ideologies and Literature* 4, no. 17 (1983).

Latcham, Ricardo. "Psicología del caballero chileno." In *El carácter chileno,* edited by Hernán Godoy, pp. 371–74. Santiago: Editorial Universitaria, 1976.

Mamalakis, Markos J. *The Growth and Structure of the Chilean Economy: From Independence to Allende.* New Haven and London: Yale University Press, 1976.

Mars, Gerald, and Michael Nicod. *The World of Waiters.* London: George Allen & Unwin, 1984.

Moreno Aliste, Cecilia. *La artesanía urbana marginal.* Santiago: CENECA, 1984.

Muñoz, Liliana. "Exile as Bereavement: Socio-psychological Manifestations of Chilean Exiles in Great Britain." *British Journal of Medical Psychology* 53 (1980): 227–32.

Pike, Frederick B. "Aspects of Class Relations in Chile." *Hispanic American Historical Review* 43 (1963): 14–33.

"Pinochet Opens Doors for some Exiles." *Latin American Regional Report,* 19 Nov. 1982: 4.

"Plebiscite Success Strengthens Pincohet's Personal Position." *Latin American Weekly Report,* 19 September 1980: 6–7.

Raczynsky, Dagmar, and Claudia Serrano. "La cesantía: impacto sobre la mujer y la familia popular." *CIEPLAN* 14 (1984): 61–97.

Rosencrantz, Hernán. "The Church in Chilean Politics: The Confusing Years." In *Chile after 1973: Elements for the Analysis of Military Rule,* edited by D. E. Hojman, pp. 65–95. Liverpool: Centre for Latin American Studies, 1985. Monograph Series No. 12.

Silva Labarca, Myre. "Mujeres chilenas exiliadas: Procesos de transformación ideológica y de comportamiento." *Chile-America* 74–75 (1981): 39–48.

Subercaseaux, Benjamín. *Chile o una loca geografía.* 16th ed. Santiago: Editorial Universitaria, 1973.

Subercaseaux, Bernardo. "El 'canto nuevo' (1973–1980)." *Araucaria de Chile* 12 (1980): 201–6.

Teodorescu Brinzeu, Pia. "The Verbal Zero Sign in Theater." *Poetics* 13 (1984): 47–56.

Valenzuela, Arturo. *The Breakdown of Democratic Regimes: Chile.* London: Johns Hopkins University Press, 1978.

Whitehead, Lawrence. "Whatever Became of the 'Southern Cone Model'?" In *Chile after 1973: Elements for the Analysis of Military Rule,* edited by D. E. Hojman, pp. 9–30. Liverpool: Centre for Latin American Studies, 1985. Monograph Series No. 12.

Index